Public enterprise economics

London School of Economics
Handbooks in Economic Analysis

EDITOR: J. J. Thomas   *Lecturer in Economics,*
                              London School of Economics
                              and Political Science

Public enterprise economics

Second edition

Ray Rees

Professor of Economics, University College, Cardiff

Weidenfeld and Nicolson   London

To Zac and Dan

© 1976, 1984 Ray Rees

First published 1976
Second edition 1984

George Weidenfeld and Nicolson Ltd
91 Clapham High Street London SW4 7TA

British Library Cataloguing in Publication Data

Rees, Ray
    Public enterprise economics. – 2nd ed. –
    (LSE handbooks in economic analysis series)
    1. Government ownership – Mathematical models
    I. Title   II. Series
    338.6′2   HD3853

ISBN 0-297-78336-X cased
ISBN 0-297-78337-8 paperback

Printed by Butler & Tanner Ltd
Frome and London

Contents

Contents

Preface to the second edition

The aim and approach of this second edition are the same as those of the first. Four of the chapters have however been completely rewritten, and a new chapter, on applications of marginal cost pricing in energy industries, has been added.

The first two chapters, which in the first edition were mainly concerned with the institutional framework of public enterprise in Britain, now deal with a more general set of issues. They examine the case for creating or perpetuating public enterprise, in the light of the purposes it is meant to serve and the alternative forms of economic organization which exist. They also discuss in some depth the question of the performance of public enterprise, and draw upon the evidence available in a number of countries. The aim is to identify those aspects of performance which seem intrinsic to the nature of public enterprise as a form of economic organization, and which are not just due to accidents of time, place or personality.

The revisions to the remaining chapters, which in the case of chapters 9 and 10 amounted to a complete rewriting, have been mainly to take account of work published since the first edition was written. I have also made a major change in the method of exposition. Each analytical chapter has an appendix giving formal derivations of the results which are explained and illustrated in the body of the chapter. The chapters themselves should be fully accessible to the 'non-mathematical' reader, who must nevertheless be prepared to work through closely argued analysis, while the appendices give a concise treatment of the theory for the 'mathematical' reader.

The approach of this book is still thoroughly normative, and I make no apologies for that. It can be regarded as an exploration of the implications of the welfare-maximization approach for the problems of resource allocation which are presented by public enterprise, as economists perceive them. To this extent it provides a set of principles which suggest how public enterprises could and should be run, and, moreover, in a decentralized way. This does not mean I am unaware that the influence of economic principles on actual decision-taking in the nationalized industries has always been patchy and uneven, and that there is evidence to suggest that it has receded in the past few years. Nevertheless, I think that, at least in part of our work, economists ought to act as if there were an eager demand for the kinds of normative principles we develop. To cease to insist on the welfare-maximization approach is to let the case go by default, and to leave the field clear to the obfuscations and fudges of accountants and the special pleading of particular interest groups. In my own experience, decision-takers in government and the industries often find economic principles valuable in helping them to solve their problems, even if they do not regard these principles as blueprints for running the industries. And at the very least, economic analysis provides 'outside observers' of the public enterprise sector with the basis for a critique of the present ways of doing things.

I am grateful to a number of people who have commented on the first edition, and in particular to David Henderson, whose comments were instrumental in my revision of chapters 1 and 2 and the addition of chapter 6. I am also grateful to Pat Watson, who deciphered and typed the redrafts with her usual cheerfulness and efficiency. This is also a good place to record my general debt to Ralph Turvey, who set me the problem which first interested me in this general area, and from whose published work I have continued to learn a great deal.

Cardiff
September 1983

Preface to the first edition

The aim of this book is to provide a systematic exposition of public enterprise economics, which goes beyond the analysis of marginal cost pricing and its applications, and incorporates the important theoretical developments of the last ten years or so. Roughly half the book is taken up with the discussion of public enterprise objectives and control, the meaning and validity of marginal cost pricing and problems of its application. In the remainder, I go on to analyse pricing and investment problems in a variety of second-best situations; consider the way in which taxation and income-distributional objectives can be incorporated into pricing policies; and conclude with an analysis of price and capacity determination under uncertainty.

The first two chapters, though more descriptive than the rest, play an essential part in placing the later economic analysis in context. In them, I have tried to set out the several objectives which public enterprises are expected to pursue, discuss the conflicts between them, and suggest how economic analysis may contribute to solutions of the problems of control. This analysis can appear metaphysical unless it is understood that the essence of the economist's approach is the search for *decentralized* procedures, which allow the several conflicting objectives to be pursued with a minimum cost of control. The continued controversy over the problems caused by excessive centralization and 'ministerial intervention' suggests that an analysis of the possibility of decentralization through the use of a pricing mechanism has much to contribute.

It will probably be clear by now that the analysis takes place mainly at the general theoretical level. I certainly share the view that the real problems of specific industries can only be solved by detailed numerical models, which represent adequately the particularities of technologies, distribution systems, etc. However, many things are taken as parameters in these models, for example prices and discount rates, which are really variables from the point of view of the industry or sector as a whole. The principles on which they should be determined can only be discussed at the more general level, in the context of theories about the working of the economy, and of explicit value judgements with respect to which optimality is defined. Subject to this, I have tried to choose problems for their relevance rather than their theoretical interest. Although the models in this book are usually simplified for expositional reasons, they are intended to capture the main features of the real problems.

The level of exposition is, in general, meant to be appropriate for second- and third-year economics undergraduates. I have assumed that the student has had a reasonably rigorous course in microeconomics, at about the level of Ferguson (1972), Baumol (1965), Stigler (1966), or Gravelle and Rees (1981), which will have included some welfare economics. This assumption relieved me of the need to provide expositions of economic theory as such, except when I wanted to suggest a specific emphasis or line of development for the purpose of analysing public enterprise problems. This is true for example of the discussions of welfare economics in chapter 3, cost curves in chapter 4, and intertemporal resource allocation in chapter 8.

The technical aspects of the book should be within reach of second- or third-year students, with the possible exception of parts of the last chapter, which will in any case be of interest mainly to the more advanced reader. I have, without apology, used some algebra and a little calculus to sharpen up the statement of results, but there is ample verbal and geometric translation. Matters of purely theoretical concern are usually dealt with in the notes. The chief prerequisite for this book is a good understanding of economic theory.

The constraint on the length of this book was certainly binding, and its shadow price derives from three major omissions. Given the emphasis on analysis, it was not possible to include descriptive material on the nationalized industries – their histories, internal problems, significance to the economy, etc. This omission does not reflect the view that such material is unimportant: I have always felt happier with generalizations when I have some knowledge of what it is that is being generalized about. Fortunately, there have recently appeared a number of books – for example Reid and Allen (1970), Reid, Allen and Harris (1973), and Thomson and Hunter (1973) – which could be used to complement the theoretical approach adopted here.

A second omission was a 'positive' analysis of public enterprise policy. A marked characteristic of the European approach to public enterprise economics is its normative character. It is implicitly assumed that public enterprises will conform to the optimality rules, once they can be found. The North American literature, on the other hand, tends to be largely positive in approach: public utilities are regarded as firms with their own goals, which they pursue subject to externally imposed constraints. This difference of course reflects the different institutional forms of state control in Europe and North America. However, it is hard to ignore the fact that, quite naturally, public enterprise managers develop their own goals. The closest broad characterization of these would appear to be in terms of growth maximization, or rate of decline minimization, but it may be that a more subtle characterization than that would be required. The relevance of positive theories of public enterprise behaviour would mainly be to the problems of decentralization and control. Why *is* such detailed scrutiny of public enterprise plans thought necessary? What *would* happen if control were very much more decentralized, allowing public enterprises, for example, to determine their own prices according to some general pricing rules? Answers to such questions, which are close to the centre of policy debate, require some theory of the objectives of public enterprises as autonomous organizations. Unfortunately, it is not possible to present one here.

Finally, the analysis in the book is entirely in equilibrium and comparative statics terms, and no attempt has been made to provide a dynamic analysis of any problem. There are several problems, particularly to do with extractive industries such as gas, oil and coal, in which a dynamic analysis has much to contribute. When time must enter in an essential way, however, the more mundane approach of two-period analysis has been adopted here. The usual procedure is to reason from necessary conditions for a static constrained maximum, to optimal policies. In doing this, the emphasis has been on providing the student with a good understanding of the reasoning which underlies the analysis, at the expense, usually, of generality and rigour.

I would like to express my thanks to my colleague, Hugh Gravelle, who read and commented most helpfully on the entire manuscript. He is not of course responsible for the ways in which I have used and misused his comments, nor for the errors which may have escaped even his attention. When writing several chapters, I also had the benefit of Mr H. Levene's views on government economic policy. The book was completed during a year spent as a visiting professor at the University of Guelph, Ontario, Canada, and I should like to thank Chairman John Vanderkamp and colleagues for the friendly and stimulating atmosphere in which I found myself. I am especially grateful to Maria Larsen, Carmelina Ridi and Irene Pereira, who deciphered and typed the manuscript. And thanks go as always to Deni, for her charm, tolerance and support.

Guelph, Ontario
July 1975

Chapter 1

Why public enterprise?

This book is largely concerned with the normative economics of public enterprise, that is, with developing principles which *ought* to be applied *if* certain objectives are being pursued. The purpose of this chapter and the next is to put this normative analysis into context, by examining in general terms the nature and limitations of public enterprise as a form of economic organization.

We should begin with a clear idea of exactly what a public enterprise is. This term is applied to an organization which produces and sells goods or services, and whose assets are owned not by private shareholders, but by a public agency. We might therefore, somewhat loosely, refer to a public enterprise as a 'state-owned firm'.

The two central characteristics of a public enterprise are clearly brought out in this definition. It is first of all a type of business organization, and its basic activities are similar in kind to those of any other firm. But because it is publicly owned, its management will usually be accountable to some part of the governmental apparatus and so is open to *direct* political influence, while there is also the strong presumption that the enterprise should be operated in the general 'public interest', in some sense, rather than have as its objective the maximization of profit.

This concept of a 'public enterprise' is of course a simplification and an abstraction from the complications of the organizational structures which exist in reality. We could, but will not, expend time and space on the issue of whether an enterprise in which the state owns a majority or minority shareholding, the rest being held by private stockholders, is 'really' a public enterprise. If the state effectively determines the decisions of the enterprise then we can regard it as if it were wholly owned.[1] Moreover, there is a wide variety of organizational forms for production activities wholly carried on by the state. In many countries postal services are supplied by a government department, in others by a separate corporation. A single 'nationalized industry' may engage in supply of a particular class of goods, but not be organized as a single enterprise – there may be a number of centres of decision-taking power, as there are in the electricity industry of the United Kingdom. Alternatively, a single public enterprise may operate in several industries, as do the large state holding companies in Italy. We find it useful to treat public production *as if* it is carried out by enterprises which are single, well-defined decision-taking units. This very much reflects the approach taken in the 'theory of the firm' in conventional economic theory. We leave, as an issue for further study, the question of whether the actual organizational forms in existence require modifications to the analysis.

Public enterprises broadly defined form a significant, though not dominant, element in the economies of most non-Communist countries, with the major exception of the United States, where a different institutional response to the problems which give rise to public enterprise has taken place. It is therefore of interest to consider the question which heads this chapter: what are the reasons for the existence of public enterprise?

1.1   Why public enterprises exist

If we take the question conceptually rather than historically, there are four basic sets of reasons for the existence of public enterprise:

(1) To 'correct' *market failure*.
(2) To alter the structure of payoffs in an economy.
(3) To facilitate centralized long-term economic planning.
(4) To change the nature of the economy, from capitalist to socialist.

Before going on to consider these in greater depth, it should be noted that they do not necessarily provide the historical reasons for all specific acts of 'nationalization'. These may have been the chance result of a politically sensitive bankruptcy, a wartime need, the attempt to preserve a sector of the economy from foreign domination, and so on.[2] However, in seeking to explain the *continued existence* of, and possible justifications for, public enterprise in those economies in which it plays a significant role, we find ourselves drawing upon the four sets of considerations just listed, and in particular the first two. We now consider them in some detail.

(1) *Market failure.* The market system is said to fail when it brings about a resource allocation which is inferior, in a certain sense,[3] to some others' which are feasible given the resources and technological possibilities in the economy. Theory suggests that market failure tends to occur in the presence of monopoly and oligopoly, when significant externalities exist, or when we have a 'common-property' resource.[4] It is then suggested that setting up a public enterprise to supply the good or service concerned is a means of 'correcting' the market failure.

The most relevant and, historically, important example of this is the case of so-called 'natural monopoly'. A natural monopoly exists when cost conditions in an industry are such that one firm can produce a particular output or set of outputs at a lower cost than is possible under any other organization of production. Where there is only one output, natural monopoly would result from significant economies of scale up to the level of market demand. Where there are several outputs, 'economies of scope' rather than, or as well as, economies of scale may give rise to natural monopoly. That is, it may be cheaper for one firm to produce the entire set of outputs than for different firms to produce subsets of them.

Natural monopoly has been a very marked feature of supply of the so-called 'public utilities' – water, gas, electricity, rail transport, telephone services – where high costs have to be incurred in establishing a supply network. It would be prohibitively expensive to have two or more competing firms constructing alternative networks so that each consumer would have a choice of supplier. A single network then has been taken to imply a single seller. If the seller is a profit-maximizing monopolist, theory predicts that price will be raised above marginal cost and output of the good will be restricted below its optimal level. To have the natural monopoly in the hands of a public enterprise may then be seen as a way of retaining the cost advantage of a sole seller while preventing the resource misallocation which would result from profit-seeking monopoly.[5]

The argument for public enterprise as a corrective of the 'static' kinds of market failure – monopoly, externalities, common-property resources – so far considered could be extended, rather more controversially, by considering the possibility of 'dynamic' market failure. This refers to the proposition that the private capital market in an economy may be insufficiently well developed, or investors in it too myopic or risk-averse, to provide adequate finance for important sectors of industry. Organizing these sectors as public enterprises and supplying them with capital raised by the state – from taxation or borrowing – is then seen as a means of compensating for the shortcomings of the private capital market.

We can illustrate this argument with two cases drawn from UK experience. In the early 1970s, two important British companies, the motorcar manufacturers British Leyland and Rolls-Royce Ltd, were on the verge of bankruptcy. The financial institutions which were the major creditors of the companies were unwilling to supply further finance, presumably because they were pessimistic about the chances that the companies would be able to return to profitability within the time horizon they considered appropriate. The general consequences of these bankruptcies – in terms of lost employment, exports, and, in the case of Rolls-Royce, technological capabilities – were considered sufficiently serious that the companies were 'nationalized', or reconstituted as public enterprises.[6] Substantial injections of capital were made, not only to restore the companies to financial viability but also, particularly in the case of British Leyland, to finance investment in new production facilities, improvements in product range, and to 'buy out' inefficient labour practices. As public enterprises, the companies have been able to rationalize and invest, whereas the scale of losses and the view taken of the time required and risks involved in their return to profitability deterred private investors from financing this process. *If*, as, at the time of writing,[7] appears to be the case, the companies do become viable, then it could be argued that the private capital market was excessively short-sighted and pessimistic relative to some notion of the social optimum.

Of course, there is considerable room for argument over these two examples. The general point however can be put in a more theoretical way, and in a form in which it will be considered more rigorously later in this book[8]: the rate of interest at which investors on the capital market discount future returns to investment lies above the socially optimal rate of discount, and this reflects market failure in the supply of capital. Public enterprise, with its associated change in the source of investment funds, may then be regarded as a means of correcting this particular market failure.

(2) *Structure of payoffs.* By a 'payoff' is meant a benefit received by some individual, which may often, though not always, take the form of income or consumption. Any one organization of production will imply a particular set, pattern or structure of payoffs to the individuals in an economy. Rather than passively accepting an existing set-up, individuals may seek to bring about changes which, in their perception, will improve their payoffs. Alternatively those who see changes as worsening their payoffs will resist them. The substitution of public for private enterprise to any significant extent would affect the structure of payoffs in the economy, as would the converse. This is particularly the case where the activity in question generates large rents, for example because of the existence of monopoly. Under private ownership these rents are likely to accrue to the owners of the firm,[9] while under public ownership they may be divided among workers, management, consumers and government by some process which reconciles the conflicts of interest among these groups. The capture of rents may therefore be an objective in creating a public enterprise; the retention of rents a factor in its continuing existence.

There are numerous examples. In several European countries tobacco and salt were supplied by state monopolies, so that the large rents could be appropriated by the state. In Canada retail sales of wine and spirits are monopolies of the various provinces, at least in part for the same reason. In the United Kingdom, the nationalization of the coal, steel, shipbuilding and rail industries was strongly supported by the workers involved, in the anticipation of better pay and conditions of work than would have been secured had the industries remained in private ownership.[10] For the same reason, denationalization of the telecommunications industry and part of the gas industry is resisted by the trades unions concerned. In

Italy, up to 1974, it was common practice for public enterprises to make donations to political parties out of their revenues, and politicians compete to induce the enterprises to make job-creating investments in their constituencies.[11] Cross-subsidization – supplying one group of consumers at a loss which is made up by profits on sales to other consumers – is very prevalent in public enterprises, and this can be viewed as a particular way of allocating the rents associated with the activity.

(3) *Centralized planning.* It is often argued that direct state control of certain key industries – what in the United Kingdom have been called the 'commanding heights of the economy' – would greatly facilitate long-term economic planning in economies in which a significant amount of private enterprise exists. The central planning represents an attempt to supplant market forces by establishing priorities for the development of particular sectors in the economy and then seeking to determine the process of resource allocation over time so as to achieve these priorities, without, however, taking *all* firms into public ownership. Control of the basic infrastructure – the energy industries, steel, transport, communications – on which the rest of the economy crucially depends, is seen as increasing the likelihood that the plan will succeed, since they can be directly developed in accordance with the plan. If this were not done – if, for example, growth of energy and transport capacity were inadequate – the plan would be very unlikely to succeed.

(4) *Socialization of production.* There has of course always been an important ideological element in the creation and defence of public enterprise. Karl Marx saw the private ownership of industrial assets – capital – as a means by which one class in the economy exploited another. Taking capital into public ownership is then seen as the means by which this exploitation is ended and a better form of society developed. Nationalization has therefore always been an important element in the programmes of socialist parties, and in *some* countries, particularly the United Kingdom and France, the major acts of nationalization were carried out by socialist governments.[12]

Having set out these explanations of the existence of public enterprise, we now consider their strength as explanations of the continued existence of public enterprises at the present time.

First, if one is not a socialist, then clearly the ideological argument for public enterprise carries no force. More strongly, if one shares the liberal ideology which underlies conventional economic theory, one would prefer private to public ownership *per se*, unless it can be demonstrated that individual welfare is increased by, in some instances, replacing private by public enterprise. Virtually the only circumstance in which this could in principle occur is where there is market failure. Thus, to the liberal, market failure is a necessary (though, as we shall see, not a sufficient) condition for public enterprise.

Interestingly enough, public enterprise as it currently exists in the non-Communist countries also comes under attack from socialist writers, the argument being that in fact it does nothing to advance socialism. Quite the reverse: public enterprise is seen as taking over activities which are so unprofitable or risky that private enterprise would not want to undertake them anyway.[13] Insofar as it is coping with the failings of the private enterprise system, it is in fact supporting the continued existence of that system, and preventing its replacement by a truly socialist economic order.

This argument does not hold in its entirety. It is by no means the case that in general public enterprises undertake only risky and unprofitable activities: for example in the United Kingdom several of the nationalized industries are highly profitable.[14] However, it is certainly true that the way in which public enterprises are operated, their financial and pricing policies and the values and attitudes of their managers, have very much in common with private enterprise. Whatever may have been the intentions of those who established the nationalized industries, they do not now appear to act as instruments for creating a socialist economy.

A similar conclusion applies to the argument that public enterprises facilitate economic planning. In fact there *is* no central economic planning of this kind conducted in the non-Communist economies, and so public enterprises have no role to play as instruments in the planning process. It is therefore hard to escape the conclusion that explanations of or justifications for the continued existence of public enterprise must be in terms of correcting market failure and achieving particular distributions of payoffs.

In relation to these, the main counter-argument is that other institutional means or policy instruments exist of pursuing these objectives, which may be more effective or less costly than public enterprise. There are three main alternatives to public enterprise:

(1) *Taxes and subsidies.* These may be used both to correct market failure and to redistribute payoffs, without the necessity for state ownership. For example, a monopoly may be induced to expand output to the optimal level by being paid an appropriate subsidy; the monopoly rents can be taxed away by a pure profits tax, which leaves a profit-maximizing monopolist's output unchanged. Investment could be stimulated by subsidies, tax credits, or a number of other fiscal devices. Risk-taking could be stimulated by allowing losses to register a tax credit. In principle, it is usually possible to design a tax/subsidy mechanism which would

induce a profit-maximizing firm to choose whatever level of output or investment is considered desirable. The main difficulties are that such mechanisms might be extremely complex and require a quantity and quality of information from the firm which, in the absence of public ownership, are unlikely to be forthcoming. Take for example the case of a monopolist owning a natural gas deposit. It may be desired to tax away the resource rents and slow down the rate of depletion of the deposit,[15] without removing the incentive to explore and develop new deposits. Given exact knowledge of the size of the reserves, the marginal costs of extraction and the monopolist's discount rate, it would be possible to design a tax/subsidy scheme to do this. However, the only source of the information is the monopolist himself, and he has an incentive to bias it when passing it on to the policy-maker, in a way which gives him the most favourable tax/subsidy regime possible. If the deposit is owned by a public enterprise, the optimal policy could be achieved directly.[16]

(2) *Anti-trust or monopolies policy*. Bodies such as the Monopolies and Mergers Commission (MMC) in the UK and the Federal Trade Commission (FTC) in the US have the responsibility of monitoring business behaviour in oligopolistic or monopolistic industries, identifying abuses of market power and recommending corrective action. They therefore present an alternative to public enterprise as a check on natural monopoly. However, such bodies tend to range widely over the whole economy, and are not well suited to provide the continuous scrutiny of specific industries which may be necessary to control market failure.

(3) *Regulation*. This is the main alternative to public enterprise. The industry concerned is left in private ownership, and a public agency is set up to regulate its prices, profits, and possibly other aspects of its operations, for example standards of safety and environmental impact. The industry raises its capital on the private capital market, but must submit proposals for price increases to the regulatory agency, which therefore may control abuse of monopoly power. In principle, and given sufficient information, the regulatory agency could ensure that the industry conformed to the criteria for efficient resource allocation (see chapter 3 below). In practice the main criterion is whether prices yield a 'fair and reasonable' rate of profit given the industry's costs. There has been little attempt by regulatory bodies in the US to apply criteria for efficient resource allocation such as those made in the UK and France in respect of their nationalized industries.

In recent years the system of regulation in the US has received a great deal of criticism. Because of the 'cost-plus' nature of the price regulation there is no incentive to efficiency, and the monopoly rents may simply be dissipated in higher costs rather than lower prices to the consumer. A subtle aspect of this problem is the so-called 'Averch-Johnson effect': if the allowed rate of return on capital exceeds the regulated industry's true cost of capital, it can increase its 'allowed' profits by expanding its capital assets beyond the efficient point – production becomes excessively capital intensive. Moreover, it is argued that regulation often works in the interests of the regulated firm(s) rather than consumers. It tends to suppress competition, particularly by restricting new entry and preserving existing monopoly power. Opinion is divided as to whether this is because the original purpose of the regulation was precisely to do this – the regulatory apparatus was supplied by vote-seeking politicians in response to a demand for it by the industry itself, which saw it as a way of protecting or enhancing its rents; or because, though initially intended to operate in the interest of consumers, the regulatory machinery has been 'captured' by the industry and, in the language of the spy thriller, 'turned round', so that it becomes a spokesman for the industry and protector of its interests. Whichever is the case, the weight of opinion among academic economists in the US seems to be critical of regulation as it works in practice.

It might well be possible, then, to achieve the purposes of public enterprise, in correcting market failure and redistributing rents, by one or a combination of taxes and subsidies, monopoly policy and regulation. The important question is that of the effectiveness of the various institutional possibilities in relation to their costs. In an ideal world, the institutional form adopted would be that which maximized the excess of benefits over costs, though precisely how these are to be defined is still an open question.

In recent years, the economic performance of public enterprises has in some countries received considerable criticism.[17] In the UK in particular serious attempts are being made to find alternative institutional forms which in general involve some degree of 'privatization' of public enterprise – the introduction of private ownership and partial denationalization. This does not of course reflect a careful assessment of the costs and benefits of alternative institutional possibilities, but rather is strongly influenced by *a priori* political beliefs. Nevertheless, perceptions of the poor performance of several public enterprises, together with the view that this may be an intrinsic aspect of the institutional form rather than a soluble problem within it, have played an important role. In the next chapter therefore we shall consider at some length the question of the performance of public enterprise.

1.2 Conclusions

Of the four explanations for the existence of public enterprise, we conclude that two of them, the correction of market failure and the distribution of rents, provide the rationale for the continued existence of public enterprise in the non-Communist economies. As we see from the responses to these problems in the US, other institutional possibilities exist and, ideally, we could conceive of the optimal institutional form as being derived from a 'comparative institutional analysis' of their costs and benefits. In any such analysis, the issue of the actual, as opposed to the expected, performance of public enterprise is central, and it is to this that we now turn.

Chapter 2

Public enterprise performance

2.1 The question of performance

In the preceding chapter it was suggested that a major justification for public enterprise is the correction of market failure, whether 'static' or 'dynamic'. We run the risk however of committing the so-called 'Nirvaana Fallacy',[1] of supposing that the alternative to imperfect markets is perfect government. In fact public enterprise may also 'fail', and the real choice is between two imperfect institutional forms. In this chapter then we try to take a realistic, though still analytical, view of public enterprise performance.

The first question we have to answer is: what do we mean by 'the performance of the public enterprise'? In general public discussion, criticism of the performance of public enterprises usually centres on their losses or, if profitable, on the level of their prices. There is naturally something of a contradiction here, when both losses and profits arouse public criticism. It suggests a general presumption that public enterprises are in some sense inefficient. Losses are then taken as an indicator of this inefficiency while profits are regarded as having been generated by use of monopoly power in pricing, rather than, as would be the case for a price-taking competitive firm, superior efficiency.

This general view has been broadly supported by the attempts economists have made quantitatively to assess public enterprise performance. In a very thorough survey of the wide range of studies which have sought to compare cost levels in public and private production in a number of countries and types of activity, Borcherding, Pommerehne and Schneider (1982) find that the large majority show higher cost levels in public enterprises than in private enterprises carrying on comparable activities.[2] A thorough analysis of cost, profit and productivity trends in the UK nationalized industries by R.Pryke (1982), suggested that, with some exceptions, the overall performance of these public enterprises had tended to be poor. On the Italian experience, Martinelli (1981) concludes:

the public corporations that once made up the most dynamic component of the Italian business sector and served as models for other industrialised nations are today riddled with managerial inefficiency and political corruption.[3]

Studies of specific areas of public enterprise operations, such as those by Burn (1978) and Henderson (1977) of the British nuclear industry, and by the Monopolies and Mergers Commission in the UK,[4] have shown significant inefficiencies in operations, planning, and price and investment policies.

Yet the picture is not all bad. Van der Bellen (1981) suggests that, following a major reorganization of Austrian industrial public enterprises into a 'holding company' structure, this quite large sector of the economy has performed well. Individual examples of public enterprises, such as Volkswagen in Germany and Renault in France, have performance records which compare favourably to any private enterprise. In France generally, though instances of conflict have arisen,[5] there seems to be satisfaction with the general performance of public enterprise, and certainly no sense of the deep-rooted malaise which seems to characterize attitudes to public enterprise in Italy and the United Kingdom. Finally, Borcherding *et al.* conclude:[6]

The literature seems to indicate that (a) private production is cheaper than production in publicly owned and managed firms, and (b) given sufficient competition between public and private producers (and no discriminative [sic.] regulations and subsidies), the differences in unit cost turn out to be insignificant.

It would therefore appear that public enterprises are capable of responding efficiently to the stimulus of competition but, in its absence, inefficiencies develop. Thus there certainly appears to be 'government failure' in areas where there would also be 'market failure'. The question then arises: what might be the explanation for the cost inefficiency of public enterprise in non-competitive situations?

There are two main explanations, which are by no means mutually exclusive. These are:

(1) The objectives which public enterprises are set are poorly defined, complex, unstable, and tend to increase cost levels and reduce profits.
(2) Failures occur in the monitoring and control of public enterprises, which allow those within them to operate in their own interests, implying high costs and low profitability.

The first of these explanations raises a question about what we really mean by 'performance'. Implicitly, the economists whose work we have reported identify this with economic efficiency,[7] though quite often there is also the presumption that heavy losses are also a sign of 'poor performance'. It could be argued that a more appropriate (and sympathetic) concept of performance would be: the extent to which a public enterprise achieves the objectives which have been set for it.

On this definition, a public enterprise could be performing very well, even if its cost levels are relatively high and losses huge, if in fact it is successfully meeting objectives which *imply* high costs and low profits. To label the enterprise a poor performer under these circumstances is essentially to adopt the value judgement that the objectives *ought* to be economic efficiency and profitability, and not those which have actually been set. This may well be a reasonable judgement to adopt; nevertheless, the discussion of performance should recognize the relativistic nature of the concept, in order to make clear that what may be being discussed is the appropriateness, in some sense, of the objectives which were set, rather than the efficiency with which the enterprise is achieving them. We shall return to this point at the end of the next section, where we examine in some detail the relation between public enterprise objectives and performance. Section 2.3 will then go on to look at the second explanation of 'poor performance', the problem of monitoring and control.

2.2 Public enterprise objectives

A requirement for rational decision-taking, as it is usually defined in economics, is a well-defined and consistent scale of preferences over the outcomes of alternative choices. In the case where a decision-taker is to choose entirely in his own interests, it is quite reasonable to assume that a scale of preference exists and is known to him. There is a wide class of situations, however, in which a decision-taker is actually making choices on behalf of someone else, and the presumption is that he will choose in the other's best interests. We refer to such a situation as one of delegated choice.[8] In any situation of delegated choice, the problem exists of ensuring that decisions actually are consistent with the preference ordering of the individual or group in whose interests they are being taken. The problem of ensuring this consistency is the problem of *control. A system of control* is a set of rules and procedures, the object of which is to achieve consistency between decisions and preferences in a delegated choice situation.

There are two sets of costs which have to be weighed in the balance, when a system of control is being designed. The first consists of those costs associated with the operation of the system itself. Resources will be absorbed in monitoring decisions, collecting and transmitting information, and examining alternatives. Delays in the implementation of decisions, which the control system might cause, also impose costs. The second set consists of the costs which arise out of non-correspondence between decisions and preferences: if the choices actually made by the decision-taker are not the 'best', from the point of view of the preference ordering which is supposed to regulate decisions, then a cost is imposed, which could be measured by the difference between the 'value' of the outcome of the optimal decision and that of the decision actually taken. This is, therefore, essentially an opportunity cost.

To see how these two sets of costs are related, let us take two extreme types of control system. In the first, the preference ordering over the outcomes of decisions in general is transmitted to the decision-taker, who is then left entirely alone to apply this to specific decisions, with no further control activity. This is then a completely *decentralized* control system, with minimal costs of operation. On the other hand, the *risk* that decisions will not be taken in conformity with the preference ordering is at its greatest. It is worth stressing that it is a risk, and not a certainty, that costs of this kind will be incurred, and the *a priori* perception of this risk will depend, among other things, on the view taken of the tendency of the decision-taker to develop his own preference ordering over the outcomes of decision, which differs from that he is supposed to adopt.

At the opposite extreme, a control system might exist in which the decision-taker must justify every decision, by presenting information on the choices he has made, and the alternatives which were available. This appraisal procedure is conducted after the decision-taker has made his choice, but before it is implemented. The only risk that decisions will not conform to the preference ordering arises from the possibility that the decision-taker will present biased information. On the other hand, the costs of operating the control system are maximal, since effectively there is duplication of decision-taking, with the 'decision-taker' acting essentially as a preliminary organizer of information. Any actual system of control, in trading-off the two kinds of costs, will end up somewhere between these two extremes.

Because of the scale and of the industrial and commercial as opposed to political nature of the decisions involved, considerable decision-taking responsibility is always delegated by government to public enterprise, and so the system is decentralized in principle. The problem arises, however, that an essential pre-requisite for effective decentralized decision-taking, i.e. a clear statement of a stable, consistent set of objectives, may not be given. There may well exist general statements about the 'aims' of a public enterprise. For example, in the statutes which set up the British nationalized industries there is usually the requirement that the enterprises should act 'in the national interest', providing 'efficient and economical supply' without 'undue discrimination' among consumers, and covering costs, including 'proper provisions to reserves, taking one year with another'. These vague phrases of course give virtually no practical guidance to decision-takers. From time to time more detailed documents are issued[9] which set out in greater detail the broad nature of the criteria and objectives which apply to the industries and some of these, in particular the rate of return required on new investment, and the enterprise requirement for outside finance, are set as numerical targets. However, the specification of precisely what the 'national interest' requires is never spelled out. There is, instead, active intervention in decision-taking itself, to ensure that ministers' concerns are taken account of. A similar situation appears to exist in France and Italy,[10] and to have existed in Austria before a recent reform in the organization of public enterprise.[11]

The fact that ministerial preferences are rarely made fully explicit, and instead become manifest only through intervention in the process of decision-taking, should be viewed not as an aberration or temporary malfunction in the public enterprise system, but rather as an intrinsic tendency within it. In the democratic systems which prevail in the countries concerned, ministers would often find it unwise and inexpedient to spell out publicly the aims they are pursuing. Indeed, they may be incapable of doing so: they can recognize the decision they prefer when confronted with the alternatives, but cannot state in an abstract way the general aims they wish to see pursued. The experience in Austria, when compared with that of the UK, France and Italy, suggests that because of the political pressures inherent in multi-party democracies, systematic ministerial intervention in decision-taking will take place *unless* there is some specific organizational set-up which prevents it.

There is then usually no clear coherent statement of preferences on which public enterprise managers may base their decisions, but only a series of official documents and acts of intervention on specific issues. For purposes of economic analysis, it is useful to try to deduce from all this a systematic description of what it is that government has been seeking to achieve, at the risk of making the real world seem more orderly and consistent than in fact it is.[12] We can distinguish four main types of objective, which appear to capture what governments have meant by 'the public interest':[13]

(1) economic efficiency;
(2) profitability;
(3) effects on income distribution; and
(4) relationship with macroeconomic policy.

We now discuss each of these in turn.

Economic efficiency
This aspect of public enterprise operations is, in the UK, the one whose desirability is frequently stressed in formal statements of ministerial preferences. It can be separated into two concepts of efficiency which are closely related.

Managerial and technological efficiency. This concerns the relationship between inputs and outputs. One production method is technologically more efficient than another if, for a given level of output, it absorbs less of at least one input and no more of any other; or alternatively if, with the same input levels, it produces more output. Similarly, one group of managers is more efficient than another, in a static sense, if they carry out a given set of managerial tasks with a smaller absorption of resources. In a dynamic sense, managerial efficiency is concerned also with readiness and ability to eliminate waste and exploit new technological and market opportunities. Other things being equal, ministers appear to prefer more technological and managerial efficiency to less. This is usually expressed in terms of the encouragement to adopt 'commercial' attitudes and methods, which is to be found in most White Papers concerned with nationalized industries.

Allocative efficiency. This concept is derived from the theory of welfare economics, and is concerned, at the most general level, with the entire allocation of resources in an economy. An inefficient resource allocation is one which can be changed in such a way as to make some people better off, and no one worse off, in terms of their own preferences. An efficient resource allocation is then one for which no such change is possible. The pursuit of allocative efficiency has many implications for public enterprise policies and, since most of the rest of this book is concerned with the analysis of these, little more needs to be said at this stage. We recognize the concern for allocative efficiency by ministerial statements which stress that prices paid by consumers should be related to the costs of supply; that important divergences between social costs and benefits on the one hand, and market prices on the other (due for example to external effects), should be taken into account; and that public enterprise investments should be evaluated in the light of the consumption and investment elsewhere in the economy which they may displace. These, and similar propositions, follow from the application of concepts of allocative efficiency to public enterprise decisions.

These two concepts of efficiency are related in the following way: allocative efficiency implies managerial and technological efficiency, but the converse does not hold, so that the existence of the latter type of efficiency is a necessary but not sufficient condition for the former. Thus, suppose an enterprise is using a technologically inefficient process which involves over-manning, so that the same amount of output could be produced with less labour and the same amounts of other inputs. Then in general, by reallocating the excess labour, it is possible to produce more of some outputs with no less of any other. As a result, everyone in the economy (including the reallocated workers) can be made better off. The technologically inefficient resource allocation was not therefore allocatively efficient. An allocatively efficient resource allocation *must* be such that no technological inefficiencies exist, by its definition. On the other hand, allocative inefficiency may coexist with technological efficiency: for example, a public enterprise may be using efficient production methods, and may be producing its output at minimum cost, but, because of an inappropriate pricing policy, its output may be 'too large'. By this we mean that at the margin, the resources used in producing the output are worth more in other uses – the value of the output to its consumers is not as great as its opportunity cost. In this case, it will again be possible to find a way to reallocate resources and make everyone (including the consumers of the over-expanded public enterprise output) better off, and so the resource allocation is not allocatively efficient. Since the two types of efficiency, though related, are not equivalent, it is worth while to maintain the distinction between them.

Profitability

We define the *gross trading surplus* of a public enterprise as the excess of its total revenue over its operating costs. Its *profit* is defined as the excess of its gross trading surplus over interest and depreciation provisions. This would, in a private enterprise, correspond to the amount available for distribution to shareholders (after taxes, which public enterprises may not pay), and so would be the object of prime concern to management. It will soon become clear, however, that it is more useful to focus on the gross trading surplus of a public enterprise, and so 'profitability' will in this context refer to the size of this surplus. There are two main reasons for ministerial concern with the profitability of a public enterprise.

(a) Finance – the net contribution the enterprise makes to the public exchequer depends, given its investment spending, entirely on its surplus. The funds for the investment spending of the enterprise have two sources, i.e. its own reserves, consisting essentially of depreciation provisions, and loans made to it by the exchequer. The exchequer in turn obtains its funds largely from public enterprise gross trading surpluses, taxation and borrowing. These funds must also finance expenditure by: (i) other public enterprises; (ii) agencies supplying public services such as health, education and defence; and (iii) agencies paying subsidies to individuals (unemployment benefit, family allowances, pensions) and to firms (investment grants, agricultural support). Given the planned investment expenditure of the enterprise, the smaller is its surplus, the greater must be taxation and/or borrowing, and the smaller must be other forms of expenditure. It does not matter therefore how this surplus is divided into 'interest', 'depreciation' and 'profit'; all that matters is its total size. This is of course in contrast to a private enterprise, where failure to meet interest payments would probably result in bankruptcy and dissolution of the company, while inadequate depreciation provisions would force the company to contract. The creditor of a public enterprise, the exchequer, will not normally declare it bankrupt, and is prepared to capitalize interest payments, or waive them altogether, and even to cover operating deficits (negative gross trading surplus) with grants and loans. The total size of the surplus is what counts to ministers, since this determines the flow of funds into the exchequer, and the extent of increased taxation, increased borrowing, and reductions in other forms of public expenditure required to finance an investment programme.

(b) Motivation – the pursuit of profitability by a public enterprise is also seen as a means of stimulating managerial and technological efficiency. Thus, we know that if a firm seeks to maximize its profit, this requires it to minimize costs at every level of output. However, the objective of profit maximization has been explicitly rejected for public enterprises because in general they have monopoly power in at least some of the markets they supply, and so profit maximization would result in policies which nationalization was expressly intended to avoid. The problem is, however, that if profitability becomes irrelevant, the incentive to hold down costs may be weakened, if not removed. By reintroducing profitability as something which must be taken into account in decision-taking, though not as something the maximization of which is the overriding goal, it is hoped to stimulate public enterprise managers to pursue efficiency, and also to provide a yardstick by which their efficiency can be measured. Of course, the argument for rejecting profit maximization as a goal also implies that a profitable public (or private) enterprise need not be an efficient one: as long as the enterprise possesses a high degree of monopoly power in at least some of its markets, satisfactory profits can be generated by raising prices rather than by increasing efficiency. This implies that 'profit targets' need not stimulate efficiency if they are unaccompanied by some monitoring of pricing policy.

Effects on income distribution
A government will generally have specific views about the distribution of real income among households in the economy. These will be reflected in the policies it adopts towards the pattern of public expenditure and taxation. Its taxation policies, and many of its expenditure policies, can be regarded as instruments through which it tries to bring about the changes it desires in the distribution of real income (subject always to the constraint that a government inherits a particular taxation-expenditure pattern and may be able to make only marginal changes in it). A major way in which income is redistributed is through the system of transfer payments: money is paid directly to the old, the sick, the unemployed, victims of criminal assaults, those with incomes below a certain level, and those with children. At least as important, however, is the provision of goods and services at subsidized prices, permitting greater consumption by certain groups of people than would be possible if they had to pay the full costs of supply. Most health and education services are of this kind, as are public housing and road use. In some cases, the prices are actually zero (state-provided education, road use, certain kinds of medical care), while in others, prices are to varying degrees below the costs of supply (public housing,

prescription drugs, dental treatment). Note also that since a lower price will (in the absence of quantity rationing) lead to a larger scale of output, the suppliers of inputs used to produce these goods and services may benefit. In particular, the suppliers of labour specific to a good being sold at a subsidized price may gain, perhaps from being employed rather than unemployed, or from having a higher wage or salary than would otherwise be the case (this assumes of course that government does not use its monopsony power as an employer to hold down these wages and so lessen the cost of subsidization). Finally, real incomes are redistributed through policies operating directly on input markets rather than output markets. Regional policy is a good example of this: constraints may be placed on the availability of particular inputs, usually land, in some areas of the country, and subsidies are paid to reduce the prices of other inputs – land, labour and capital – in other areas. The object is to change the spatial distribution of real income by changing the spatial distribution of economic activity. In summary, the instruments by which a government redistributes real income are direct money transfers, subsidized supply of outputs, and constraints and subsidies in supply of inputs, along with the system of taxation.

Since public enterprise decisions will often have significant effects on income distribution, they impinge upon a government's income distribution policies, and so these effects will be a relevant attribute of those decisions. Indeed, more positively, public enterprise operations may be used as policy instruments, since they may appear to provide means of redistributing incomes in desired directions more cheaply and effectively than other instruments of public policy. Examples of this abound, and some will be presented and discussed in this and later chapters.

Macroeconomic effects
A major concern of government is macroeconomic policy, and again, since public enterprise decisions may appear to impinge on this, their potential macroeconomic effects become a matter of concern. Again, certain variables under public enterprise control may actually be viewed positively as instruments of macroeconomic policy. In formulating macroeconomic policies, attention is generally focused on four target variables: the level of unemployment; the rate of inflation; the surplus/deficit on the balance of payments; and the rate of growth of potential national output. The instruments by which the values of these variables are influenced are primarily those of monetary and fiscal policy, although such measures as direct administrative intervention in markets ('prices and incomes policy') have also been adopted from time to time. Several aspects of the operations of public enterprises, and in particular their investment, employment, price and wage policies, appear to affect the values of the target variables. The investment expenditures may, through the usual multiplier effects, influence the aggregate level of economic activity in the

short run, and in the longer run help determine the rate of growth of productive potential. Also these investment expenditures, in conjunction with gross trading surpluses, affect the government's financial requirement and so its need for borrowing and taxation, which in turn affect fiscal and monetary policy. Since public enterprises supply goods and services which account for a significant proportion of household expenditures and industrial costs, increases in their wages and prices may be thought to have correspondingly significant effects on the rate of inflation. The balance of payments may be affected both directly and indirectly by public enterprise policies. Public enterprises typically provide most of the basic infrastructure of the economy – energy, steel, transportation, and communications – and so the efficiency with which they operate will determine in part the international competitiveness of the economy. More directly, public enterprises may be extensively engaged in export markets and their purchasing decisions may also have important balance-of-payments repercussions, a good example being the aircraft procurement policies of state-owned airlines such as Lufthansa, Air France, and British Airways. Given the many instances in which ministers have intervened in public enterprise pricing and investment decisions, in the interests of prevailing macroeconomic policies, we conclude that the definition of 'the national interest' extends to these macroeconomic effects.

This classification of objectives is intended to bring some logical order to a confused scene, but it should be stressed that relative emphasis on them differs across countries, and within a given country at different times. Moreover, it is important to distinguish between the apparent importance of an objective, as suggested by the prominence it receives in official statements, and its actual importance in practical decision-taking. Thus in Italy, the main emphasis has been on avoiding making workers redundant and on creating employment in specific regions of the country, particularly the Mezzogiorno.[14] These would be classed as income distributional and macroeconomic policy objectives, and little attention appears to have been paid to economic efficiency or profitability. In the UK, on the other hand, a great deal of attention has been paid to the development of economically efficient criteria for public enterprise pricing and investment. At the present time, profitability is a major concern,[15] with a willingness to accept whatever consequences for price inflation, unemployment and income distribution that are implied by increasing the financial contributions of those industries which are profitable and reducing the burden of those which are not. At other times, for example in the early 1970s, public enterprise prices were held down in the presumed interests of counter-inflation policy, with considerable damage to profitability, i.e. the macroeconomic objective dominated. Moreover, although considerable prominence has been given to economic efficiency in official pronouncements, it does not appear that the criteria which implement this objective have been widely or systematically adopted, and certainly not 'enforced', among the public enterprises themselves.

It would therefore appear that the 'government' has multiple objectives of quite a complex kind. Let us consider some examples, taken from the UK experience, of how these objectives conflict with each other, in the sense that increased achievement of one may worsen that of another.

(1) *Economic efficiency and income distribution.* There are several instances in which efficiency has been sacrificed in the interests of increasing or maintaining incomes of particular groups. For example, the decision taken by the Macmillan government to divide a proposed new steel complex in two, locating one part at Ravenscraig in Scotland and the other at Llanwern in Wales, sacrificed economies of scale in the interests of increasing Scottish income. The various measures of support for the coal industry throughout the 1960s – including a tax on fuel oil and 'compulsory coalburn' by the electricity industry – raised energy costs in the UK economy generally, in the interests of slowing the rate of decline of the coal industry, and thus making the real incomes of coal-miners higher than they would otherwise have been. The persistence of over-manning in several public enterprises can be viewed as a tacit decision to distribute real income to particular groups of workers at the expense of economic efficiency.

(2) *Profitability and income distribution.* In general, reduced technological efficiency implies lower profitability, and so the foregoing examples are also relevant here. Some examples which do not appear to imply technological efficiency losses (but which may imply allocative efficiency losses) can also be given. The supply of public enterprise outputs to particular groups of consumers at prices below cost increases their real incomes but reduces profitability. For example, many rural and commuter rail services incur a loss, as does the air service to the Scottish Highlands and Islands. The overall nature of the income redistribution implied by such policies depends on the way in which the below-cost provision of services in financed. If an enterprise must meet an overall target surplus, and receives no government subsidy to compensate for loss of profitability on below-cost operations, its prices on profitable services must be correspondingly higher. Hence, real income is distributed away from consumers of profitable services, to those benefiting from services provided at a loss. If this 'cross-subsidization' exists to any large extent, it must be assumed that the minister accepts it as a form of income redistribution which is consistent with his government's policies. On the other hand, the losses may

be subsidized by an *actual* or *implicit* payment from the exchequer, in which case the income is redistributed away from taxpayers in general (or from those who would have benefited from forms of public expenditure which have had to be reduced to finance the subsidies) and towards those benefiting from the below-cost services. An *actual* payment is a sum credited to the accounts of the enterprise by the exchequer: the enterprise can be thought of as acting as a 'contractor' for the government, supplying the services and presenting two bills for their cost, one to the government and the other to the consumers. An *implicit* payment is made if the government reduces the target surplus which the enterprise is expected to achieve, by an amount corresponding to the loss it sustains on the services provided at the government's request. Clearly, in terms of the net contribution which the enterprise makes to the exchequer, it makes no difference *in principle* whether the subsidy is implicit or actual – the financial effects of providing the below-cost services are precisely the same. However, recalling the motivational aspect of the concern with profitability of a public enterprise, there may be in practice a difference in terms of the effects on motivation of managers, and of the ability to use profitability as a yardstick of performance.

(3) *Profitability and macroeconomic policies.* The pursuit of profitability may also conflict with macroeconomic policies, the most striking example being the use of public enterprise price and wage policies as instruments in a formal or informal prices and incomes policy. The policy of the government in 1972 and 1973, which involved resistance to trades-union wage demands at the cost of strikes, reduced the profitability of the coal and electricity industries in those years, because the losses incurred during the strikes were not made up by cost savings from wage settlements lower than would have been achieved without the strikes. Similarly, the policy of restricting price increases of public enterprise outputs throughout 1972 and 1973, at a time when costs were rising sharply, actually led to operating deficits for hitherto profitable enterprises. Constraints which have been placed on aircraft purchasing of the air corporations, forcing purchase of British aircraft when American aircraft would have been cheaper, provide an example of the conflict between profitability and balance-of-payments support.

(4) *Economic efficiency and profitability.* Although increases in *managerial and technological* efficiency will, other things being equal, increase profitability, so that no conflict exists in that respect, there may be a conflict between *allocative* efficiency and profitability. There is first the point that allocatively efficient pricing and investment policies will *imply* a particular surplus for the enterprise, which may be greater or less than that considered desirable. Turning the point around, if the

enterprise is required to earn a specific surplus, then there is nothing to guarantee that the implied prices and outputs will be allocatively efficient. A particular instance of this, much discussed in the literature, is the case where marginal cost pricing is allocatively efficient, and is applied in an industry subject to increasing returns to scale, thus leading to a loss. It may also occur, however, where there is thought to be a divergence between social costs and benefits on the one hand, and revenues and costs calculated at market prices on the other, so that optimization in terms of the former may lead to a loss. For example, it is argued that reductions in traffic congestion and consequent time savings to travellers justify loss-making public transport systems, because of the overall excess of social benefits over social costs.

(5) *Economic efficiency and macroeconomic policy.* The two most important examples of this type of policy conflict are provided by short-term cuts in public enterprise investment expenditure, and restraint of price increases. The first tend to be imposed when efforts are being made to contain total government expenditure, as for example in the late 1960s. The major problem is that by the nature of the investment programmes of public enterprises, a very high proportion of expenditure in the current and following year is committed to projects already in progress. Hence, significant cuts in expenditure for those years disrupts project planning, causes completion delays, and ultimately raises capital costs. Within a time horizon of at least two years, public enterprise investment is neither a cheap nor flexible instrument of short-term control of aggregate demand. The policy of public enterprise price restraint, which was applied, with varying degrees of stringency, from the late 1960s up to 1974, can be expected to distort the pattern of resource allocation. It implies falls in public enterprise prices relative to other prices in the economy, which have usually not been subject to similar controls. Thus, demands and outputs will tend to be higher than would otherwise be the case, implying that, at the margin, resources absorbed by public enterprises would have a greater value in other uses. Closely related is the fact that since public enterprise gross trading surpluses have been lower than they would have been in the absence of the policy, outputs such as health and education, which are also financed by public expenditure, may have been correspondingly smaller.

Given such conflicts between objectives, the only way in which decentralized decision-taking could take place is if a clear and consistent set of 'trade-offs' or relative weights were assigned by the minister and transmitted to the enterprise manager. We have already suggested that the type of political system in which public enterprise is typically embedded does not function like this. A further difficulty is that the implicit treatment of 'the government' as a single individual is itself an over-simplification. The 'government side' actually consists of a number of politicians and administrators with different priorities or emphases which they give to the various objectives. The balance of power may shift among members of this group, or its composition may change as a result of elections, political reshuffles, career changes, and so on. As a result the implicit weights given to the various objectives, which are the outcomes of some sort of bargaining process within the group, may change quite sharply over time. These implicit weights may in any case be kept deliberately vague, in order to minimize conflict within the group: the very attempt to make them explicit creates conflict.

What conclusions about the performance of public enterprise can we draw from this fairly lengthy discussion of their objectives? There appear to be three.

(1) Even assuming that clear, consistent and stable objectives were set for public enterprises, these objectives may quite well imply higher costs and lower profits than would follow from sole concern with economic efficiency. An enterprise could be performing satisfactorily in the broader sense, meeting its income-distributional and macroeconomic objectives, and yet be judged as performing poorly by the kinds of studies discussed in the previous section. In that case, such studies are really identifying the *opportunity cost*, in terms of economic efficiency, of setting the public enterprise other objectives. However, it is always open to the economist to push the argument one stage further, to suggest that lower cost methods of meeting these other objectives exist (for example income redistribution through the tax system) or that they are basically misconceived and ought not to be adopted. For example we might argue that to seek to develop national self-sufficiency in nuclear technology is essentially a misguided objective; or to use public enterprise prices as a means of trying to control price inflation is cost-ineffective and likely to fail. But clearly here the discussion must take place at a more fundamental level than that of public enterprise performance as such.

(2) Where 'wider' objectives than economic efficiency and profitability are pursued, they tend not to be stated in a clear, consistent and stable way, and so the necessary basis for efficient decentralized decision-taking does not exist. Judging by the experience in the British and Italian public enterprises, the consequence is poor performance even on the broader definition, associated with higher opportunity costs in terms of losses of economic efficiency and profitability, than would be the case under a stable system of objectives. This seems to be inherent in the nature of the political processes and the way public enterprises interact with them, rather than matters of

particular personalities, temporary aberrations, etc. To that extent we can regard this as a failing of public enterprise viewed broadly, as a system of political control of industrial activity.

(3) The objectives differ in the nature and extent of the political intervention they imply. As the theory set out in the rest of this book will suggest, the objectives of economic efficiency and profitability can be met within a decentralized framework of targets and pricing and investment criteria. *Some* types of income-distributional objective can be met in this way, e.g. the desire to moderate prices if a large proportion of output is bought by poor consumers. On the other hand, constant struggle between warring political factions to direct the flow of investment into areas which yield them political payoffs leads to the kind of intervention which is inconsistent with decentralization. In some circumstances, macroeconomic objectives might be capable of being expressed in a stable, consistent form to permit decentralization. If, however, macroeconomic policy itself is unstable, partly because of underlying difficulties in performance of the economy and partly because of fairly frequent changes of government and/or policy doctrine, then this instability will naturally be imported into the public enterprise sector and make decentralization impossible. This appears to have been very much the case in the UK over the period from the early 1960s to the present, and may explain the difference in experience of public enterprise there, to that in Austria, France, Germany and Sweden. It follows that unless there is the kind of stable macroeconomic performance and political consensus about income distribution which Van der Bellen (1981) shows has been the case in Austria, institutional change to permit decentralization can only succeed if it effectively reduces the set of objectives public enterprises are made to pursue. It is perhaps the implicit recognition of this which has caused the almost total rejection of institutional change by successive governments in the UK.[16]

2.3 Incentives and control

The preceding section sought to explain public enterprise performance in terms external to them, that is, in terms of the costs imposed by the nature of their objectives and the political intervention needed to implement them. We now consider a second explanation which may, at first sight, seem to contradict the first, but in fact is complementary with it. This is that the control and monitoring process of public enterprise is sufficiently weak that it allows interest groups within the public enterprise to pursue their own objectives, which tend to imply inefficiency and high costs. It may seem contradictory to argue that there is considerable political intervention in public enterprise policies yet weak control, but in fact one reinforces the other.

The main forms of control of public enterprise are evaluation by a government department of investment programmes and of specific large investment projects, before the expenditure is incurred; and monitoring of profitability which may, as in the UK, take the form of financial targets. In respect of monitoring of investment, government departments rarely have sufficient information to appraise the programmes in detail, and much of the information they do have is provided by the enterprise. So-called 'appraisal optimism' – the biasing upward of demand and revenue forecasts and biasing downward of costs – is recognized, by all parties, as a common feature of public enterprise investment programmes. The only possible corrective to such optimism – the tying of managerial rewards and punishments to realization of the projected returns to investment – is however absent.[17] There is no systematic retrospective comparison of forecasts with outcomes for investment projects and programmes and no sanction applied to management for obviously over-optimistic decision-taking. The way in which over-optimistic forecasting may show up is in failure to meet profit targets. But these tend to be only loosely related, if at all, to the forecasts underlying investment programmes, part of the reason being the difference in time-scale, which is short-term for profit targets and long-term for investment programmes. Moreover, the specific acts of intervention to secure the 'wider aims' of income distribution and macroeconomic policy, since they tend to increase costs and reduce profits, undermine the monitoring role of the targets. The intervention is used by the public enterprise management to explain failure to meet targets. *Qualitatively* this may be justified, but it will always be difficult to obtain sufficient information to isolate *quantitatively* the effect of the intervention on enterprise performance.[18] Thus there may be considerable slack in the constraints imposed by the control mechanism.

Recall that the type of public enterprise with which we are primarily concerned is that with some degree of monopoly power in at least some of its outputs, since one subject to effective private-sector competition is unlikely to pose problems.[19] Such enterprises then will generate rents, which could be distributed to consumers in the form of lower prices, higher quality, better service, and so on; which could be appropriated by government as revenue for the exchequer; or which could be absorbed by the two major interest groups within the enterprise, 'managers' and 'workers'. We could hypothesize that the basic motivations of managers and workers in public enterprises are no different to those in private enterprises. Managers will be interested in their salaries, perquisites, status, security, and the quietness of their lives. Workers prefer more income to less and less effort to more. There is an additional dimension on the labour side, however, which is too important to be ignored in public enterprise: the existence of trade unions, which conduct all negotiations on behalf of the workers. A trade union will to some extent reflect its members' preferences for higher wages and more leisure, but will also often be concerned with the size of its membership, or the total number of workers in the enterprise, partly because its political influence depends on this,[20] and partly also because of its influence on the salary, status and security of the leadership. In the UK, for example, a number of unions are entirely specific to a public enterprise: their membership consists of a subset of the workers in the enterprise, for example, the National Union of Railwaymen (NUR), the National Union of Mineworkers (NUM), and the Amalgamated Society of Locomotive Engineers and Footplatemen (ASLEF). Hence such unions will prefer a larger to a smaller workforce, and will be prepared to trade this off for wage increases.[21]

The question then arises: if the managers and workers together control the decision-variables of the enterprise – prices, wages, employment, investment – subject to constraints imposed externally by government, what will be the outcomes of these decisions given the above view of managers' and workers' motivations? Some formal analysis[22] makes a number of predictions, which seem to be borne out by casual observation and 'stylized facts'[23] about public enterprise:

(a) labour productivity will tend to be lower than is consistent with efficient production – there will be overmanning and excessively labour-intensive production;

(b) the profit constraint will be met by charging 'what the traffic will bear', i.e. profit mark-ups will be higher on outputs with less elastic demands;

(c) prices will be as low, and outputs as high, as is feasible, given the labour costs implied by the wage rates and employment levels 'won' by the union, and the capital and profit constraints imposed by government;

(d) 'tightening' the profit constraint will in general raise prices, reduce outputs, and reduce labour costs through lower wage rates and employment levels;

(e) 'tightening' the capital constraint will increase labour costs and overall production costs, raise prices and reduce outputs.

A number of other aspects of public enterprise decision-taking can be explored with this kind of model, but hopefully enough has been done to show the nature of the approach.[24]

2.4 The property rights explanation

In the previous two sections we have examined in some depth the explanation of public enterprise performance in terms first of all of their objectives and the way these are operationalized, and secondly of the interests of the effective decision-takers within an enterprise. It could be argued, however, that we have still not given a *fundamental* explanation of why a publicly owned enterprise might be expected to be less efficient than a privately owned enterprise undertaking the same activities. The answer must, trivially, be the form of ownership, since that is the only thing which differs, but what is it *precisely* about the nature of ownership which causes the difference? The answer suggested by the 'property rights' approach[25] to economic behaviour is the impossibility of transferring ownership rights among individuals in the public sector as compared to the relative ease of such transactions with private assets. In other words, we have a point familiar from the literature on the 'theory of the firm'[26]: shareholders may express their dissatisfaction with the flow of benefits they receive from a private enterprise by selling their shares, thus affecting the market value of the company and placing a constraint on managers. The owners of public enterprises – the taxpayers – cannot transfer their 'shares' in them. The political mechanism is relatively unresponsive to the wishes of taxpayers (and consumers in general) and cannot provide an effective substitute, in ensuring that a public enterprise will act in the interests of its (ultimate) owners.

It should be noted that the difference is one of degree and not kind. The 'market in corporate control' may not function perfectly, and private shareholders in large companies may find it costly and difficult to monitor managers and ensure that decisions are entirely in their interests. Moreover, there is competition between political parties for taxpayers' support, which may make the control of public enterprise to some extent responsive to their interests. Nevertheless the degree of difference in the extent to which each form of enterprise acts in its owners' interests is likely to be large.

It does not follow from this that the solution to the problem is necessarily to restore a public enterprise to private ownership. Although it may then operate more in accordance with its owners' interests, this need not represent an improvement in welfare overall. For example, to take a natural monopoly and restore it to private ownership will, if it acts fully in accordance with its new owners' interests, lead it to maximize profit by restricting output and raising price: the market failure follows from its pursuit of its owners' interests. The 'property rights explanation' therefore should be regarded as giving an interesting slant on the reason for 'public enterprise failure' rather than a prescription for restoring private enterprise.

2.5 Conclusions
The evidence appears to suggest that public enterprises tend to be less economically efficient and less profitable than comparable private enterprises. Where comparable private enterprises do not exist, detailed studies of the economic performance of public enterprises, in the UK and Italy at least, suggest that economic performance

on the whole had been poor. This experience is not, however, universal. Austria, Germany and France provide examples of successful and efficient public enterprise.

We considered two main explanations of public enterprise performance. The first was in terms of the objectives which are set for them, and suggested that, since they typically extend beyond economic efficiency and profitability, an enterprise could be performing well, in the sense of meeting its full set of objectives, but could appear to be performing poorly on the narrower criteria of costs and profitability, because of the trade-offs among objectives. However, in the UK and Italy particularly, the precise way in which these objectives have been applied has caused poor performance overall. The second explanation was in terms of the scope provided by the control system for managers and workers in public enterprise to pursue their own interests, which will in general imply less than optimal efficiency, among other things. These two sets of explanations complement each other, and it is for further empirical work to try to evaluate their validity and relevance.

Finally, we would make the point that to take the theory and evidence on public enterprise performance as an argument for replacing public by private enterprise – denationalization or privatization – may be to commit the 'Nirvaana Fallacy' in reverse. Although there may be 'government failure', this does not necessarily imply that the market will do better. We still need a comparative institutional analysis for each given situation, and the result will depend partly on the possibilities of effective competition following privatization and partly, as the Austrian experience suggests, on the possibility of correcting the 'government failure' by improving the framework within which public enterprise operates.

Chapter 3

Welfare economics and public enterprise policy

3.1 Welfare economics

Most of what economists have written about public enterprise pricing and investment policies has been concerned with allocative efficiency, and so can be regarded as an application of welfare economics. In this chapter, we examine some basic propositions of welfare economics, and consider their main implications for public enterprise policies. Of course, no attempt will be made to provide a complete exposition: we shall simply set out as clearly as possible those propositions relevant to our purposes.

We can best begin with a definition due to Dr E. J. Mishan:[1] welfare economics is that branch of study which tries to formulate propositions by which we may *rank on a scale of better or worse*, *alternative situations* open to the *economy*. The key words in the definition are italicized, and we shall expand upon the definition by interpreting them.

The choice of a *scale of better or worse* requires a set of ethical or value judgements, which are necessarily subjective. In trying to formulate propositions which will be applicable *in general*, economists have tended to adopt a set of value judgements which appear to be mild and generally acceptable. We call these the *Paretian* value judgements.[2] They take the following form:

(1) Individuals are held to be the best judges of their own welfare, so that we accept that a person is better off in situation *A* than in situation *B* if he prefers *A* to *B*.

(2) Situation *A* is better than situation *B*, if at least one individual in the economy is better off at *A* than at *B*, and no one is worse off.

The property of the first value judgement is that it avoids paternalism, while that of the second is that it avoids the need to make *interpersonal comparisons*, i.e. to evaluate against each other the well-being of different individuals. These properties confer a particular kind of generality on the propositions which can be derived from the value judgements, since to incorporate specific paternalistic judgements and interpersonal comparisons into the analysis would limit its scope. This generality is, however, bought at a cost: if, in situation A, some individuals are worse off, while others are better off, than in situation B, we cannot say whether A is better or worse than B. A and B are in this case *non-comparable*, and so the ranking of 'alternative situations' may be incomplete.

A criticism which could be levelled at the Paretian value judgements is that although they may be general in a logical sense, they do not describe the kinds of value judgements which are in fact generally held, particularly by policy-makers. The most important difference is that people generally do have ethical or political views which lead them to make interpersonal comparisons. These may be based on a comparison of the intensities or magnitudes of gains and losses, or on some views about the individuals or groups who deserve to gain or lose, related to the levels of welfare they already enjoy. For example, given some initial state of the economy, B, suppose that we generate a new state, A, by taxing the very rich and giving the proceeds to the very poor. Many people would say that A is better than B, perhaps because they think the gain in well-being to the poor exceeds the loss to the rich, or because in any case they think the poor more deserving than the rich, since they are absolutely worse off. On Paretian grounds, on the other hand, A is neither better nor worse than B: they are not comparable.

Although accepting the validity of this criticism, we find it most useful to proceed *initially* on the basis of the Paretian value judgements; we shall, however, subsequently give careful attention to the consequences of assuming that a policy-maker does make explicit interpersonal comparisons.

The *alternative situations* referred to in the definition depend on the problem under study. Most generally, we take the 'alternative situations' to be the entire resource allocations available to the economy, where a resource allocation can be thought of as a set of quantities of goods consumed and inputs supplied by all households, and goods produced and inputs used by all firms. However, in specific contexts, we may define the alternatives quite narrowly: for example, cost-benefit analysis is usually concerned with applying welfare propositions to situations with and without some specific investment project. In this book, the alternative situations consist generally of different levels of outputs, prices, inputs, and investment of public enterprises. The propositions we shall develop are designed to answer such questions as: How should the energy market be divided among coal, gas, electricity and oil? Should the price of rail transport be higher or lower in peak hours than at other times of day? Should public enterprises be allowed to undertake investments with lower rates of return than would be acceptable in the private sector? What is the appropriate size of labour force for the steel industry? Often, we shall analyse such questions at the level of the individual enterprise, but sometimes more general, and hence more complex, models will have to be constructed.

The word *economy* does not require a definition, but it is italicized in order to stress the following: the propositions we derive are not *initially* about some real-world economy 'out there', with its actual prices, outputs, buyers and sellers. Analysis can only take place in terms of a *model* of the economy, i.e. an abstract system of variables and relationships which, it is hypothesized, capture certain elements of the real economy. In formulating a model, we necessarily have to make simplifications and abstractions, which render tractable the complex reality. It follows that different models may be good or bad representations of reality. Propositions are first formulated in the context of some model of the economy. If we then apply a proposition to the real economy, we would have more confidence in its correctness, the better the representation of reality its associated model appears to be.[3] Thus, we can distinguish between the *validity* and the relevance of a proposition.

A proposition is *valid* if it is correctly deduced, without logical error, from its premises. A proposition is *relevant* if it is not only valid, but also likely to be helpful and correct in its application to reality. This point is worth making because, as we shall see, much of the theoretical discussion in public enterprise economics has centred on the validity of propositions whose relevance was small, which was in turn due to the fact that they were derived from a model of the economy which is a poor approximation to reality. For example, the following two propositions are valid but may not be relevant to all circumstances:

(a) allocative efficiency is achieved (in a *first-best* model of the economy) if prices are equated to marginal costs; and
(b) allocative efficiency is achieved (in a first-best model of the economy) if public-sector investments are discounted at a rate equal to the marginal rate of return in the private sector.

These propositions have been much debated in the literature. The debate often tended to confuse their validity with their relevance. The critical phrase is the one in parentheses: its presence establishes both the validity and the limited relevance of the propositions. The fact that it is usually omitted from statements of these propositions has been responsible for much fruitless debate. We now consider what exactly is meant by a first-best economy.

3.2 The first-best economy
The inelegant term 'first-best' is chosen to contrast with the concept of the 'second-best'. A first-best economy is defined as follows:

(1) There is a given population of individuals, with given tastes, which do not change.[4]

(2) Time is divided into equal discrete periods, indexed $t = 0, 1, 2, \ldots$, where $t = 0$ is the present. Within each time-period, production and exchange take place, exchange being organized through a system of markets. This establishes a complete resource allocation, and a system of relative prices,[5] within each period.

(3) In addition to the markets for goods and services, a capital market is held at each period, in which are exchanged dated claims to future wealth called *bonds*. Borrowing is the act of selling bonds; to lend is to buy bonds. The price in the capital market is expressed in terms of an interest rate r: a claim to one unit of wealth today exchanges for a claim to $1 + r$ units in one period's time.

(4) All markets, including the capital market, are perfectly competitive.

(5) At any point in time, all economic agents (consumers and firms) know the prices which will be established on markets at all future dates.[6] Consumers know their tastes over all future consumptions, and the endowments of goods and services they will have in each future period. Firms know with certainty all future technological possibilities.

(6) There are no external effects in any period, i.e. there are no direct interdependences external to the price mechanism between economic agents.

In this first-best economy, consumers can at $t = 0$ draw up a plan specifying their net consumptions of every good in every time-period, and their borrowing or lending (bond sale or purchase) in each period. Firms can draw up a plan specifying net productions, investment, and finance in every time-period. Because of assumption 5, all such plans are consistent, in the sense that planned demands for any one good equal planned supplies for any one good at the price which everyone expects to prevail.

A rather simpler version of the model is obtained if we take only $t = 0$, and ignore all subsequent time-periods. We could then analyse the price system and resource allocation on the basis only of assumptions 1, 4 and 6. Such an *atemporal* model would be useful for certain purposes, particularly for deriving some 'short-run' welfare propositions, and for examining in the simplest context the consequences of relaxing the assumptions of perfect markets and no externalities. If we wanted to say anything about investment and 'long-run' pricing problems, however, we would have to consider more than one time-period, and this in turn requires assumptions to be made about the structure of the capital market, and about knowledge of future prices, tastes and technology.

The first-best economy is obviously a highly abstract model of the real economy. However, it has, in one form or another, been the basic model of microeconomic analysis. Here, we are concerned with the welfare propositions derived from this model.

3.3   Some welfare propositions

Recall the Paretian value judgements, which hold one 'situation' to be better than another if at least one person regards himself as better off, in terms of his own preferences, and no one regards himself as worse off. Let us define 'situation' as a resource allocation in the first-best economy. Suppose, given some initial resource allocation B, it is possible to find another allocation A at which someone is made better off and no one worse off. Then A is called *Pareto preferred* to B. Suppose we make the change to A, and then find that there is no other resource allocation which is Pareto-preferred to A; in other words, we cannot find a way to make someone better off and no one worse off, by moving to another attainable resource allocation. Then, A is called a *Pareto-optimal* resource allocation, since, according to the Paretian value judgements, we have achieved the best resource allocation we can. The following propositions[8] can be shown to be valid:

(I) In a first-best economy, a market equilibrium resource allocation is always also a Pareto-optimal resource allocation.

(II) Any resource allocation which is Pareto optimal can be attained as a market equilibrium resource allocation by choosing an appropriate initial distribution of wealth.

A diagram will help illustrate these propositions. Suppose there are only two individuals[9] in the economy. Let the well-being or *utility* which the first receives from any given resource allocation be denoted by u_1, and that received by the second by u_2. Then, values[10] u_1 and u_2 can be plotted along the axes of Figure 3.1, as shown, so that any point within the axes represents a pair of values $(u_1 u_2)$.

The line $F_1 F_2$ in the figure has the following interpretation: given the resources which are available to the first-best economy, it shows, for any given value of u_1, the greatest value of u_2 which can be achieved. To find any one point on the line, set u_1 equal to some value, say u_1^0, then choose that resource allocation which maximizes u_2 out of the set of all resource allocations which generates u_1^0, and finally find that value of u_2 implied by this resource allocation. The whole line is obtained by repeating this procedure for all values of u_1 in the interval $[OF_1]$. The line will be called the *utility possibility frontier*, since it shows the 'outermost' values of utilities which can be obtained in this economy. It can be shown, using 'standard' assumptions, that the frontier *must* have a negative slope: in moving along it, we can

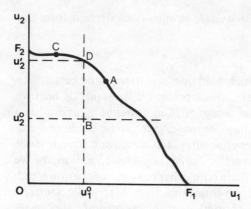

Figure 3.1

only make one individual better off by making the other worse off. Also, using these same assumptions, it can be shown that each point on or below the line corresponds to one and only one resource allocation, so that although strictly speaking such points are pairs of numbers $(u_1 u_2)$, we will often refer to them as 'resource allocations'.

We first can show that the set of points on the line $F_1 F_2$ correspond to Pareto-optimal resource allocations, while the set of points below the line correspond to Pareto non-optimal allocations (the points above the line are of course unattainable). Thus, consider point B in the figure. This cannot be Pareto optimal since, holding u_1 at u_1^0, we can, by changing the resource allocation, increase u_2 from u_2^0 to u_2'. Thus, we make the second individual better off and the first no worse off. Alternatively, we could make them *both* better off by changing the resource allocation so as to move to some point north-east of B, such as A. This clearly holds for all points below the line $F_1 F_2$. Therefore, no such point can be Pareto optimal. However, given any point on the line, such as D, no other point is attainable at which one individual is made better and the other no worse off. Changes can only be made which make both worse off, or one better off at the other's expense. Since this is true of *all* points on the line $F_1 F_2$ they all correspond to Pareto-optimal resource allocations.

Propositions I and II above can now be expressed in terms of Figure 3.1 as follows: in a first-best economy, an equilibrium resource allocation corresponds to a point on the line $F_1 F_2$, such as A, D or C; while any point on the line can be attained as an equilibrium resource allocation given an appropriate initial distribution of wealth. Thus the line $F_1 F_2$ corresponds to *both* the set of Pareto-optimal allocations *and* the set of possible market-equilibrium resource allocations.

Since our main concern is with questions of economic policy, we can now derive some policy implications from these propositions. The first of these is as follows: if a policy-maker in a first-best economy holds the Paretian value judgements and is content to achieve any Pareto-optimal resource allocation, then his best policy is simply to leave the market mechanism entirely alone – he is in fact redundant. The reason is of course that left to itself the market mechanism will produce an equilibrium which is a Pareto optimum.

Suppose, however, that included among the firms in the economy are some which are public enterprises.[11] The policy-maker will have to formulate specific policies to determine their pricing and investment decisions. What should these be? First we note the following: in order to be Pareto optimal, a resource allocation must satisfy certain necessary conditions.[12] The necessary conditions will be satisfied in a market economy if the following conditions are in turn satisfied:

(a) all consumers and firms face the same price for each good, borrow or lend at the same interest rate, and always act as price-takers; and

(b) all firms set output levels so as to equate marginal cost to market price (which is the same for all producers of the same good), and set input levels so as to equate the marginal value product to price.

In a first-best economy without public enterprises, these conditions are satisfied. They will be satisfied in a first-best economy *with* public enterprises if the policy-maker instructs the enterprises to adopt rule (b): they should adopt marginal cost pricing policies and employ inputs, including capital goods, up to the point at which their marginal value products equal market price.[13] In this way, given that the necessary conditions are also *sufficient*, a Pareto-optimal resource allocation on the boundary of $F_1 F_2$ will be achieved.

We can note here an important point. Suppose that 'initially', i.e. before he has received the advice of his economists, the policy-maker has instructed public enterprises simply to 'break even', which implies that they would equate prices to average costs. Assuming non-constant returns to scale, it can be shown[14] that the necessary conditions for a Pareto optimum are then violated, which in turn implies that the economy will be at some point such as B in Figure 3.1. Hence, his economists will advise the policy-maker that he can make everyone in the economy better off by instructing the public enterprises to adopt the new rules of marginal cost pricing and net present value maximization. If they were to do so, we would get a change in resource allocation, with prices rising in diminishing returns industries, and falling in increasing returns industries, and with corresponding changes in investment expenditures. *There is no guarantee, however, that the economy will thereby move* from B to A or D. All we know is that once the necessary conditions are satisfied, the economy will be at some point on $F_1 F_2$ (assuming those conditions are also sufficient). The economy could very well have moved in fact to *C*, at which someone is worse off and someone is better off. It follows in this case that the decision *to implement* the pricing and investment rules can not be justified on Paretian grounds, since *B* and *C* are non-comparable on the Paretian value judgements. It is important to make the distinction between *being* at a resource allocation which satisfies the necessary conditions, and *having to move* from a resource allocation at which the conditions are not satisfied, to one at which they are. In the latter case, a specific move which follows from implementation of the rules may not be justified on Paretian grounds; rather, the valid proposition is that given the initial allocation, there exists *some* way of changing the allocation which makes everyone better off. However, more may be involved in this change than a simple instruction to implement certain general rules which are known to hold at an optimum. This important question of the *transition* to an optimum will be considered further below. There we will show how the apparent paradox – that a move to a Pareto-optimal resource allocation may not be justifiable on Paretian grounds – can be resolved.

To return to the basic policy implications: we have so far asserted and illustrated the validity of the propositions on which they are based; what now of their relevance? The propositions follow from the premises first, that the policy-maker is a Paretian, and second, that the economy is first-best. The realism of these premises determines the relevance of the propositions. Let us examine them in turn.

3.4   The distribution of welfare

The policy-maker is likely to have specific value judgements which lead him to make interpersonal comparisons of utility. To put this another way, he will be prepared to compare situations in which some individuals lose and some gain, and the basis of his comparison will be ethical or political views he holds about who *should* lose and who should gain. However, given that these views meet a certain fairly plausible condition, this observation does not lead to a rejection of our earlier Paretian analysis, but rather to an extension of it. This condition takes the following form: an increase in any one individual's utility, all other individuals' utilities remaining unchanged, must always be regarded by the policy-maker as a good thing. Note that satisfaction of this condition does not rule out the possibility that the policy-maker would be prepared to make someone worse off *in order to* make someone else better off (soak the rich to help the poor); but it does rule out the possibility that he would want to make someone worse off *for its own sake*, with no corresponding improvement for anyone else. The condition is obviously satisfied if the policy-maker is a Paretian, but we assume it also to be satisfied by the value judgements of a policy-maker who is prepared to make interpersonal comparisons, and consequently explicit choices of who should gain and who should lose. We immediately can draw an important conclusion: an optimal (from the point of view of the policy-maker's value judgements) resource allocation must still correspond to a point on the line F_1F_2 in Figure 3.1, and so must still satisfy the necessary conditions for a Pareto optimum. To see this, we note that our policy-maker will always approve of a move which makes at least one individual better off and none worse off, just as if he were Paretian, and so he would always favour a move from any point below the line, such as B in Figure 3.1, to an *appropriately chosen* point on the line, such as D or A. We can now say something more. Because of his readiness to make explicit interpersonal comparisons, the policy-maker is able to rank resource allocations which a Paretian would find non-comparable; in particular he is able to choose among different points on the line F_1F_2, and identify that or those he prefers. Thus, the policy-maker might *reject* the move from B to C on the grounds that he prefers the utility pair at B to that at C. He would *accept* the move from B to D, but he might well *prefer* the move from B to A on the grounds that it produces a 'better' distribution of utilities between the two individuals.

What are the policy implications of this analysis? The answer hinges upon the assumption we make about the means available to the policy-maker for bringing about redistribution of wealth and therefore utility. The crucial question is whether or not he can make *lump-sum redistributions of wealth* to any required extent. A lump-sum redistribution consists of a set of payments to some individuals, financed by taxes on others, where these payments and taxes are not regarded by households and firms as being affected by any decisions they may take. This rules out income-related taxes and payments, as well as indirect taxes and subsidies, since these affect the prices which households and firms face on markets, and cause them to adjust accordingly. An example of a lump-sum tax would be a tax on pure economic rent, earned by a good or service in perfectly inelastic supply, while a lump-sum payment would simply be an outright gift to specified individuals, where the gift must not depend on some activity within the individuals' control. The important feature of lump-sum redistribution consists of a set of payments to some individuals, financed conditions for a Pareto optimum. In the case of taxes on incomes or outputs, the price a buyer pays will differ from the price a seller receives, and so the Pareto-optimum conditions will not be fulfilled.

Let us suppose, therefore, that by lump-sum redistribution the policy-maker can achieve any desired distribution of wealth. In addition, recall that the resource allocation which he regards as optimal will be in the set of Pareto-optimal allocations. We can then apply proposition II given earlier, which stated that any Pareto-optimal allocation can be attained as a market equilibrium, given a choice of the appropriate wealth distribution. The planner can allow the market mechanism to determine an allocation of resources, while he uses a system of lump-sum redistribution to bring about the distribution of utilities he prefers. This can be explained in terms of Figure 3.1 as follows: suppose the market mechanism initially establishes a resource allocation corresponding to point C. The policy-maker finds this outcome unattractive, and so redistributes wealth in a lump-sum way, away from individual 2 and towards individual 1. This will, of course, cause a change in the pattern of market demands and supplies and so a change in resource allocation. But, given that the market determines the new equilibrium, this must be on the line $F_1 F_2$ to the right of point C. By a sequence of such redistributions, the policy-maker could arrive at his preferred utility distribution. We conclude that in a first-best economy, if lump-sum redistribution is possible, then even when the policy-maker has explicit views about the distribution of welfare, the market mechanism is allowed to operate with only minimal intervention in the form of lump-sum redistribution.

We can immediately draw a similar conclusion for the case in which some firms in the economy are public enterprises: by introducing the marginal cost pricing and net present value maximization rules, the policy-maker ensures that a Pareto optimum is achieved. He then achieves his preferred welfare distribution by lump-sum redistribution. This also allows us to resolve the paradox suggested earlier to the effect that a move from a Pareto-non-optimal to a Pareto-optimal resource allocation may not be justifiable on Paretian grounds. Thus, suppose as before that the implementation of the rules moves the economy from point B to point C in Figure 3.1. The policy-maker may prefer B to C, but by lump-sum redistribution he is able to move to point A, which he prefers to both. Hence, *if it can always be accompanied by appropriate lump-sum redistribution*, introducing the first-best pricing and investment rules will always be an optimal policy.

3.5   The second best
When we review the assumptions which define the first-best economy, it is clear that they abstract from important features of the real world. It is the unrealism of the first-best economy which leads us *a priori* to doubt the relevance of the propositions on policy derived so far. There is a need for further analysis to establish the extent to which the propositions so far derived retain their optimality properties in more realistic models of the economy. This analysis should also suggest how, if at all, we may extend these propositions so as to give them a higher degree of relevance. The term 'second-best' is applied to an economy in which at least one of the assumptions defining the first-best economy is violated. The result of this violation is to invalidate proposition I given above: the market mechanism will not in general achieve a Pareto-optimal resource allocation, implying that given the technological possi-

bilities and resource availabilities in the economy it would be possible to make some people better off and no one worse off than in the market allocation. Since the policy propositions so far derived depend heavily on proposition I, we would expect significant differences in economic policy in a second-best economy. We now go on to consider these differences, particularly as they relate to public enterprises.

To begin with, let us consider the divergences between the first-best model and reality. The most important of these are: market imperfections arising from monopoly and oligopoly; widespread external effects; and uncertainty, in that all economic agents must take current decisions in the light of incomplete information about future prices, tastes and technology.[15] A somewhat separate but closely related set of issues concerns the policy-makers' involvement in the economy. State economic activity does not consist only of wealth redistribution. The state provides public goods, such as defence and 'law and order'. In financing the provision of such goods, and also in pursuing its policies towards wealth redistribution, the government imposes taxes and pays subsidies which are *not* lump-sum. It does not appear to be feasible to design a system of lump-sum taxes and subsidies on the scale required to meet the government's redistributive policies and needs for finance. The income and output taxes which are in fact used, in themselves lead to violations of the conditions for a first-best optimum. As a result, the separation between the achievement of an optimum resource allocation by the market mechanism and of a desired distribution of welfare by wealth redistribution breaks down. There is now an interdependence between the redistribution policies and the necessary conditions for an optimum, in the sense that the latter cannot be defined independently of the policy-maker's preferences over alternative distributions of welfare.

Thus we have the problem of deriving propositions which can form the basis for economic policy in a second-best economy. In chapters 6 to 10 below, we carry out some detailed analyses aimed at solving this problem. To illustrate the general nature of the analysis of the second best, we consider here a simple model of an economy which contains a number of monopolies. As a mnemonic, we call it the M-economy. The purpose of the following discussion is to bring out certain important general features of second-best problems, which should not be lost sight of in the later, more detailed analysis, easy though it is to do so.

The M-economy

Suppose that the policy-maker in this economy is able to identify the set of *first-best* Pareto-optimal resource allocations,[16] and that these correspond to the line F_1F_2 in Figure 3.2. We would generate this line essentially in the same way as before. Taking as constraints *only* the technological possibilities and resource availabilities in the economy and ignoring its institutional structure (in particular that some firms are monopolies), we could find the resource allocations which maximized u_2 for each given value of u_1 in the interval $[OF_1]$. As proposition I previously stated, a *first-best* economy would achieve a market equilibrium resource allocation on the line F_1F_2. However, the M-economy contains 'deviant sectors', in the form of profit-maximizing monopolies, and the result is that the necessary conditions for a first-best Pareto-optimal resource allocation are not satisfied. Hence, the economy is at some point below F_1F_2, such as M in the figure. Can a policy be devised which will improve the situation? The answer depends crucially on the assumption we make about the *policy instruments* open to the policy-maker. Two cases can be distinguished:

(a) The policy-maker is able to influence directly the price-output decisions of the monopolists. Then, in this case, it is possible to define a subsidy policy, or a policy of price regulation, which will actually lead the economy to achieve a *first-best* Pareto optimum, and hence a resource allocation on the line F_1F_2 in Figure 3.2. In this case, it can also be shown that the first-best rules for public enterprise pricing and investment are *still valid*. The direct correction of the behaviour of the deviants means that the rest of the economy can be treated as if the M-economy were in fact first best. This can be illustrated with a simple model. In Figure 3.3(a) and (b) we

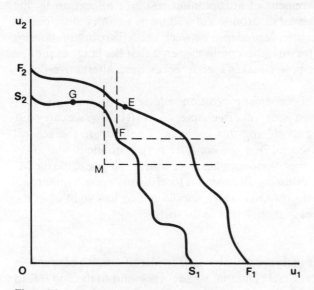

Figure 3.2

show demand, marginal revenue, and marginal cost curves of two private-sector industries, and in Figure 3.3(c) we show the demand and marginal cost curves of a public enterprise. Suppose that initially the economy is the first-best equilibrium, with prices (p_1^0, p_2^0, p_3^0), and outputs (q_1^0, q_2^0, q_3^0). Now suppose that industries 1 and 2 become monopolized, with no change in marginal costs. To maximize profits, the monopolists raise price to p_1^* and p_2^*, respectively, and outputs correspondingly fall to q_1^* and q_2^*. For simplicity, we assume that cross-elasticities of demand between the first two industries' outputs are zero, so the price increases have no effects on the positions of the first two demand curves. Suppose, however, that both goods are substitutes for good 3, the public enterprise output. Then, the increase in p_1 and p_2 will cause increased demand for good 3, so that the demand curve shifts upward, say to D_3'. If the public enterprise continues to set price equal to marginal cost, its output will be q_3^*. Assuming continued full employment in the economy, the effect of the monopolization has been to release from the first two industries the resources which were required to produce outputs $(q_1^0 - q_1^*)$, and $(q_2^0 - q_2^*)$, respectively, and these are then absorbed into industry 3 to produce the output increase $(q_3^* - q_3^0)$. The resulting set of outputs (q_1^*, q_2^*, q_3^*) and the associated resource allocation is not Pareto optimal; it corresponds to a point such as M in Figure 3.2. The reason is, of course, that price ratios are unequal to marginal cost ratios, and, in particular

$$\frac{p_1^*}{p_3^0} > \frac{MC_1}{MC_3} \quad \text{and} \quad \frac{p_2^*}{p_3^0} > \frac{MC_2}{MC_3}. \tag{3.1}$$

We know, therefore, that it is possible to make everyone better off in this economy by reallocating resources out of industry 3 and into industries 1 and 2. One way of putting this is to say that consumers of goods 1 and 2 would be prepared to bribe consumers of good 3 to release resources: the former consumers could fully compensate the latter for their loss of consumption, and still have a gain in utility. The market mechanism fails to organize such exchanges, however, because of the intervention of the monopolists who control industries 1 and 2. This is the situation which confronts the policy-maker in the M-economy. Since we assume that he can act directly on the monopolies, we have the result that by a suitable choice of policy he can attain a first-best resource allocation. Thus, suppose the policy-maker can enforce on the monopolists a marginal cost pricing policy. Their prices fall to p_1^0 and p_2^0, respectively, demand for good 3 falls to D_3, and the initial first-best situation is reattained. In effect, we have an economy consisting of two regulated monopolies and a public enterprise, with marginal cost pricing as the optimal policy for each of them. An alternative policy to regulation would be the subsidization of consumption of goods 1 and 2 by just enough to make the price which consumers pay

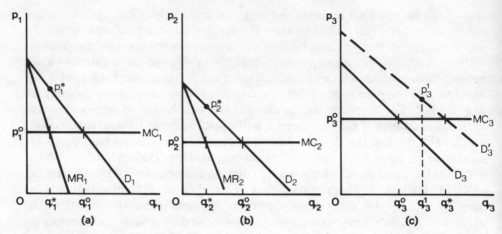

Figure 3.3

(= market price *minus* subsidy) equal to marginal cost in each industry. This again would cause increases in demand for goods 1 and 2, a reduction of demand for good 3, and a reallocation of resources in the desired direction. With the appropriately chosen subsidies, a resource allocation which satisfies first-best Pareto-optimality conditions would be achieved, and so once again marginal cost pricing would be appropriate for the public enterprise. Note that the two policies described here have the effect of moving the economy from a point such as M in Figure 3.2 to (probably different) points on $F_1 F_2$. These movements will involve changes in the distribution of welfare as compared to point M. Therefore, the comments made earlier in relation to the *transition* to a point on $F_1 F_2$ still apply. Such a transition can only be justified on Paretian grounds if it represents a move to a point north-east of M, such as E in Figure 3.2; on the other hand, if lump-sum redistributions are possible, some way can always be found of making a transition which makes everyone better off.

(b) Suppose now that the policy-maker in the M-economy cannot influence the price-output decisions of the monopolies directly, but can *only* do so through the policies of the public enterprises under his control. Thus, the pricing policies of the enterprises are the *only available instruments* of second-best policy. He will want to choose these policies in such a way as to achieve a Pareto optimum, but *subject to the constraint* that the monopolists are free to determine their own behaviour. A detailed analysis of this problem is given in chapter 6. Here we note and illustrate two important results:

(i) For any one public enterprise, the second-best Pareto-optimal pricing rules will differ from the first-best (marginal cost pricing) rule, *except* in the case where changes in its prices do not affect the price-output policy of any monopolist.[17]

(ii) The Pareto-optimal second-best resource allocation will be inferior to first-best resource allocations, and hence the policy of indirectly influencing monopolies through public enterprise policies is inferior to that of direct regulation of monopolies. Thus, in Figure 3.2, let the line $S_1 S_2$ correspond to the set of resource allocations which can be achieved by an *indirect* policy. It is possible to make everyone better off, moving from point M to a point such as F on $S_1 S_2$, by adopting the appropriate second-best public enterprise policy. It would be possible to do better still, however, for example achieving the move to E, if a *direct* policy of regulation could be adopted.

Propositions (i) and (ii) can be further illustrated by Figure 3.3. Given the resource allocation with prices (p_1^*, p_2^*, p_3^*) and outputs (q_1^*, q_2^*, q_3^*), the planner is aware that welfare gains can be made by reallocating resources from industry 3 to industries 1 and 2. Since he is constrained to act only on good 3, he can instruct the public enterprise to raise its price, say to p_3^1. This will cause demand to fall along D_3' to q_3^1. Since goods 1 and 2 are substitutes for 3, their demands will increase, and resources will be diverted into their production. The problem of determining the final optimal position in the three industries is quite a complex one and will be analysed further in chapter 6: it cannot be usefully handled with Figure 3.3. However, the figure should give the flavour of the result: by varying the price of good 3, the planner is able to cause demand variations and price changes (as the monopolists adjust their profit-maximizing positions to the changes in demands) in the other markets, until finally a resource allocation is achieved, such that no consumer can be made better off without making another worse off, *given* the policy instrument (public enterprise price) available to the policy-makers. This, then, is the second-best Pareto optimum.

3.6 Conclusions

In this chapter we have examined the welfare economics foundations of public enterprise pricing and investment policies. Assuming a Paretian policy-maker, and a first-best economy, we have the proposition that optimal rules for a public enterprise involve marginal cost pricing and net present value maximization, using as discount rate the market interest rate. Where a policy-maker is prepared to make explicit interpersonal comparisons of welfare, these rules are still applicable, *provided that* his value judgements satisfy the 'Paretian condition', *and* that lump-sum wealth redistribution is possible. When we allow the existence of monopolies, we find that the set of first-best Pareto optimal resource allocations is in principle still attainable, if the policy-maker is able to adopt appropriate policies. These involve direct intervention in monopolized markets, or subsidies, to ensure that prices equal marginal costs. If these policies are adopted, then public enterprises can be treated *as if* they were part of a first-best economy, and therefore the rules already described apply. If the possibility of such policies exists, then the economy is in a sense only *weakly* second best: the market system alone would not achieve a first-best optimum, but the system, reinforced with the appropriate corrective policies, could. A *strictly* second-best situation arises when there exist constraints on the set of policy instruments the planner may use, which preclude or inhibit direct intervention in monopolized markets. In that case, we can speak of 'uncorrected' sectors of the economy. The problem is to define optimal public enterprise policies given such uncorrected sectors. The first conclusion is that the optimal second-best policy for a public enterprise is the same as in the first-best, if price and output decisions for the public enterprise do not affect the equilibrium position of *any* decision-taker in an uncorrected sector. If this condition is not met, then in general the second-best policy will differ from the first-best, so that marginal cost pricing rules are inapplicable. Also, in general, the welfare position reached by the optimal second-best policies will be inferior to those of the first-best. An obvious question therefore concerns the constraints on policy instruments: why is it the case that public enterprise policies are taken to be the only policy instruments in the second-best economy? This question is taken up in chapter 6, where, after the analysis of the intervening chapters, we shall be in a better position to answer it. We note here only the general point: the strictly second-best situation arises out of the constraint on policy instruments, and, in analysing second-best problems, it is essential to specify the policy instruments which we take to be available.[18]

Chapter 4

Marginal cost pricing and partial equilibrium

The discussion in the previous chapter took place mainly at the level of the entire economy, that is, at the general equilibrium level. It was concerned with the relation between some general propositions of welfare economics, developed essentially for entire resource allocations, and public enterprise pricing and investment policies. However, when we come to consider the implementation of optimal policies, the general equilibrium level of analysis is rather *too* general and abstract. We encounter problems concerned with the particular features of products, technology and demand, which are much more fruitfully handled at the partial equilibrium level, the level of the individual enterprise or market. In chapter 5 we shall examine in a partial equilibrium context some problems which arise when the attempt is made to apply marginal cost principles to the pricing policies of public enterprises. First, however, it will be useful to clarify the meaning of marginal cost pricing, within the neat and simple framework of the standard textbook analysis.

In the light of the remarks in the previous chapter it may seem surprising that we should now be concerned with marginal cost pricing, since in general this rule may not be applicable in a strictly second-best economy, which is what we take the real economy to be. However, there are two strong arguments for examining the attempts to apply marginal cost pricing: the first is that it constitutes much of the core of what is currently 'public enterprise economics', and it is worthwhile to know this core before one tries to extend it; the second is that although second-best optimality generally requires departures from marginal cost pricing, the optimal prices will usually be related in some way to marginal costs, and hence the problems of the determination of marginal costs will still remain. One way of viewing the attempts to apply marginal cost pricing is as an elucidation, in various situations, of the structure of marginal costs, and as such they are relevant to second-best rules. And of course, there may still be some real-world situations in which marginal cost pricing is indeed optimal.

4.1 The derivation of marginal costs

We assume we are in a first-best economy, with no market imperfections or externalities and, of particular importance in this partial equilibrium analysis, complete certainty about future demand and technological conditions. Recall that time is divided into equal discrete periods which we can conveniently call 'years'. We shall consider the application of marginal cost pricing policies, beginning at the first instant of the year 0, and continuing indefinitely. For simplicity, we assume there are only two inputs, L and K. The first can be varied at will, while the second takes time to vary: an order is placed, the required quantity is delivered, installed, and then can be brought into production. It is convenient to assume that all this takes one 'year': a decision taken at the first instant of year 0, to add a certain increment ΔK to the amount of K available for production, will result in that increment's availability at the first instant of year 1. K can be thought of as capital, and L any variable input.

Output is a flow, and so must always have a time dimension: we can only speak of production at a rate of so many units *per unit time*. Here, it will be convenient to define the time unit as the period already identified, the year, which is also the time it takes to expand input K.

In relating costs to output, we make a distinction between the characteristics of L and K. The inputs of L required for production throughout the 'year' are paid for as they are used up: they are labour services supplied to, or raw materials consumed by, the enterprise, for which immediate payments are made. K, on the other hand, is a durable input, which is owned by the enterprise. It yields productive services over a number of years, but no direct payment is made for them. Rather, its cost has two components: first, in supplying productive services through the year, it undergoes wear and tear which reduces its productivity, and which represents a cost. The value of this cost is reckoned as follows: at the beginning of the year t, the market value[1] of one unit of K will be some number denoted by V_t. At the end of the period (beginning of the next) this value will be V_{t+1}. The difference $\delta_t = (V_t - V_{t+1})$, which can be called 'depreciation', gives the first component[2] of the cost of using one unit of K over the period t. Secondly, in acquiring one unit of K, the enterprise will borrow to finance the cost of acquisition, or use funds which it could otherwise lend. Given a perfect capital market, the yearly interest cost of these funds, from whatever source, will be rP_t given by the market interest rate r times the price of one unit of K in the year in which K is installed. The annual cost of one unit of K is then $rP_t + \delta_t$, the annual interest cost involved in its acquisition, plus the fall in value resulting from its use in one year's production. Much complexity is avoided if we assume δ_t and P_t invariant both with respect to t and to scale of K.[3] Hence, we can define the *annual rental*, $n = rP + \delta$, as the price of one unit of K in each year.

The decision situation which we shall analyse is this: the enterprise is located in time at the first instant of year 0. It must take two kinds of decisions: it must set a price for year 0, which will determine actual sales, costs, profits, etc. in that year, and it must form a *plan* which specifies the price it will set in year 1, and the amount of the inputs L and K it will require to produce the resulting output.[4] If the implied amount of K differs from that currently available, it must institute an 'investment programme', which will be carried out in the course of year 0, and result in the desired amount of K being available at the first instant of year 1. Thus, it actually *implements* in year 0 an investment programme and a pricing policy for that year, and the former is based on a *plan* it makes about price and output in year 1.

The crucial difference between the problem of setting price for year 0, and the problem of choosing a planned price for year 1, is that in the former the enterprise must take the quantity of K as fixed, while in planning for year 1 it can regard K as variable. This has an important effect on the way in which costs will vary with output in each year. Given the prices of the two inputs, n for K and, say, w for L, total costs C are computed as $C = nK + wL$, for any input quantities K and L. Now when planning for year 1, K is variable, and so the enterprise can proceed in the following way: for some given rate of output in year 1, it can find those quantities of K and L which produce it at the lowest possible cost.[5] Valuing these cost-minimizing input quantities at their respective prices, and adding, gives the total cost of producing this rate of output *when both inputs are variable*. Performing this computation at each possible rate of output leads to a relationship between total costs and output in year 1. When planning for year 0, however, K is fixed at some level K_0 in which case its associated costs are also fixed[6] at nK_0. Variations in output can only be achieved by varying L, and likewise cost variations only arise from changes in L. Within this constraint, it will be possible to find the least-cost amount of L with which to produce each rate of output in year 0, and the corresponding total cost can then be calculated. Because of the different circumstances, we would expect the cost–output relationship or *cost function* in year 0 to differ from that defined on outputs planned for year 1. However, these two cost functions will be related in a specific way. Figure 4.1 analyses this relationship.

In the figure, the curve OC_1 shows the relation between rate of output in year 1 and total costs, given that both inputs can be varied. Its shape is determined by technological assumptions commonly made in economics: as the rate of output q_1 in year 1 is increased from a value of 0, costs first rise less than proportionately with output, reach a point of inflexion, and then rise more than proportionately with output. The initial stage is said to correspond to 'increasing returns to scale', and the latter stage to 'diminishing returns to scale'. By its derivation, the curve shows the lowest possible total cost, given the state of technology and input prices,[7] n and w, at which each rate of output q_1 can be produced.

Let ouput $\bar{q}_0$ in the figure have the following property: it is that rate of output for which the fixed amount of K, K_0, is in fact the cost-minimizing amount. Told the year before that $\bar{q}_0$ was to be produced in year 0, the enterprise would have chosen

K_0 as the appropriate value for that output. It follows that the cost of producing $\bar{q}_0$ in year 0 is the same[8] as it would be in year 1, and is shown by the vertical distance $\bar{q}_0\alpha$. Suppose, however, that the enterprise considers producing other rates of output in year 0. This can only be done by varying L, with K_0 fixed, and so deviations from the least-cost input combinations must result.

It follows that the cost of producing some rate of output $\hat{q}_0 \neq \bar{q}_0$ in year 0 must be greater than the cost of producing an equal rate of output $\hat{q}_1 = \hat{q}_0$ in year 1. Hence the curve relating total costs in year 0 to output in year 0 must lie above curve C_1 at all points except α, as shown by the curve C_0 in the figure. Moreover, the greater the difference between $\hat{q}_0$ and $\bar{q}_0$, the greater will be the divergence from the optimal input proportions (the less appropriate will K_0 be). This explains why C_0 diverges steadily from C_1 as we move rightwards or leftwards from point α in the figure. At zero output in year 0, no L would be used, and so costs would consist only of nK_0,[9] as the figure shows.

We can generalize this argument: assume a different level of fixed K, say K_0', implying a different level of output $\bar{q}_0'$, for which capacity in year 0 is optimally adjusted. By repeating the argument we could generate a second year 0 cost curve, which would have the same general properties as C_0. An example is shown in the figure as C_0'. By choosing every possible output, $\bar{q}_0, \bar{q}_0', \bar{q}_0'', \ldots$, we could generate an

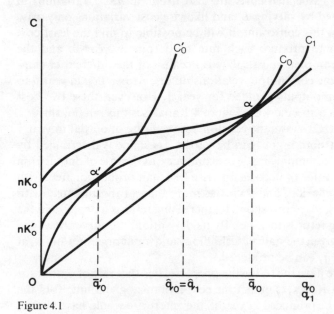

Figure 4.1

infinity of such curves, each lying above the curve C_1 except at just one point. The year 1 cost curve C_1 would then be *the envelope* of the year 0 cost curves C_0, C_0', C_0'', ...

In analysing pricing policy we need to have curves of marginal and average costs. The shapes of these curves are implied by the total cost curves shown in Figure 4.1 by virtue of the following facts:

(1) At any level of output, *marginal cost* is given by the value of the slope of the tangent to the *total cost* curve at that output level; for short-run marginal cost we take tangents to the short-run total cost curve; for long-run marginal cost we take tangents to the long-run total cost curve.

(2) At any level of output, *average cost* is given by the value of the slope of the ray drawn from the origin to the corresponding point on the total cost curve (this is because: the slope of the ray = vertical distance/horizontal distance = total cost/output); for short-run average cost we take a ray to the short-run total cost curve, for long-run average cost we take a ray to the long-run total cost curve.

Using these facts we can then show how the relationships between all four cost curves – short-run and long-run marginal and average costs – follow from the relationships between the total cost curves. This is done in Figure 4.2. In the upper part of the figure are shown two short-run total cost curves which touch the long-run total cost curve, C_1, at α' and α'' respectively. By drawing a sequence of tangents to C_1, at increasing output levels, we would see that long-run marginal cost first falls then rises, giving the U-shaped curve MC_1 in the lower half of the figure. Likewise, by drawing a sequence of rays to C_1, such as $O\alpha'$, $O\alpha$ and $O\alpha''$ shown in the figure, we see that average cost falls up to output $\bar{q}_0$ and then increases, giving AC_1 in the lower half of the figure. The ray $O\alpha$, which is the flattest of all rays to C_1, is also the tangent to C_1 at $\bar{q}_0$. Hence at this point, the minimum long-run average cost is equal to long-run marginal cost. Thus MC_1 cuts AC_1 at $\bar{q}_0$ in the lower diagram. The reader can confirm that the shapes of the pairs of short-run curves MC_0', AC_0' and MC_0'', AC_0'' follow in a similar way. We turn now to our main concern, the relation between the short- and long-run average and marginal cost curves.

The key proposition is: *at an output at which the fixed amount of K is in fact the optimal amount, long-run marginal cost is equal to short-run marginal cost, and long-run average cost is equal to short-run average cost.* This is shown in the lower half of Figure 4.2 by having: MC_0' intersect MC_1 and AC_0' touch AC_1 at $\bar{q}_0'$; and MC_0'' intersect MC_1 and AC_0'' touch AC_1 at $\bar{q}_0''$.

The proposition follows from the fact that at outputs $\bar{q}_0'$ and $\bar{q}_0''$ respectively, the relevant short-run total cost curves are tangent to the long-run curve for reasons we have already explored. Thus in the upper part of Figure 4.2, at point α' both C_0' and C_1 have the same tangent, their slopes are equal at that point and this implies the equality of short- and long-run marginal costs there. Similarly the ray $O\alpha'$ is common to both curves, and so long-run average and marginal costs are also equal. The same is true at output $\bar{q}_0''$.

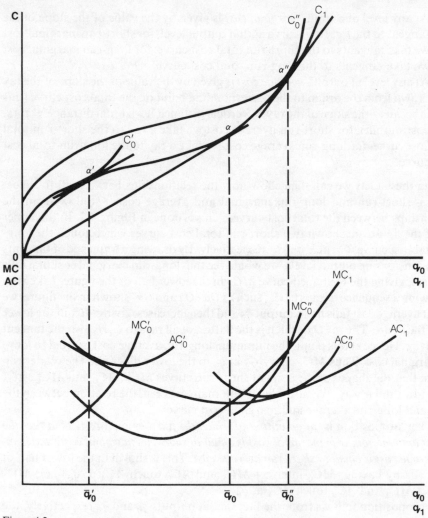

Figure 4.2

4.2 Marginal cost pricing

We can now apply this analysis of cost curves to the question of 'marginal cost pricing' in a partial equilibrium context. Recall that the problem really has two aspects:

(a) to set at the beginning of year 0 a price which will prevail in that year; and
(b) to choose at the beginning of year 0 an investment programme, based on *planned* price and output in year 1.

We now see how these problems are solved.

To be able to discuss pricing policies at all, we must assume that the enterprise has knowledge of its demand curves in *both* years 0 and 1. These are graphed, along with the marginal cost curves, in Figure 4.3(a) and (b).

Consider first the analysis for year 1. In Figure 4.3(b), D_1 is the demand curve which will prevail in that year, and MC_1 is the relevant marginal cost curve, since it is based on the assumption that both K and L are variable. The principle of marginal cost pricing implies that planned output should be q_1^* and planned price p_1^*, since then the market-clearing price equals marginal cost. Corresponding to planned output q_1^* will be cost-minimizing input quantities K_1^* and L_1^*. Since K_0 is the amount of K available at the beginning of year 0, the enterprise must carry out investment[10] in year 0 of the amount $K_1^* - K_0$.

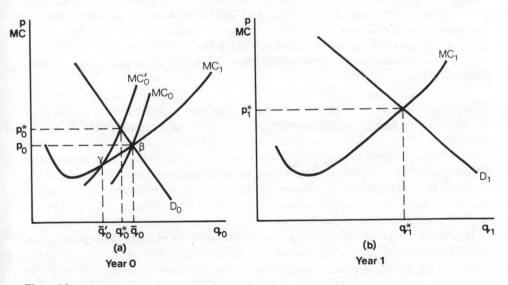

Figure 4.3

Consider now the choice of price and output in year 0, shown in Figure 4.3(a). Given the demand curve D_0, does marginal cost pricing imply choice of the price and output pair $(p_0 \bar{q}_0)$, at the intersection of D_0 and MC_1? The first step in the answer is to note that the MC_1 curve is irrelevant for year 0 decisions. It relates to the possibility of varying *both K and L*, but *K* is fixed in year 0. If the output which has been planned for this year, back in year $t = -1$, was in fact $\bar{q}_0$, then, *because the relevant curve, MC_0, must pass through point β*, the pair $(p_0 q_0)$ *is* appropriate. Suppose, however, that the output $\bar{q}'_0$ had been planned: the demand curve D_0 has turned out to be higher than expected. The installed *K* will be at the level K'_0 appropriate to $\bar{q}'_0$. Hence, the relevant marginal cost curve, given that *K* is fixed at K'_0 in year 0, must be that passing through point γ in Figure 4.3(a), since this is the point on the MC_1 curve corresponding to output $\bar{q}'_0$. This marginal cost curve is denoted by MC'_0 in the figure. It follows that the appropriate price and output for year 0 are p_0^* and q_0^*, since these correspond to the intersection of the demand curve with *that marginal cost curve which relates to variations in year 0 output*.

This discussion can be summarized as follows: marginal cost pricing requires that the price which will prevail over a particular period be equal to the marginal cost of varying output *within that period*. Output variations within the current year are constrained by fixed *K*; variations within future years are not. At a given point of time, two sets of decisions are being taken. Given the demand curve prevailing in the current year, a price–output pair has to be set. Given the demand curve expected to exist in the future year, future price and output have to be planned, and the corresponding investment programme determined and set in motion. The planned price and output will actually be implemented in the future year, if the assumptions about demand and costs upon which they are based turn out to be correct. Otherwise not.

The analysis of this section has been concerned with the meaning of 'marginal cost pricing' in a partial equilibrium context. We have not so far tried to justify or rationalize it in partial equilibrium terms: the validity of marginal cost pricing was considered in the previous chapter in terms of a general equilibrium analysis, and this is always the most appropriate framework for such questions. Illustrations and explanations can conveniently be given in partial equilibrium terms, but they are not rigorous and may mislead because we are not forced to make explicit the full set of assumptions and postulates on which the analysis is based. It is hard to avoid such explicitness at the general equilibrium level, as we saw in the previous chapter.

Bearing this in mind, we now translate the rationale for marginal cost pricing into partial equilibrium terms. We assume that there is some unit of account in which prices of all goods are measured. Now, from consumer theory, we have the important result that the price of a good gives a measure of the subjective value, to each consumer, of the marginal unit of consumption of that good.[11] In addition, marginal cost gives a measure of the value of the output sacrificed by supplying the marginal unit of the good. Now suppose that output were set at a level at which price exceeded marginal cost. This implies that consumers value the marginal unit more than the sacrifice involved in producing it, and hence are prepared to bid resources away from other uses in order to expand production of the good concerned. If, on the other hand, output were at such a level that marginal cost exceeded price, the value of the resources used in producing the marginal unit exceeds the value of that unit to consumers. In that case, there exist consumers of other goods prepared to bid away resources. Only if price just equals marginal cost is the value of the marginal unit to consumers just equal to the value of what has to be sacrificed to provide it. In that case only, will it not be possible to move resources about and (provided appropriate lump-sum compensations are paid) make some people better off and no one worse off. To reduce the argument almost to a slogan: the intention of marginal cost pricing is to impose on the consumer the cost of providing his marginal unit of consumption, so as to cause him to adjust his total consumption to the point at which the value of the marginal unit to him is just equal to its cost.

This kind of reasoning is persuasive, and incorporates at least two important ideas which are often not perceived by those who determine resource allocation in reality. First, there is the significance of a market price as a measure of marginal valuations, as a device for transmitting information on marginal costs, and as a means of rationing available output among consumers. Secondly, there is the emphasis on the concept of opportunity cost.

However, in some ways the reasoning is *too* persuasive. It does not make clear the welfare value judgements on which it is based; the implicit assumptions about compensation which must be made; and the fact that its validity is totally dependent on the existence of a first-best economy. In a second-best economy, the marginal social benefit of an output may no longer be measured by its market price, and the marginal social cost may no longer equal the marginal cost incurred by the enterprise or firm. Since the *correct* principle on which to determine a public enterprise output is the equality of its marginal social benefit with marginal social cost, the intuitively appealing argument just set out breaks down in either of these cases.

There is a history of criticism of the marginal cost pricing 'doctrine' almost as long as that of the doctrine itself. We now consider briefly the main strands of this criticism.

4.3   Criticisms of marginal cost pricing
There have been many criticisms of marginal cost pricing, some of which have been

trivial or wrong, but some of which have been valid and important. These latter emanate from a set of problems which can be grouped under three main headings.

Problems of application
The neatness and simplicity of the textbook analysis, based on the smooth 'well-behaved' cost curves of Figures 4.1, 4.2 and 4.3, is very useful for clear discussion at the conceptual level, but is seldom encountered in reality. We often find, for example, discontinuities arising from capacity restrictions, indivisibilities, and jointness of production and costs, which present difficulties to the definition of marginal cost. As we would expect, gaps or breaks in relevant curves mean that concepts based on small movements along those curves have to be applied with some care. This has been a fruitful area for the generation of paradoxes and conundrums, for example, what is the marginal cost of the $N+1$st rail passenger when the capacity of a train is exactly N? And the following 'paradox': 'once a bridge has been constructed, its capital costs are bygones, and marginal cost pricing requires a price of (virtually) zero (since the costs imposed by one trip across a bridge are very small); hence, the marginal cost price *before* the event, when capital costs are variable, must differ from that *after* the event, when it is fixed; moreover, the capital costs will never actually be recovered in revenues, given the marginal cost price which will be charged once the bridge is built, even though before the event it appears that they will be.' Such riddles are useful to solve, since we invariably learn something about both the theory and the world in doing so. They also make good examination questions. It cannot be said, however, that the problems of application of marginal cost pricing invalidate the principle: rather, they preclude unthinking application of the textbook model, and require the results to be worked out again from first principles in the context of an aoppropriate model. These results cannot really be viewed as departures from the marginal cost principle, but rather as extensions of it. We see this in the next chapter.

Objections arising from the theory of second best
These were introduced in the previous chapter, and will be extensively discussed in chapters 7, 8 and 9. They stem essentially from the non-correspondence of the first-best economy with the real world, and establish the inapplicability of the marginal cost pricing principle under a wide range of circumstances. Criticisms based on second-best theory are therefore fundamentally damaging to the principle.

Objections to the assumption of certainty
Common to the analysis of marginal cost pricing in this chapter, and the later second-best analysis, is the assumption that future demands, technology and prices

are known with certainty at the point in time at which decisions and plans are made. In a sense, relaxation of this assumption is the most fundamental step of all, since it requires us to reformulate our theories of the consumer and the firm; to consider institutions such as insurance and stock markets, which have no place in a world of certainty; and to change the conceptual framework around which both first and second-best theories are constructed. Thus, criticisms of the assumptions of perfect knowledge in our earlier analysis are quite far-reaching, since they require a major change in the model before we can even begin to assess their importance for the results. Some aspects of the problems presented by uncertainty are considered in chapter 10.

The extensions to the analysis necessitated by each of these sets of criticisms are considered in subsequent chapters. Some examples of the criticisms which are here called 'trivial or invalid' are:

(1) marginal cost pricing invariably implies that the enterprise operates at a loss, and so is unacceptable;
(2) the marginal cost pricing principle is ambiguous, since there exists more than one marginal cost, each corresponding to some particular group of inputs which are being held fixed, and price cannot be equal to all of them at once;[12]
(3) the analysis of marginal cost pricing cannot handle changes in future demands, prices and technology (assuming these are known with certainty);
(4) the analysis assumes unrealistically that the enterprise is starting up from scratch, and does not have a hodge-podge of plant and equipment inherited from past decisions;

and so on. Proofs of the triviality or invalidity of these propositions should be quite possible with the help of the principles set out in this chapter and the next, and are left to the reader as an exercise.

Appendix to chapter 4

In this Appendix we formulate the basic pricing model which will be used repeatedly throughout the rest of this book. Here it will be used to derive the marginal cost pricing rule.

Let q_0 denote the total output of a public enterprise in period 0 ('this year'), and $p_0 = p_0(q_0)$ the inverse demand function. The standard measure of consumer benefit which is used in partial equilibrium welfare analysis is

$$B_0(q_0) = \int_0^{q_0} p_0(q_0)dq_0 \qquad (A.4.1)$$

i.e. the integral under the usual (Marshallian) market demand function. If short-run total cost to the enterprise $C_0(q_0)$ is a measure of social cost, then net social benefit $S_0(q_0)$ is simply

$$S_0(q_0) \equiv B_0(q_0) - C_0(q_0) \qquad (A.4.2)$$

and maximization of S_0 with respect to q yields the conditions:

$$p_0(q_0^*) - C_0(q_0^*) = 0 \qquad (A.4.3)$$

$$p_0(q_0^*) - C_0''(q_0^*) < 0 \qquad (A.4.4)$$

at the optimal output level q_0^*. The first-order condition is of course the short-run marginal cost pricing rule, while the second-order condition will certainly be satisfied, given a downward-sloping demand curve, because short-run marginal cost is always taken to be increasing over some range, due to the law of diminishing returns.

Turning to the plan for price and output in period 1 ('next year'), it will be useful to take a more fundamental view. The purpose of the analysis will be to establish two important propositions:

(1) If next period's demand can be accurately forecast, so that capacity can be optimally adjusted to the output which will be produced, short-run and long-run marginal cost pricing are equivalent.
(2) If the level of the enterprise's investment is chosen by maximizing the net

present value of social benefits, this is equivalent to setting output so as to equate price with long-run marginal cost.

The first proposition is directed at a question which is sometimes posed, of whether 'short-run marginal cost pricing' or 'long-run marginal cost pricing' is 'correct'. By the former is meant setting price where the demand curve meets the short-run marginal cost curve. By the latter is meant setting price where the demand curve meets the long-run marginal cost curve. As the discussion surrounding Figure 4.3 in this chapter sought to make clear, this question reveals a confusion about what is meant by marginal cost. If price is to be set for the current period, and capacity is fixed, then the relevant marginal cost is short-run marginal cost and 'marginal cost pricing' means nothing other than short-run marginal cost pricing. Since prices are only actually *set* for the current period – they are *planned* for future periods – marginal cost pricing always involves short-run marginal cost. When planning future price and capacity, and therefore current investment, by definition long-run marginal costs are relevant. Planned price and capacity will be set where the expected future demand curve cuts the long-run marginal cost curve and if the demand forecast turns out to be right, short-run marginal cost will also equal this price (see Figure 4.3).

Of course, as the following chapter makes clear, ('short-run') marginal cost pricing may create problems in the form of losses or indeed profits, and undesired income distributional effects. These must, however, be taken as requiring explicit modification of the marginal cost pricing principles and not as an argument for substituting 'long-run' for 'short-run' marginal cost pricing in the current period.

The second proposition seeks to establish the connection between what an investment planner might do in practice and the textbook model of pricing and investment planning (as in Figure 4.3(b), for example). Investment planning usually takes the form of maximization of the discounted future benefits of investment. We can show that in the type of enterprise envisaged here, and in the absence of uncertainty, this is nothing more nor less than setting future capacity and planned price where the future demand curve cuts the long-run marginal cost curve.

Let $f(K, L)$ be the enterprise production function, with $f_K, f_L > 0$, $f_{KK}, f_{LL} < 0$, and assume it is unchanged over time. If K is fixed at K^0 in the current period, then optimal price and output are determined by maximizing $B_0(q_0) - wL$, subject to the constraint $q_0 = f(K^0, L)$, where w is the wage rate. This yields the condition:

$$p_0 = \frac{w}{f_L} = C'_0 \qquad (A.4.5)$$

or marginal cost pricing for the current period.

The investment planning problem can be formulated as follows. Let $B_1(q_1)$ be the consumer benefit function for period 1 (given the underlying period 1 demand function). Then the net present value of social benefit is given by:

$$S = [B_1(q_1) - wL_1](1+r)^{-1} - v[K - K^0] \tag{A.4.6}$$

where v is the price of one unit of K, and the values of L_1 and K are to be determined. This is a standard net present value formula, with of course $v[K - K^0]$ the value of current investment. Maximizing S, again subject to the production function constraint, yields the conditions:

$$p_1 = \frac{w}{f_L} = C_0' \tag{A.4.7}$$

$$p_1 = \frac{(1+r)v}{f_K} = C_1' \tag{A.4.8}$$

Here $(1+r)v$ is the price or 'rental' of 1 unit of capital for one period, and so the ratio $(1+r)v/f_K$ is simply a ratio of factor price to marginal product, or marginal cost. Thus maximization of net present value of benefits and marginal cost pricing are equivalent. Moreover, given the value of capital, say K^* determined by conditions (A.4.7) and (A.4.8), if, when period 1 arrives, demand is as expected and so K^* *is* optimal, then the value of f_L in (A.4.5) will be the same as that in (A.4.7) and $C_0' = C_1'$, which could be expressed by saying that short-run and long-run marginal cost pricing are equivalent. Note finally that conditions (A.4.7) and (A.4.8) imply

$$\frac{w}{(1+r)v} = \frac{f_L}{f_K} \tag{A.4.9}$$

i.e. K^* and L_1^* satisfy the condition for cost-minimizing choice of inputs, something else which is implied by the benefit-maximization approach.

We conclude this Appendix with a comment on the benefit function $B(q)$. This is of course the measure of 'Marshallian consumer surplus', around which there is some controversy. The interested reader is referred to Deaton and Muellbauer (1980, Ch. 7), Hausmann (1981) and Willig (1976). For the purposes of this book, we do not need to involve ourselves in this controversy. The formulation is a simple way of generating conditions on optimal prices in a partial equilibrium context. The forms of these conditions can be validated by a more general and less objectionable, but more complicated, analysis. Knowing that is enough for present purposes.

Chapter 5

Marginal cost pricing in practice: fixed capacity, peak-load pricing and indivisibility

When the attempt is made to apply marginal cost pricing principles to some particular enterprise it is usually necessary to extend the structure of the theory in order to deal with specific features of outputs, demands and costs. In this chapter and the next we consider the major kinds of extensions to the theory which have been necessary.

We shall consider in this chapter three main sets of problems. First, we take the situation in which the technology of an enterprise is such that, once capacity is installed, a maximum output level is defined, which cannot be exceeded at any cost. This is the 'fixed-capacity case', which appears to be typical of most public enterprises. The central problem is that of the indeterminacy of marginal cost at capacity output, but we also encounter the important issue of the relative desirability of rationing by price as opposed to rationing by non-price methods. In considering this issue we are led to extend the principle of marginal cost pricing to incorporate the principle of rationing by price. Secondly, we take the situation in which demand on an enterprise may vary from minute to minute in a systematic way over a given time-period – the so-called 'peak-load pricing problem'. There are really two interdependent problems here: that of determining the optimum number and lengths of sub-periods into which to divide the whole period, such that price within each period is uniform, while prices between periods differ; and that of determining optimal prices for these periods. Finally, we consider the problem of plant indivisibilities, which again make marginal costs indeterminate in certain respects. We see that 'marginal cost pricing rules' can still be defined and implemented, the main difference to other cases being that marginal calculations cannot be used to define optimal investment programmes: we become involved in comparisons of total benefits with total costs which, as cost–benefit analysis has shown, are much more difficult to make than marginal calculations based on market prices.

5.1 Fixed-capacity plant

The theoretical model of the previous chapter assumed what is called *flexible capacity*. There was a particular rate of output for which capacity was optimally adjusted (e.g. $\bar{q}_0$ in Figures 4.1 and 4.2), but it was possible to increase output beyond this point by increasing the variable input. A situation which is often encountered, however, is that in which the installed plant has a given rate of capacity output which cannot be exceeded at any cost. We call this *fixed-capacity plant*. This situation should be distinguished from that of plant *indivisibilities*, which exists when increments to capacity can only be made in discrete finite amounts, rather than in infinitely divisible amounts. Indivisibilities are important in practice – indeed indivisibilities and fixed capacity often occur together – and will be considered below. The analysis is helped by taking one problem at a time, however. We assume, given installed capacity, that although a particular rate of output cannot be exceeded in any one time-period (the 'year'), installed capacity can be expanded by any amount, however small, with a gestation period of a year.

Except for the fixed-capacity assumption, the basic situation is assumed the same as in the previous chapter. The enterprise is at the first instant of year 0, it must choose a price and output for that year, and also an investment plan. This investment plan is in turn derived from the planned price–output pair for year 1. The important difference between years 0 and 1 is that in the former output variations can be made only within the limitations of fixed capacity, whereas in the latter output variations can be planned allowing all inputs to vary. The cost parameters are also the same. One unit of L costs w; one unit of K costs the interest cost, plus δ, the annual 'wear and tear' cost, or depreciation, so that the annual capital rental is again n. Hence annual costs are $C = wL + nK$, where the first component varies with output in a given year, while the second is fixed within a year but variable between years.

Let us first consider the total costs associated with variations in output in year 0. The curve C_0 in Figure 5.1 embodies the assumption we shall make: at zero output, variable costs are also zero, so that total costs in year 0 are nK_0, with K_0 again the value of installed K at year 0. The segment ab of C_0 shows how total costs increase as L and output are increased up to the capacity limit $\bar{q}_0$. It is assumed that variable costs rise proportionately with output: a given increment in output always requires the same increment in L, and, since w is constant, always causes the same increment in cost.[1] At the capacity output rate, C_0 becomes vertical; costs go to infinity, which is another way of saying that more output cannot be obtained at any cost. Note that the slope of C_0 is well defined and constant over the interval $O \leqslant q < \bar{q}_0$. However, at $q = \bar{q}_0$, there is a kink in the curve, which implies that the slope of C_0 is not defined at that point.

Now consider the line OC_1. This is the total cost curve which relates to output variations in year 1, when K can be regarded as variable. Hence, at zero output, zero costs are incurred, and, as output increases, total costs are assumed to increase proportionately, i.e. there are constant returns to scale. The OC_1 line is smooth and continuous because it is assumed that there are no indivisibilities – capacity can be planned in quantities which can be written out to as many decimal places as we like. Hence, at every point on the line, the slope is well defined and constant. C_0 and C_1 must meet at $\bar{q}_0$.[2] Choice of output $\bar{q}_0$ to be produced in year 1 would imply total costs given by point b on C_1. If, once the corresponding capacity is installed, output falls from $\bar{q}_0$ this will cause costs to fall but at a slower rate than along C_1 since *only* the input L can be reduced. Hence, the curve for year 0 output variations corresponding to capacity $\bar{q}_0$ must meet C_1 at point b and must also meet the vertical axis at the point a, as shown, where total costs are nK_0.

To discuss pricing policy, we translate the total cost curves of Figure 5.1 into the marginal cost curves of Figure 5.2. The slope of the line OC_1 in Figure 5.1, a constant, is shown as MC_1, and the slope of the segment ab of C_0, also a constant, is shown as MC_0. The vertical segment of MC_0 at $\bar{q}_0$ indicates that marginal cost is undefined at that point. Note that since OC_1 is steeper than the segment ab of C_0, MC_1 exceeds MC_0. Given the installed capacity, an increment in output can be achieved only with an increment in L, and, as long as $q < \bar{q}_0$, this increment costs less than it would if capacity had also to be expanded. However, it still remains true, as Figure 5.1 shows, that the *total* cost of producing outputs below q_0 is less when it

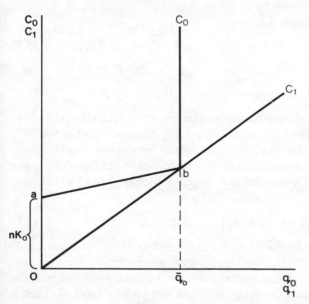

Figure 5.1

is possible to vary both inputs, than when it is possible to vary only one of them.

The classic example of a public enterprise with cost curves such as those shown in Figures 5.1 and 5.2 is a bridge. We could think of output q, as representing the number of trips made across the bridge per year. In Figure 5.1, nK_0 would be the annual capital cost of building a bridge of capacity $\bar{q}_0$, while the remaining costs incorporated in the line ab would consist largely of maintenance and toll collection. Then, given the assumption that all costs increase proportionately with traffic flow across the bridge, MC_0 in Figure 5.2 would measure maintenance and toll-collection cost per vehicle and MC_1 would consist of this *plus* capital cost per vehicle. *Before* the bridge is built, the capacity flow of vehicles can be varied continuously by varying the size and design of the bridge but, once built, capacity is fixed at $\bar{q}_0$. Thus, when the bridge is being planned the problem is to decide on the optimal capacity (size and design) and associated price or toll. If the bridge is already built then we have simply to decide on the toll. Although the following analysis is meant to apply in general to all kinds of public enterprise which have this rigid capacity characteristic (as most of them do), it will be instructive and interesting to consider the interpretation of the analysis in terms of the bridge example.

Since MC_0 in Figure 5.2 is essentially marginal operating or 'running' cost, while MC_1 is this plus capital cost, it will be useful to denote the running cost by v and capital cost by β, so that in Figure 5.1:

$$C_0 = vq_0 + \beta\bar{q}_0 \quad \text{for} \quad 0 \leqslant q_0 \leqslant \bar{q}_0, \quad \text{and} \quad C_1 = (v+\beta)q_1. \quad (5.1)$$

While in Figure 5.2,

$$MC_0 = v \quad \text{for} \quad 0 \leqslant q_0 < \bar{q}_0 \quad \text{and} \quad MC_1 = v+\beta. \quad (5.2)$$

In Figure 5.3 we analyse the determination of marginal cost prices. In (a) and (b) are shown alternative possibilities for year 0. In (a), the demand curve in year 0 is D_0, and, since the relevant marginal cost for output variations in year 0 is $MC_0 = v$, price will be set equal to v, on marginal cost pricing principles. Note that this implies a large loss for the enterprise. At a price of v, actual output is q_0^*, and so the loss, revenue *minus* total costs is

$$vq_0^* - [vq_0^* + \beta\bar{q}_0] = -\beta\bar{q}_0 \quad (5.3)$$

or the whole of capital costs. In this case this is an unavoidable consequence of marginal cost pricing. The justification of this policy in partial equilibrium terms is as follows: suppose that in year 0 the enterprise were to set price greater than v, for example equal to $v+\beta$ (at which, however, it would still make a loss). At such a price, the quantity demanded will be q_0' in the figure implying an excess capacity of

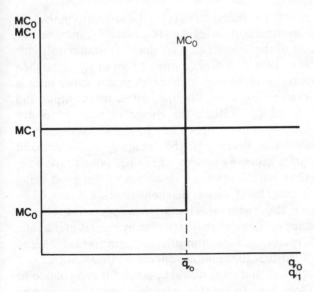

Figure 5.2

$(\bar{q}_0 - q_0')$. The marginal social cost of increased output, v, is below the value which consumers place on the marginal unit of consumption, which is measured by the price. Hence, net social benefits are increased by increasing output, and utilizing otherwise idle capacity; the capital costs β are 'bygones', they do not vary with output in year 0 and so should be ignored.

This argument, although perfectly acceptable in a first-best economy, ignores the fact that the 'policy-maker' may not be indifferent to the amount of net revenue accruing to the exchequer from the public enterprise. The fact that no interest payments are being made by the enterprise implies that (since the government must itself service the debt it issued to finance the investment of the enterprise) the policy-maker must increase taxes or borrowing, or reduce other public expenditure. In a first-best economy, the finance could be raised by lump-sum taxation, and so (provided the policy-maker does not dislike the resulting change in wealth distribution) the deficit could be met in this way. This would imply no loss of allocative efficiency elsewhere in the economy. However, in a second-best economy financing the deficit may have welfare effects which need to be taken into account in the pricing decision. Hence, the straightforward and appealing marginal cost pricing argument may not apply. This criticism raises in a partial equilibrium context the issues of wealth distribution, indirect taxation, and the second best, discussed earlier in chapter 3.

Figure 5.3(b) also relates to year 0, and differs from (a) in the assumption that the demand curve D_0' intersects the 'vertical portion' of the MC_0 curve.[3] A price set at v would now imply excess demand of the amount $q_0'' - \bar{q}_0$, since maximum output is fixed at $\bar{q}_0$. If excess demand is to be avoided, price must be set at p_0^*, since then demand exactly equals $\bar{q}_0$. This suggests the important point that whether price is set at v, p_0^*, or indeed some intermediate level, does not affect total output and consumption, which cannot exceed $\bar{q}_0$. Rather, the choice between p_0^* and v determines the way in which available output will be rationed among consumers. If price is set at v (or any other value below p_0^*), the resulting excess demand necessitates some sort of non-price rationing system – queuing, points rationing, random allocation – which will in part depend on the nature of the good being produced.[4] Pricing at p_0^*, on the other hand, means that consumption is secured by those most willing to pay for it, i.e. those who value it most in money terms. There is a strong presumption among many economists that rationing by price is preferable, and this stems from two sets of arguments. First, non-price rationing is likely to lead to a loss of allocative efficiency, in that the resulting allocation of output among consumers will not be Pareto-optimal, and there would be scope for everyone to be made better off by further reallocation. To see this, note that under rationing by price, households choose their consumption in such a way that the money value of everyone's marginal unit of consumption is the same, being equal to the market price. Under a non-price rationing scheme, a different allocation of the given total

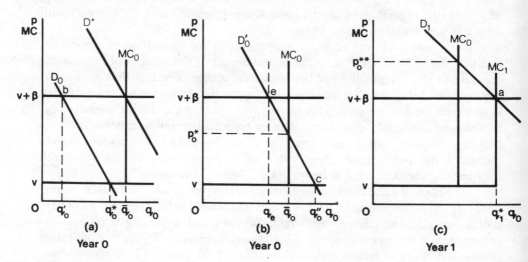

Figure 5.3

output among households is likely to result. It follows in that case that some households will value their marginal consumption at more than the price, and some at less, so there is scope for 'gains from trade'; everyone can be made better off by appropriate exchanges of money for some quantities of the good. Thus, non-price rationing is allocatively inefficient, while price rationing is allocatively efficient. Secondly, as a mechanism for allocating output, a non-price rationing scheme is likely to absorb more resources than would rationing by price. If, by the 'costs of a non-price rationing scheme', we mean both the loss in allocative efficiency and the resource costs of the scheme, then the economists' conclusion is that non-price rationing is more costly than rationing by price.

Support for non-price rationing derives basically from the view that income is inequitably distributed: rationing by price implies consumption by those most *able* to pay for it, and so is an inequitable rationing device unless there is a 'fair' distribution of income. We have, in fact, a close parallel to the discussion of first- and second-best economic policies in chapter 3. If the policy-maker is neutral toward the distribution of welfare, or if he can achieve any desired distribution by lump-sum transfers, then rationing by price would be an optimal policy. In a second-best world, however, there may be circumstances in which allocative efficiency will be traded off for distributional equity, which in the present case might imply that price may not be used as a rationing device. Since the optimality of marginal cost pricing is conditional on the existence of a first-best economy in general, it seems appropriate to regard marginal cost pricing as being equivalent to rationing by price in the fixed-capacity case. Hence, the price p_0^* in the figure is that which is consistent with the marginal cost pricing rule.

There is, for year 0, a third possibility, which is shown in Figure 5.3(c). Suppose that in year 0, demand were as high as D_1. As we shall see, if demand were expected to continue at this level the enterprise would plan to expand capacity. However, in year 0 this is not possible. Then, if price is to be used to ration available output, it will have to rise to p_0^{**}, which also generates a profit for the enterprise, since $p_0^{**} \bar{q}_0 > (v + \beta) . \bar{q}_0$. Thus, we can state the marginal cost pricing rule for year 0: when there is fixed capacity equate price to v *unless* there is excess demand at this price, in which case price should be raised to whatever level is necessary to restrain demand to capacity output. As was pointed out, however, there are issues concerned with profitability, rationing and the distribution of welfare which have to be resolved before this conclusion can be accepted. These are discussed further in chapter 8 below.

Figure 5.3(c) can also be used to analyse the planned price–output decision for year 1. Assume now that D_1 is the demand curve which the enterprise expects to prevail in year 1 (it can be assumed that demand is expected to grow from D_0 or D_0', or that it will remain constant at D_1, depending on which of the three year 0 cases so far considered actually prevails). The relevant marginal cost curve for planning year 1 price and output decisions is MC_1, since K can be treated as a variable in planning one year ahead. It follows that the price planned for period 1 will be equal to $v + \beta$, and planned output will be q_1^*, since D_1 intersects MC_1 at a. Therefore in order to increase capacity from $\bar{q}_0$ to q_1^*, the enterprise will have to set in motion the required investment programme in year 0. Then, when a year has elapsed and the enterprise finds itself at the first instant of year 1, it will have a fixed capacity of q_1^*. It will then have to *set* a price for year 1, in the light of the demand which actually exists, and choose a *planned* price and output for year 2, which will imply a year 1 investment programme; and so the cycle repeats itself. If demand in year 1 turns out to be less than D_1, then we have similar results to those shown in Figure 5.3(a) and (b); marginal cost pricing, or rationing by price, will imply that price in year 1 will actually be set below $v + \beta$, the planned level, and losses will be made. If demand turns out to be higher than D_1, the price which restrains consumption to equal capacity output must be above $v + \beta$, and profits will be made. Thus we have the result that when marginal cost pricing policies are applied under fixed-capacity conditions with constant marginal costs, overestimation of demand always leads to losses, and underestimation of demand always to profits. Correct estimation of demand leads to neither profit nor losses.

Let us now reinterpret this analysis in terms of our example of a bridge. Suppose the bridge has not yet been built – we stand, as it were, at the first instant of year -1. We know for certain the values v and β, so we can draw the cost curves in Figure 5.3. Our demand forecasters estimate that the demand curve will remain the same in each future year, and estimate it as the curve D^* in Figure 5.3(a). It follows that, on marginal cost pricing grounds, we choose the capacity of the bridge at $\bar{q}_0$ and set about building this, and plan to charge a toll equal to $v + \beta$ or long-run marginal cost. We expect the bridge therefore to break even: total revenue will equal total costs including capital charges (this is essentially a consequence of the constant-cost assumption).

If our demand forecasters are right then our pricing plan in year 0 and each succeeding year will be implemented and demand will just match capacity. If they are wrong, then Figure 5.3 suggests the prices which may be charged if marginal cost pricing is to be applied. If there had been a very large overestimate, because demand turns out to be D_0 in Figure 5.3(a), then the toll will be set at v, the maintenance and toll-collection costs per vehicle, and no contribution at all will be made to capital charges. If demand has been less seriously overestimated, as in (b) of the figure, then the toll is set so as to ration demand to capacity and revenues make a partial contribution to capital costs (though this is incidental to the purpose of rationing by price). If demand had been underestimated, as in (c) of the figure, the toll which rations demand to capacity (avoids traffic-jams at the approaches to the bridge) is above long-run marginal cost and yields a profit. In this case, if we can be assured that demand will remain at this level, we will plan an expansion of bridge capacity to q_1^* in the figure, which, by assumption, will take a year to carry out.

Now consider the financial and political consequences of marginal cost pricing for the bridge. If demand turns out to have been overestimated ((a) or (b) of the figure), the bridge authority's accountants will be aghast at the fact that capital charges are not being covered. These 'financial obligations' will still have to be met in *some* way, if not by the bridge authority then by whatever agency of central or local government is ultimately responsible for the authority's finances. If this cannot be done by lump-sum taxes, then it may well be desirable, on grounds of efficient resource allocation as well as financial orthodoxy, that users of the bridge pay higher tolls than v, or p_0^*, in order to reduce the distortions created elsewhere in the economy by the need to finance the deficits.

On the other hand, consider the case shown in Figure 5.3(c), where demand has been underestimated. Although a capacity expansion is being planned, this may take quite some time to carry out (recall that our designation of this period as a 'year' is purely for convenience), and in the meantime tolls are high and profits are being made. Users of the bridge, and their political representatives, may well protest. It will be argued that low-income families cannot afford to use the bridge. There will be great pressure to restrict the toll, possibly to the 'break-even' level $v + \beta$. The economist will argue that the consequence of this will be excess demand, congestion and queuing, with greatly increased time and petrol costs for bridge-users. A better solution would be to identify 'the poor' and use some of the profits to subsidize them directly. Nevertheless, the economic inefficiency of non-price rationing might be judged an acceptable price to pay to ward off the political clamour or to avoid the income-distributional consequences of the 'market-clearing' toll p_0^{**}. In any debate on public enterprise prices, the economist's voice is rarely the only one to be heard, and is often not the loudest or most attended to.

5.2   Peak-load pricing

In the analyses of this chapter and the last, we have worked with an arbitrarily chosen time-period, the 'year', over which a uniform price would be charged for all units sought in that period. The actual nature of the time-profiles of demands for many public enterprise outputs requires us now to examine more closely the question of defining the time-periods for which uniform prices are set.

It has been observed that for many outputs there is a systematic pattern of demand fluctuations within a given period, this pattern repeating itself from period to period. The duration of the fluctuations is too short to permit capacity to be varied to match them, while the high cost or technological infeasibility of storage rules out this way of reconciling fluctuating demand with smooth production. In effect, output can only be 'stored' in the form of capacity to produce it. Thus, we could think of the demand cycle as completing itself within a 'day', as compared to the 'year' it takes to vary installed capacity. Denote the demand in the mth minute of the day by D_m, where $m = 1, 2, \ldots, 1440$. If we were to plot demand, minute by minute, against each successive minute of the day, we would typically observe a pattern of peaks and troughs of the general form shown in Figure 5.4. Such a general pattern characterizes daily demand for most energy supplies and transport services, especially rail and bus services, and electricity and gas supply. The problem is that demands at all minutes are met from the same installed capacity, and so there are corresponding fluctuations in capacity utilization.[5] If sufficient capacity is provided to 'meet the peaks', then the rest of the time varying amounts of it are lying idle. On the other hand, since the demand at each minute will depend on the price which prevails in that minute (as well as those prices set in other minutes, in general), pricing policy could be used to 'flatten' the peaks and raise the troughs, so as to get a more even rate of capacity utilization with a lower overall level of capacity. The peak-load pricing problem is, then, in its most general form, that of determining optimal values for a sequence of prices $p_1, p_2, \ldots, p_m, \ldots, p_{1440}$, and an overall capacity level. In a first-best economy, necessary conditions for Pareto optimality in

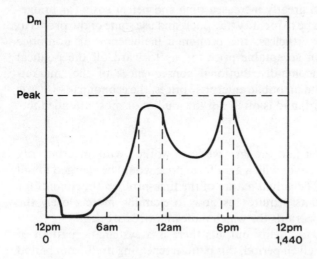

Figure 5.4

this case require marginal cost pricing. Hence, we can regard the problem as essentially one of applying marginal cost pricing to a system of fluctuating demand.

It is useful to have a general solution to this problem.[6] However, there are two reasons for not pursuing this general solution here: greater insights into the meaning of the results are obtained by taking a simple case; and, in practice, it is not yet feasible to have a system of prices which change 'by the minute'. We have often ignored in economic theory the fact that operating a pricing mechanism incurs costs, and in the present context this fact becomes very relevant. To have 1440 prices for electricity per day would require complex and costly metering equipment; a railway ticket office at which fares changed every minute has vast comic possibilities. In practice, the day is divided into relatively few time-periods, within which uniform prices are set. This suggests that the peak-load pricing problem consists of two interdependent parts: we have to find the optimal number of pricing periods, given the costs associated with pricing structures of varying complexity, and we have to determine optimal total capacity and uniform prices within these periods.

Although it is possible to solve this problem in one grand step,[7] again we will gain greater insight, as well as remaining within the constraints set for this book, by proceeding in a more pedestrian way. First, in this section we shall assume that the daily demand pattern is as shown in Figure 5.5. The day can be divided into two 12-hourly periods, during each of which demand in each minute is the same. Assuming negligible costs of simple two-period price differentiation, there is then no need to worry about determining the optimal structure, since the demand pattern does this for us: we have only to determine the price to set in each period. Analysis of this problem will bring out the main elements of peak-load pricing problems, and suggest immediate applications. We then in the next section consider the problem of determining the number of pricing periods, and the optimum uniform price in a period, given that demand may actually not be constant within it.

Let q_1 be total output produced in the 12-hour period with lower demand in Figure 5.5, and q_2 that produced in the 12-hour period with higher demand. We assume that we have fixed-capacity plant and, for simplicity, that all relevant marginal costs are constant. The key to the analysis is the appropriate definition of the units in which costs are measured. As before, we take the annual per unit interest cost as rP, and the annual 'wear and tear' or depreciation on a unit of K to be δ. We can express these in terms of 12-hourly periods as follows: since there are 8760 hours in the year, $\delta' = \delta \times 12/8760$ is the depreciation for one 12-hourly period. Likewise, let r' be the 12-hourly interest rate.[8] Then, the cost per 12-hourly period of adding one unit of K is $n' = \delta' + r'P$. If $\tilde{\tilde{q}}$ is the 12-hourly output of one unit of K, then the 12-hourly capacity cost per unit of output is $\beta' = n'/\tilde{\tilde{q}}$. Likewise, let v' be the cost of the amount of L required to produce one unit of 12-hourly output. We assume v', the

12-hourly 'running cost', is the same in each period. We can then write the cost functions for periods 1 and 2, respectively, as

$$C_1 = v'q_1 + \beta'q_1^0 \quad \text{for} \quad O \leqslant q_1 \leqslant q_1^0 \tag{5.4}$$

and

$$C_2 = v'q_2 + \beta'q_2^0 \quad \text{for} \quad O \leqslant q_2 \leqslant q_2^0, \tag{5.5}$$

where q_1^0 and q_2^0 are, respectively, the 12-hourly capacity outputs in periods 1 and 2. But we must have that $q_1^0 = q_2^0$, since the installed capacity is the same in each period. We call this common 12-hourly capacity output q^0. The total *daily* costs of the enterprise are simply the sum of costs in each 12-hourly period, and so are given by

$$C = C_1 + C_2 = v'(q_1 + q_2) + 2\beta'q^0. \tag{5.6}$$

The problem faced by the enterprise is similar to that considered in the previous section, with the added dimensions of price differentiation between outputs q_1 and q_2. It must, at the first instant of year 0, set prices for q_1 and q_2 which will hold for each respective 12-hour period throughout that year, *given* the available 12-hourly capacity q^0. It must also plan the prices and outputs for year 1, in the light of its expectations about 12-hourly demands in that year, and given that it can regard capacity as a variable for that year. These planned prices and outputs will then

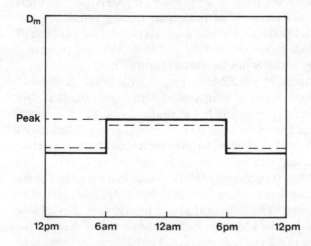

Figure 5.5

determine an investment programme to be carried out in year 0. The analysis of this problem is set out in Figure 5.6, which shows the situation in year 0.[9] Capacity is fixed at q^0, and D_1 and D_2 are the demand curves for output in the two periods. On marginal cost pricing principles, the price in period 1 will be set equal to v', implying an output of q_1^*, which is below capacity. If we accept that available output should be rationed by price, then price in period 2 will be set at p_2^*, since then demand, at point a on D_2, is equal to capacity q^0. The fact that D_2 is higher than D_1 implies that the price at peak demand is above that at off-peak. However, if D_2 had intersected the horizontal section of the MC_0 curve, *both* prices would have been set at v'. The arguments here are precisely those set out in the previous section. In the case shown in Figure 5.6, the enterprise makes a daily loss: its revenue each day is $v'q_1^* + p_2^*q^0$, so, given its daily cost as in equation (5.6), its net loss is

$$L = v'q_1^* + p_2^*q^0 - v'(q_1^* + q^0) - 2\beta'q^0 \tag{5.7}$$

$$= [p_2^* - (v' + 2\beta')]q^0. \tag{5.8}$$

The daily capacity cost is $2\beta'q^0$, since the 12-hourly capacity cost is $\beta'q^0$. Hence, this daily loss can be regarded as the daily capacity cost less the excess $(p_2^* - v')q^0$ of revenue over running cost made on peak output. Off-peak output simply covers

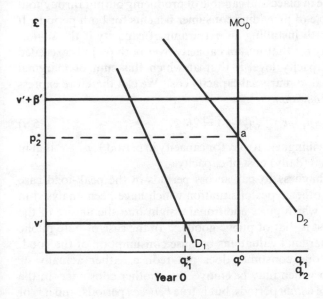

Figure 5.6

running costs, and makes no contribution to capacity costs. The arguments set out in the previous section concerning finance of such losses are directly applicable here. Note again, however, that these losses are due to past overestimation of demand. It is quite conceivable that demands could have been underestimated: for example the demand curves D_1 and D_2 could intersect the vertical portion of MC_0 at points above the line $v' + \beta'$ which implies that rationing by price would generate a profit. Thus, the losses or profits are attributable to marginal cost pricing *in the presence of incorrect demand estimation* in the past, rather than marginal cost pricing as such.

We now consider the problem of choice of planned prices and capacity for year 1. The important concept we have to introduce here is that of the consumers' *willingness to pay for capacity*. Recall that at any given level of output of a good, we can interpret the price, p, as the consumers' valuation of, or willingness to pay for, the marginal unit of their consumption. If we subtract from this price the cost of the *variable* inputs required to produce the marginal unit of output, we can interpret the amount remaining as the consumers' willingness to pay for the *capital costs* incurred in producing the marginal unit, i.e. their marginal willingness to pay for *capacity*. In the present case, therefore, we would define $p_1 - v'$ as consumers' marginal willingness to pay for capacity to produce output in period 1, and $p_2 - v'$ as consumers' marginal willingness to pay for capacity to produce output in period 2. Now a unit of capacity will be in place and capable of producing output throughout the entire day, i.e. it is capable of providing consumer benefits for both periods. It follows that it would be worth installing an extra unit of capacity if the *sum* of consumers' willingness to pay for that unit of capacity over both periods exceeded its cost, and the optimal capacity level is that at which this sum of marginal willingness to pay is just equal to marginal capacity cost. We can therefore express this as the *optimal capacity condition*:

$$(p_1 - v') + (p_2 - v') = 2\beta' \qquad (5.9)$$

where $p_1 - v'$ is the marginal willingness to pay for capacity in period 1, $p_2 - v'$ that in period 2, and $2\beta'$ the marginal (daily) cost of capacity.

The fact that we *sum* willingness to pay across periods in the peak-load case suggests analogies with two other types of situation which have been analysed in economics, consideration of which gives additional insight into the nature of the 'peak-load problem'. The first is that of public goods.[10] In the case of pure public goods we sum consumers' marginal valuations because consumption of the good, say a radio broadcast, by one consumer does not reduce, either actually or potentially, the consumption which may be enjoyed by another consumer. In the peak-load case, this is not true *within* periods, but is true *between* periods, and it is of course across periods that the summation is taking place. One consumer's utilization of capacity, i.e. consumption, within one period displaces someone else's consumption during that period but does not pre-empt anyone's consumption during the other period. Thus consumption in different periods is not 'rivalrous' and so marginal willingnesses to pay should be summed.

The second analogous situation is that of *joint products*.[11] By rearing a sheep we produce both mutton and wool. The value of the sheep is the sum of the value of the mutton and the value of the wool. In the same sense, a unit of capacity is available to produce output in each period, the outputs in each period are its joint products, and so the value of the unit of capacity is the sum of the values of its outputs.[12]

The condition in (5.9), which states that the optimal level of capacity is that which equates the sum of marginal willingness to pay across periods with the marginal capacity cost, is the central element in the analysis. From it we can deduce the marginal cost pricing policy. Consider Figure 5.7. In the lower part (b) of the figure are shown the demand curves for the two periods, D_1 and D_2, and the marginal

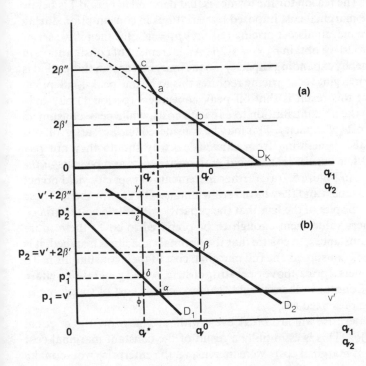

Figure 5.7

operating cost v'. Ignore the rest for the moment. If we subtract v' from each price along D_1, to the *left* of point α, we obtain a 'demand-for-capacity curve' or 'willingness-to-pay-for-capacity curve', $p_1 - v$ for period 1. This is clearly just the portion of D_1 lying above v' in the figure. The corresponding curve for period 2, $p_2 - v'$, is just the portion of D_2 above v'. If we then sum these demand-for-capacity curves vertically, we obtain the curve D_K in the upper half of the figure, and this curve shows how $(p_1 - v') + (p_2 - v')$, or the left-hand side of condition (5.9), varies with capacity. The kink in this total-demand-for-capacity curve occurs at point a in Figure 5.7(a) because D_1 cuts v' at point α in Figure 5.7(b), i.e. $p_1 - v' = 0$ at that point. Thus to the right of point a, D_K simply measures $p_2 - v'$.

Suppose that marginal (daily) capital cost is at the level shown by the line labelled $2\beta'$ in Figure 5.7(a). Then condition (5.9) is satisfied at point b, implying an optimal capacity of q^0. The optimal prices then follow immediately. We should have:

$$p_1 = v' \quad \text{and} \quad p_2 = v' + 2\beta', \tag{5.10}$$

as shown in the figure. The reason for the former is that demand in period 1 is below capacity, therefore the marginal cost imposed by variations in consumption during this period is v'. Hence marginal cost pricing requires $p_1 = v'$. But then if we set $p_1 - v' = 0$ in condition (5.9) we obtain $p_2 = v' + 2\beta'$. An increment of consumption in period 2 can only be met by expanding capacity, so the marginal cost in this period is $v' + 2\beta'$, and therefore marginal cost pricing requires this to be the 'peak-load' price.

The main feature of this result is that off-peak consumers (period 1) pay only operating costs and make no contribution to capacity costs, while peak consumers (period 2) pay all the costs of capacity. This may be considered 'unfair'; after all, off-peak consumers are also benefitting from capacity so why should they not pay something towards it? The answer is that what matters are costs and benefits *at the margin*. Beyond point a in Figure 5.7(a), further increments of capacity yield no net benefit to off-peak consumers and they have zero willingness to pay for them. These increments are made – in spite of the fact that the capacity will lie idle half the day – because peak consumers value them enough to be prepared to cover their entire cost. Under these circumstances, to ensure that the optimal capacity is installed, it is necessary to charge peak consumers the full marginal cost of their consumption. To charge off-peak consumers a price above operating cost, v', would generate a welfare loss, since the value of output to them would then exceed the cost of supplying it, which is v' when capacity is fixed at q^0.

Note also that the enterprise will just break even, with revenues $p_1 q_1 + p_2 q^0$ equal to costs $v' q_1 + (v' + 2\beta) q^0$. This is essentially a result of the constant marginal cost assumption, however. If marginal costs were increasing, the enterprise would make a profit; if decreasing, a loss.

In the situation analysed so far, the 'peak-load' phenomenon does not disappear. Off-peak consumption is still below that at peak, and so the load curve would still have the general shape of that shown in Figure 5.5. Thus it should be emphasized that 'flattening the load curve' is not an end in itself. Rather, as a result of charging optimal prices we obtain the optimal load curve, which in the present case is *not* flat. To further flatten the curve would require a higher price for peak consumption and/or a lower price for off-peak consumption, and the reader should return to Figure 5.7 to show the welfare losses which would result from this.

However, it *is* possible that the optimal policy would imply a flat load curve, i.e. 100 per cent capacity utilization at all times. To see this, refer again to Figure 5.7 and suppose that marginal capacity cost is now higher, at $2\beta''$. This intersects the demand-for-capacity curve at c, implying an optimal capacity level of q^*. Now, if we set $p_1 = v'$, there would be excess demand in period 1, and so we have to raise price to p_1^* to ration demand to capacity. Likewise, the appropriate peak price is p_2^*, which is less than $v' + 2\beta''$ by exactly the amount by which p_1^* exceeds v' (confirm!). This follows of course because the condition in (5.9) must be satisfied. In this situation consumption in both periods is equal to capacity, and both prices contain an element of capital cost. This is because demand in *each* period is capacity-constrained. The enterprise again breaks even.

This latter case is often referred to as the *shifting-peak* case. This is because an attempt to follow the rule of setting $p_1 = v'$ and $p_2 = v' + 2\beta''$ would result in the off-peak demand exceeding the peak demand, and so the peak-load pattern is reversed. In contrast, the first case we considered, where optimal prices *do* take this form, is usually known as the *firm-peak* case. Clearly, essentially the same principles apply to each. Which we observe in practice depends on the relationship between the position of the D_K curve in Figure 5.7(a) and the level of marginal capacity cost.

5.3 Uniform pricing and the pricing structure
To restate the problem: if we take the minute as the smallest time unit in which to measure demand, and take as the most general case that in which demand varies from minute to minute, marginal costs may then vary accordingly. The 'peak-load pricing problem' now becomes that of determining a schedule of prices $p(m)$, $m = 1$, $2, \ldots, 1440$, and a level of capacity. However, such a schedule of prices would be prohibitively costly to implement, and so we have to consider the problem: what is the optimal set of periods into which to subdivide the 'day', such that within each period a single price prevails, whatever the consequent variations in output and marginal cost? We now turn to the problem of the 'decomposition of the load curve'.[13]

We could solve this problem in its full generality, but this involves some heavy mathematics. In the interests of maximizing insight rather than generality we take the following simple approach: our intuition tells us that the optimum pricing structure will have been found when the costs of adding one more pricing period exceed the benefits from doing so. We take the costs of operating the pricing structure as a straightforward function of the number of pricing periods: this will determine the costs of measuring (metering) consumption, providing information on prices, changing prices, computing bills, making mistakes, etc. Hence, the analysis resolves itself into an examination of the benefits of introducing $n+1$ pricing periods where previously there were n. We take the simplest possible case, where $n = 1$. Then the problem becomes that of analysing the welfare losses arising from setting a uniform price over a period within which there are two levels of demand, since the elimination of these losses constitutes the benefit to introducing price differentiation. The essential results can be obtained most simply by taking the model of the previous section, with the added conditions that a uniform pricing constraint rules out the possibility of peak/off-peak differentiation.

We again have the type of load curve of Figure 5.5, with the demand curves and cost structure exactly as shown in Figure 5.6. However, we now have a uniform price constraint: only one price may be set over the entire period. The welfare loss arising from this constraint will be found by comparing the price–output solutions with and without it. We have already analysed the latter, so we now consider the former.

We want first to consider the problem of setting a price in year 0, with capacity output for each 12-hourly period in the year fixed at q^0. As it turns out, we obtain some rather special, though interesting, results for the fixed-capacity case, and so to put them in context let us digress briefly to consider the (logically) more general flexible capacity case. In Figure 5.8, the marginal cost curve MC_0 shows the 12-hourly marginal cost of outputs q_1 and q_2, respectively. The demand curves D_1 and D_2 relate to periods 1 and 2, respectively. The optimal uniform price over the two periods p^* is shown in the figure, implying an output of q_1^* in period 1 and q_2^* in period 2. The property of the optimal uniform price p^* and outputs q_1^* and q_2^* is that they satisfy the condition

$$p^* = W_1 MC_0(q_1^*) + W_2 MC_0(q_2^*), \tag{5.11}$$

where the weights W_1 and W_2 are positive and sum to 1. This condition says that the optimum uniform price p^* is set equal to a weighted average of marginal costs in each period, where these marginal costs are calculated at the demands generated by the uniform price. The weights W_1 and W_2 are given by:

$$W_1 = \frac{\Delta q_1/\Delta p}{(\Delta q_1/\Delta p)+(\Delta q_2/\Delta p)} \qquad W_2 = \frac{\Delta q_2/\Delta p}{(\Delta q_1/\Delta p)+(\Delta q_2/\Delta p)}$$

where $\Delta q_i/\Delta p$, $i = 1, 2$, is the slope of the demand curve D_i *with respect to the price axis*. Before analysing this condition in detail, we note some straightforward implications:

(1) If marginal costs in each period are constant at the same value $\overline{MC_0}$, then:

$$p^* = (W_1 + W_2)\overline{MC_0} = \overline{MC_0}. \qquad (5.12)$$

In other words, we have the obvious result that uniform pricing with fluctuating demand involves no departure from marginal cost principles when marginal costs are the same.

(2) If the demand curves have the same slopes at the optimum point, then $W_1 = W_2 = \frac{1}{2}$ and so we have

$$p^* = \frac{MC_0(q_1^*) + MC_0(q_2^*)}{2}, \qquad (5.13)$$

i.e. the optimal uniform price is simply the arithmetic mean of the two marginal costs.

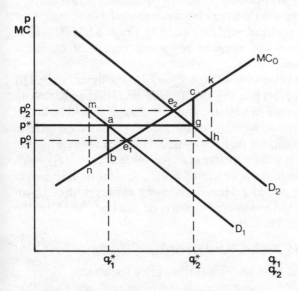

Figure 5.8

(3) If marginal cost increases with output, and $q_2^* > q_1^*$, then since $W_1 + W_2 = 1$, we have

$$MC_0(q_2^*) > p^* > MC_0(q_1^*), \tag{5.14}$$

i.e. the uniform price must lie between the two marginal costs. Moreover, we can rearrange (5.11) to obtain:

$$p^* - MC_0(q_1^*) = (-)\frac{W_2}{W_1}[p^* - MC_0(q_2^*)] \tag{5.15}$$

which implies that the period in which the demand curve is steeper relative to the q axis, or flatter relative to the p axis, will have the higher divergence of price from marginal cost (recall that the Ws are in terms of slopes relative to the p axis).

The derivation of the uniform-pricing condition in (5.11), and its implications, are illustrated in Figure 5.8, where it has been assumed that the marginal cost curve in each 12-hour period MC_0 is linear, and that the demand curves D_1 and D_2 are parallel straight lines and therefore have everywhere the same slope. Now if peak/off-peak price differentiation could be practised, marginal cost pricing would imply prices p_1 and p_2, respectively, corresponding to intersection points e_1 and e_2. We can best see the effects of a uniform-pricing constraint by supposing that initially these two prices did prevail, but then uniform pricing was imposed. Now, recall that the marginal value of output to consumers is measured by price, while its cost is measured by marginal cost. Then, the marginal net social benefit of output is measured by price *minus* marginal cost.

Now suppose that the uniform price were set initially at p_2^0 in the figure, so that $p_2^0 - MC_0(q_2) = 0$, while $p_2^0 - MC_0(q_1)$ is given by the distance mn. This means that an increment in q_1 would yield a net gain in welfare. Thus the change should be made. This change can only be brought about by reducing the uniform price below its level p_2^0. Extending this reasoning, we can see that at any uniform price above p^* in the figure, the value of $(p_1 - MC_0(q_1))$ will be greater than the value of $(MC_0(q_2) - p_2)$, indicating that a further reduction in the price will generate a greater welfare gain in period 1 than the welfare loss in period 2. Hence, assuming appropriate compensation were paid, a Pareto-preferred position can always be reached. At p^*, on the other hand, we have that $ab = cg$, i.e. that

$$p^* - MC_0(q_2^*) = MC_0(q_2^*) - p^* \tag{5.16}$$

so that no net welfare gain would be made by a further price reduction.

Using similar reasoning, we could begin with a uniform price at p_1^0, and show that the marginal welfare gain from reducing q_2, measured approximately by kh, exceeds the marginal welfare loss from reducing q_1, which is zero, and so such a reduction would be Pareto optimal, again assuming appropriate redistribution. Extending this reasoning would again lead to p^* as the uniform price at which the marginal welfare gain in period 2 is just equal to the marginal welfare loss in period 1. Thus, we have that p^* is the Pareto-optimal uniform price, since any other price holds out the possibility of Pareto improvement.

Because of the assumption of parallel demand curves, we have in this case that the uniform price is the arithmetic mean of marginal costs in the two periods, as was earlier shown to be the case. The figure also enables us to show the welfare gains from introducing peak/off-peak price differentiation. If the uniform price p^* were replaced by the prices p_1^0 and p_2^0 in periods 1 and 2 respectively, then the welfare gain in period 1 is approximately the area abe_1, while that in period 2 is the area cge_2. Hence the sum of these areas should be set against the cost (per day) of operating a pricing mechanism which would permit such price differentiation. Note that the sum of these areas will be greater: (a) the steeper the marginal cost curve MC_0, and (b) the greater the difference between the heights of the demand curves.

Moreover, as we would expect, the effect of a uniform-pricing system is to lead peak output to be greater, and off-peak output to be less, than under a peak-load pricing system, as can be seen in Figure 5.8.

Since period 2 consumers are better off at g than they would be at e_2, while period 1 consumers are worse off at a than they would be at e_1, the uniform-pricing system could be thought of as 'discriminating' against off-peak consumers and in favour of peak consumers.

The notion that the uniform price should be set so that the marginal net social benefit, price *minus* marginal cost, is equal in absolute value in each period, is intuitively appealing. However, as equation (5.15) shows, this is not quite true in the general case, but rather only in the special case we have just examined. As (5.15) shows, in general the price–marginal cost divergences will be different in each period. The reason is that the instrument by which we adjust outputs and welfare losses in the two markets is the uniform price p and so the relevant optimality condition is that the marginal net welfare losses, *with respect to changes in the uniform price*, must be equal. Equality of marginal net welfare losses with respect to price is equivalent to that with respect to output if and only if the effect on output of a change in the uniform price is the same in each market, i.e. if and only if the demand curves have the same slopes.

The foregoing discussion of optimum uniform pricing has prepared the way for analysis of the problem in the fixed-capacity case. We find in this case some results which differ in an interesting and empirically important way from those just derived. First, we analyse the problem of setting price in year 0, with capacity given. Figure

5.9 shows three logical possibilities. In (a) we have the case in which the demand curves in both periods intersect the horizontal portion of the MC_0 curve, i.e. there will be excess capacity in both periods. In that case, we can conclude immediately from the previous analysis that the uniform price will be set at v', since marginal cost is the same in each period. Hence, in this case, there is no departure from the principle of marginal cost pricing.

In (b) we have that both demand curves intersect the 'vertical portion' of MC_0. In this case, the following problem arises: if the uniform price is set below p_2^0 in the figure, there will be excess demand in period 2, while if it is set above p_1^0, there will be a welfare loss in period 1. In analysing the nature of an optimal choice, we must therefore take into account the costs and feasibility of using non-price rationing methods, and weigh these against period 1 welfare losses. Thus at one extreme, suppose that demand can be *costlessly* restricted to capacity in a way which ensures that units of output are acquired by the people who would be prepared to pay the most for them. In this case, the optimum solution is to set the uniform price *no higher than* p_1^0 in Figure 5.9(b). The reason for this is that at any higher price, period 1 consumption would be less than capacity $\bar{q}^0$, and there would be a welfare loss measured at the margin by the excess of price over v'. Now if, on the other hand, price were set at p_1^0 (or indeed at any value down to v'), this welfare loss would be avoided. A price of p_1^0 would imply that in period 2, since output cannot exceed $\bar{q}^0$, there would be excess demand of the amount ab. The assumption of costless non-

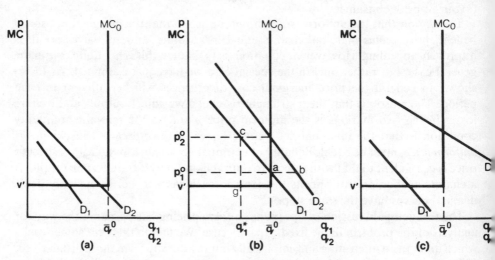

Figure 5.9

price rationing, however, implies that period 2 demand could be restricted to capacity without cost. Hence, the policy of setting price at p_1^0 and restricting demand in period 2 to capacity would generate no welfare loss, as compared to a uniform price greater than p_2^0. Thus, we have the optimal uniform price[14] as p_1^0.

This conclusion obviously depended on an extreme and unrealistic assumption about non-price rationing. Let us now choose its opposite, and assume infinite costs of *any* amount of non-price rationing, however small. It follows that a uniform price at any value below p_2^0 in Figure 5.9(b) would involve infinite costs arising out of the consequent need to restrict demand in period 2 to capacity $\bar{q}^0$. The conclusion must be that p_2^0 is the optimal price, since at that price no non-price rationing costs are incurred, while the total welfare loss (as compared to the previous case with price at p_2^0) is incurred by period 1 consumers, and is approximated by the area *cga* in the figure.

These two extreme cases serve to bring out the main issues. Any uniform price in the interval $p_2^0 > p^0 > p_1^0$ must involve welfare losses in period 1 and excess demand in period 2. Therefore, the optimal uniform price now depends on a comparison of the costs of non-price rationing on the one hand, with the period 1 welfare losses on the other. The costs of non-price rationing will depend on the level of desired demand q_2 and on the level of capacity, q^0, and of course only exist if $q_2 > q^0$. We could then introduce the *rationing cost function*

$$R = R(q^0, q_2). \tag{5.17}$$

This rationing cost function measures the two kinds of costs arising out of non-price rationing which we discussed in the previous section: the resource costs of administering the rationing mechanism; and the welfare losses which arise out of the inequalities among consumers' marginal valuations of output. The precise form of the R-function will of course depend on the particular non-price rationing system adopted,[15] but for present purposes we need consider only its general properties. We would expect an increase in capacity with demand fixed to reduce the extent of non-price rationing and hence rationing costs, while an increase in demand with capacity fixed, would increase these costs. Thus let MB_{q_0} represent the *marginal rationing cost saving* from a *capacity increase* and MC_{q_2} the *marginal rationing cost increase* from a *demand increase*.

In the cases shown in Figure 5.9, capacity is fixed. A small change in the uniform price changes desired demand in period 2 (though not actual consumption because this is restricted to capacity) and this change in demand then changes rationing costs by MC_{q_2}. The optimal uniform price p^* must then satisfy the condition

$$(p^* - p_1^0) \cdot \frac{\Delta q_1}{\Delta p} = MC_{q_2} \frac{\Delta q_2}{\Delta p} \tag{5.18}$$

where $\Delta q_1/\Delta p$ is the slope of D_1, and $\Delta q_2/\Delta p$ is the slope of D_2 (with respect to the p axis). This condition has a straightforward interpretation. The term on the left-hand side is the marginal welfare loss in period 1 with respect to changes in the uniform price. The term on the right-hand side is the marginal rationing cost with respect to the uniform price. The optimal uniform price is such as to equate these. Only in the case in which the marginal rationing cost is zero, would the uniform price be set at p_1^0. In general it would not be, and so we would expect welfare losses in both periods. It follows from this that the introduction of peak/off-peak price differentiation will have two effects: it will, in allowing prices to be set at p_1^0 and p_2^0 in the respective periods, first eliminate the welfare losses of period 1 consumers, and secondly avoid the costs of non-price rationing in period 2. Thus, the sum of these savings should be set against the costs of operating the pricing mechanism.

The third case, shown in Figure 5.9(c), has D_1 intersecting the horizontal portion of MC_0, and D_2 intersecting the vertical. Apart from a few details, this case leads to the same conclusions as that just considered. It is left to the reader to provide the analysis, and, in particular, to justify the conclusion that the optimal uniform price condition is now

$$(p^* - v')\frac{\Delta q_1}{\Delta p} = MC_{q_2}\frac{\Delta q_2}{\Delta p}. \tag{5.19}$$

We can now conclude this discussion of uniform pricing in the context of fixed-capacity plant by examining the problem of planning price and capacity for year 1, when price differentiation for peak and off-peak demands cannot be made. Of particular interest will be the implications for the investment programme of the enterprise.

Here, we do not consider the 'shifting peak' case discussed in the previous section; instead we leave the reader to extend to this the analysis now given for the case in which off-peak output will be less than capacity. (See also the Appendix to this chapter.) In Figure 5.10, we again assume parallel demand curves, D_1 and D_2, respectively. Recalling our earlier solution for peak-load pricing, we know that if price differentiation were possible, planned capacity would be set at $\bar{q}^0$, with planned price in period 1 at v' and in period 2 at $v' + 2\beta'$. However, the uniform-pricing constraint precludes this solution. We therefore have to solve the problem from first principles, taking this constraint into account.

In contrast to the cases just considered for period 0, we now have *two* instruments with which to determine consumers' welfare, namely the (uniform) price and capacity. We take them one at a time. Suppose first that we have fixed capacity at its optimal level and want to know what price to set. But this is precisely the problem we have just solved – determining optimal price with given capacity – and so the optimal condition for price is again (5.19). Given capacity, the optimal uniform price equates marginal welfare loss $p - v'$ in period 1 with marginal rationing cost MC_{q_2} in period 2 (each appropriately weighted by the slope of the demand curve). A change in price leaves consumption in period 2 unaffected (because this is fixed at the level of capacity), and changes only excess demand and therefore rationing costs. This then has to be traded off against the welfare effects of a price change in period 1.

Now suppose that price is fixed at its optimal level, and consider the effect of a small increase in capacity. Assuming that period 1 demand is below capacity, this has no welfare effect in that period. But it has two effects on welfare in period 2. Since consumption in this period is constrained by capacity, a capacity increase allows an equal increase in consumption. Denote the benefit arising out of this marginal consumption increase by MB_{q_2}. The *net* benefit of the *capacity* increase is then $MB_{q_2} - v'$. In addition to this, the increase in capacity (with price and therefore demand in period 2 given) reduces rationing costs, by an amount MB_{q_0}. Thus the overall marginal benefit of a capacity increment is $(MB_{q_2} - v') + MB_{q_0}$, and the optimal capacity level equates this to the marginal capacity cost $2\beta'$. Thus we have as the optimal capacity condition:

$$(MB_{q_2} - v') + MB_{q_0} = 2\beta'. \qquad (5.20)$$

The two conditions (5.19) and (5.20) taken together then imply the kind of solution illustrated in Figure 5.10. Since in (5.19), $MC_{q_2} > 0$, the optimal uniform price p^* is certainly above v^*. How far above will depend on the value of MC_{q_2}, which will also be influenced by the level of capacity. The figure shows optimal capacity at $\hat{q}^0$, which is above the first-best level of $\bar{q}^0$, and implies excess demand in period 2 of $q_2^* - \hat{q}^0$. This what is perhaps the most plausible kind of solution, but one in which optimal capacity would be *less* than $\bar{q}^0$ cannot be ruled out. The argument goes as follows: *if* available output in period 2 *were* allocated according to willingness to pay, then at capacity $\hat{q}^0$ the marginal benefit of consumption MB_{q_2} would be given by $\hat{p}_2$, the coordinate of $\hat{q}_0$ on the demand curve D_2 in Figure 5.10. In that case (5.20) would become:

$$\hat{p}_2 = v' + 2\beta' - MB_{q_0} \qquad (5.21)$$

and, since $MB_{q_0} > 0$, this must imply a capacity level above $\bar{q}^0$, because at that point we would have $\hat{p}_2 = v' + 2\beta'$. However, when rationing is *not* according to willingness to pay, the marginal benefit of consumption MB_{q_2} will in general differ from $\hat{p}_2$, its value depending on precisely *how* available output is allocated, i.e. on the non-price rationing mechanism. Marginal output may be allocated to consumers who value it at more than or less than $\hat{p}_2$; this depends entirely on the mechanism. However, if MB_{q_2} at any output level either exceeds the corresponding

p_2 level or, if below, is reasonably close to it, then, since $MB_{q_0} > 0$, (5.20) will imply that capacity is larger as a result of the uniform-pricing constraint. A more rigorous treatment of this question is given in the Appendix to this chapter.

To summarize the conclusions from this analysis of uniform pricing under conditions of fluctuating demand: except in the case of perfectly costless non-price rationing, there are invariably welfare losses arising from the deviations of price from marginal costs in each period. When capacity is fixed, the overall welfare loss is the sum of the loss of consumption benefits to off-peak consumers, and the costs of non-price rationing of peak demand (which may not all be borne by the enterprise).

When capacity is variable, the welfare loss is the sum of loss of consumption benefits to off-peak consumers, costs of over-expansion of capacity, and non-price rationing costs. All these losses would be avoided by a system of peak/off-peak price differentiation, and so should be compared with the costs of introducing and operating such a system. Note that we have been discussing an *optimal* uniform-pricing system. It is possible to argue that any uniform-pricing system in fact in use would not be optimal. Then, this implies that the welfare losses set out above *understate* the true losses from uniform pricing, since they refer to the case in which these are minimized. This of course strengthens the case for price differentiation.

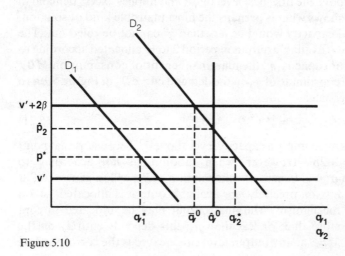

Figure 5.10

The main purpose of the analysis was to bring out the basic elements of a general solution to the problem of 'decomposition of the load curve'. If there were 1,440 different demand curves, rather than just two, the analysis would be the same in kind. However, the simple analysis set out here probably has more practical relevance than the general one. It is unlikely that more than two or three pricing periods would in practice be justified, and so a simple analysis is adequate. Moreover, in many parts of the public sector the major gain would probably be realized by introducing just two pricing periods where currently there is one, with sharply diminishing returns accruing to further complexity. Hence, the analysis presented here is likely to be directly applicable.

Finally, the analysis of the optimal uniform price is itself of immediate relevance to the peak-load pricing problem. Once optimal pricing periods have been determined, it is probable that there will be some fluctuations of demand within them. Hence, the price set for each period will itself be a uniform price, and the present analysis has suggested how this could be determined.

5.4 Indivisibilities

The assumption of continuity, or infinite divisibility, which underlies most of economic analysis is always an approximation: everything in reality is measured in finite units. In many contexts, where the basic unit of measurement is small relative to the aggregate, this approximation is acceptable. However, it may happen that the aggregate is small relative to the unit, in which case marginal analysis based on the 'nicely calculated less or more' may not be applicable. Indivisibilities imply discontinuities and therefore the absence of well-defined slopes on which marginal analysis is based. Here we consider the problems which arise when we try to apply marginal cost pricing rules to public enterprises whose capacity can only be increased in relatively large indivisible units. Examples abound: if the capacity of a railway coach is x passengers, to carry the $x + 1$st requires another coach; to increase the capacity of a cross-channel ferry service requires another ship; if existing airports are at capacity, expansion requires a new runway and terminal facilities; and so on. Note that two kinds of situation may exist here: there may be an absolute technological or physical barrier to relatively small capacity increments; or, though technically feasible, it may be extremely costly to make small increments. Many 'indivisibilities' are likely to be of the latter kind. It would be quite possible to design the one-man railway coach or to launch the one-passenger cross-channel ferry service, but they would be 'prohibitively' expensive ways of adding to capacity. The question of the appropriate scale of expansion therefore becomes an economic problem, with the technological indivisibility an extreme case, in which the costs of marginal increments are infinite. Here, however, we analyse only this extreme case.

We take the fixed-capacity situation of the first section of this chapter and assume that there are no peak-load problems: demand is uniform in every minute of the year, and so we again choose the year as the time unit in terms of which to express the rate of production. Again, it is assumed to take a year to expand capacity. Now, however, capacity can only be expanded in fixed, indivisible amounts $\bar{K}$. Thus, if the enterprise has at the beginning of year 0 a capacity of K_0, its capacity in year 1 can only take on the possible values $K_0, K_0 + \bar{K}, K_0 + 2\bar{K}, \ldots$, or in general $K_0 + \lambda\bar{K}$, $\lambda = 0, 1, 2, \ldots$. We assume essentially the same cost conditions as in the first section of this chapter, except for the amendments made necessary by the existence of indivisibilities. The total cost curves for various levels of capacity will be as shown in Figure 5.11. The output rates q_0, q_1 and q_2 represent the respective capacity levels K_0, $K_0 + \bar{K}$ and $K_0 + 2\bar{K}$. The dotted line C is hypothetical; the only points on it which are actually available are b_0, b_1 and b_2. The total cost curves become vertical at those points because of the rigid capacity assumption. The intercepts a_0, a_1 and a_2 represent capacity costs nK_0, $n(K_0 + \bar{K})$ and $n(K_0 + 2\bar{K})$, respectively. Segments, a_0b_0, a_1b_1 and a_2b_2, reflect the assumption that total costs vary proportionately with output as output increases towards capacity.

To analyse the problem of setting price and output in year 0 would add nothing to the analysis in the first section, and so we consider only the planning problems of the

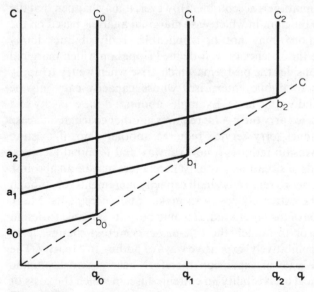

Figure 5.11

enterprise. At the beginning of year 0 the enterprise must forecast a demand curve for year 1, choose planned price, output and capacity, and determine its investment programme. Clearly, at the root of the problem is the question of the *timing* of new investment: in what year is it optimal to make the great leap from one capacity level to another? We analyse the determinants of the answer with the help of Figure 5.12. Capacity output in year 0 is $\bar{q}_0$, and the cost 'curves' take the now familiar form for the fixed-capacity case.[16] Let D_1 be the estimated demand curve for year 1. In the light of this, the enterprise can adopt one of two alternative investment plans. It can choose not to invest, in which case capacity output remains at $\bar{q}_0$; or it can make the increment K to capacity so that capacity output increases to $\bar{q}_1$. Each of these implies a corresponding pricing policy. In the first case, rationing available output by price implies that price should be set at p_1^*. In the second case, the principle of marginal cost pricing requires that price be set at v, equal to marginal running costs. Given that these pricing policies *would* accompany the corresponding investment choice, how do we determine which choice should be made?

First, consider the benefits to consumers arising from the expansion. As before, $B(q)$ measures the money value of benefits received by consumers from output q. Then, if capacity is expanded, the gain which consumers would receive from the output increase is given by

$$\Delta B = B(q_1^*) - B(\bar{q}_0). \qquad (5.22)$$

The costs imposed by the increase are first the increase in variable costs, given simply as $v_1^* - q_0$), which is the shaded area $aq_1^*\bar{q}_0d$ in the figure; and secondly the capacity costs, which depend *not* on the increase in output, $q_1^* - \bar{q}_0$, but the increase in *capacity*, $\bar{q}_1 - \bar{q}_0$, and so are given by $\beta(q_1 - \bar{q}_0)$. Hence, the criterion for undertaking the capacity expansion, namely that consumer benefits exceed costs, could be written as

$$B(q_1^*) - B(q_0) > \beta(\bar{q}_1 - \bar{q}_0) + v(q_1^* - \bar{q}_0). \qquad (5.23)$$

If this criterion is not satisfied, then no investment should be made in year 0, though of course the decision can be re-examined at the beginning of year 1 in relation to the demand estimate for year 2.

Take as an approximation to the value of the change in benefits ΔB the area $aq_1^*\bar{q}_0c$ under the demand curve. Then, netting out the increased variable costs (= additional total expenditure by buyers) gives the 'consumer surplus' adc as the benefit gain, to be compared to the increased capacity cost $\beta(\bar{q}_1 - \bar{q}_0)$. The point in time at which the capacity expansion should be made is then that at which the area of net benefit gain, adc, is just equal to the increased capital cost, area $defg$. Note that, in Figure 5.12, the area $adeb$ is common to both the extra consumer benefit and the extra capital cost. Thus the comparison boils down to one between triangle *bec* and area *abfg* in the figure. Clearly then, in the case shown in the figure, the discrete capacity increment would not be warranted because the net gain in consumer benefit is less than the extra capital cost.

However, if demand is steadily growing over time then a point will come at which an expansion will be warranted; Figure 5.13(a) illustrates. The equality of the areas of the triangles *abc* and *ade* ensure that the condition of equality between net benefits and net capital costs is satisfied. In Figure 5.13(b), the implications of this investment criterion for the pattern of prices over time is shown, on the assumptions that each successive increment in capacity is of the same size, and demand grows smoothly at a constant rate – with the slope of the demand curve unchanged – over time. The pattern shown in Figure 5.13(a) is repeated indefinitely, with t_1^*, t_2^* ... showing the points in time at which it is optimal to expand capacity. Just before capacity is expanded, the price required to ration demand to capacity is again p_1^*, then immediately the new capacity comes on stream the rationing price falls to p_2^*. As demand grows, so this price must rise steadily until another capacity expansion takes place and again there is an abrupt cut in price.

Clearly, the optimal time-paths of price and capacity involve fluctuations in prices which could be very marked. The steeper the demand curve, and the larger the

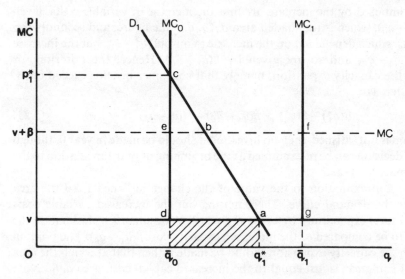

Figure 5.12

size of capacity increment, the wider apart will be the upper and lower limits of price, p_1^* and p_2^* (though p_2^* can never be below v); while the faster the growth rate of demand, the faster will be the rate of increase in price and the more frequently capacity increments will be made. At each point in time at which price is less than the average incremental cost $v + \beta$, the enterprise will make a loss, but of course it makes a profit when price exceeds $v + \beta$, which it must for some of the time. The *present value* of profits may then be positive or negative in general, depending on the respective differences between the upper and lower price limits and $v + \beta$, and also on the length of time prices are above or below this level. What is certain is that, over time, profits will also fluctuate markedly.

These fluctuations in prices and profits might well be a very undesirable aspect of the optimal solution to the planners who actually control the public enterprise. The time-horizons over which financial outcomes are appraised may be far shorter than the interval between capacity expansions ($t_2^* - t_1^*$, say), and so the enterprise may appear to be persistently making losses (the $p(t) < v + \beta$ phase) or persistently making 'excessive' profits (the $p(t) > v + \beta$ phase). The rate of growth of prices may be regarded as excessive, the sudden plunges in price viewed as disruptive,[17] and there may be strong resistance to the high prices required to ration demand to capacity just before an expansion is undertaken. However, any other pricing pattern

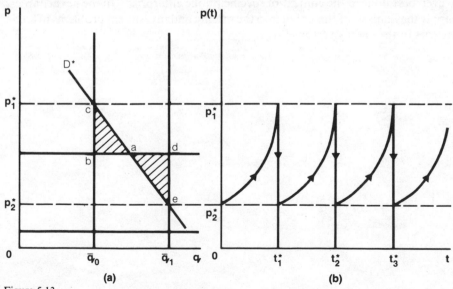

(a)   (b)

Figure 5.13

will involve welfare losses. If the price floor p_2^* is raised, this will involve under-utilization of capacity and welfare losses just after the new capacity comes on stream. If the price ceiling p_1^* is lowered then with unchanged timing of capacity expansion there will have to be non-price rationing in the period before a capacity expansion. More probably, capacity will be expanded prematurely, so that capital costs, in present value terms, are higher than they should be. Likewise short-run profit constraints, both minima and maxima, will imply distortions to prices and corresponding welfare losses, without necessarily changing the net present value of the entire time-stream of profits. Thus the optimal 'smoothing' of the price fluctuations and the associated timing of capacity expansions would have to trade off these kinds of welfare losses against the savings in costs which are thought to arise from having a more stable sequence of prices.

5.5   Conclusions
In this chapter we have considered three sets of problems which arise when the attempt is made to apply marginal cost pricing principles in practice. This treatment of these problems is by no means exhaustive. We have not tried to discuss the difficulties of estimating the cost and demand functions on which to base pricing policies, which are very large topics in themselves. Nor have we covered all the problems of defining cost, demands and outputs in practical situations. This is, however, best done in the context of specific public enterprises. In the next chapter, we apply the analysis of this chapter to the pricing and investment problems of some industries in the energy sector.

Appendix to chapter 5

1 Fixed-capacity plant

For this problem the benefit functions are just as in the Appendix to chapter 4: $B_0(q_0)$ for period 0 and $B_1(q_1)/1+r$ for period 1, with $B_0'(q_0) = p_0(q_0)$ and $B_1'(q_1) = p_1(q_1)$. The cost functions are

$$C_0 = vq_0 + \beta\bar{q}_0 \quad \text{for} \quad q_0 \leqslant \bar{q}_0 \tag{A.5.1}$$

$$C_1 = (v+\beta)q_1 \tag{A.5.2}$$

where $\bar{q}_0$ is fixed capacity and the capacity-constraint condition in (A.5.1) is an essential element of the period 0 problem.

Optimal price and output for period 0 are found by maximizing $B(q_0) - C_0$ subject to the capacity constraint, and this yields

$$p(q_0^*) = v + \lambda^* \tag{A.5.3}$$

$$q_0^* - \bar{q}_0 \leqslant 0 \qquad \lambda^* \geqslant 0 \qquad \lambda^*[q_0^* - \bar{q}_0] = 0 \tag{A.5.4}$$

as the necessary conditions, with λ^* as the dual variable associated with the capacity constraint. If $q_0^* < \bar{q}_0$, we have $\lambda^* = 0$ from (A.5.4), and so $p^* = v$ in (A.5.3). If $\lambda^* > 0$, the capacity constraint binds, and $q^* = \bar{q}_0$ from (A.5.4). Hence the value of this shadow price λ^* is given by

$$\lambda^* = p(\bar{q}_0) - v \gtrless \beta. \tag{A.5.5}$$

If $\lambda^* > \beta$, the marginal value of capacity exceeds its marginal cost and a capacity expansion would be warranted. If $\lambda^* = \beta$ then $p^* = v+\beta$, and the short-run capacity output $\bar{q}_0$ is also the long-run optimal output. If $\lambda^* < \beta$ then a capacity reduction is warranted. Clearly $\lambda^* = p^* - v$ lends itself to the interpretation as a 'marginal willingness to pay for capacity' at the period 0 optimum. (The reader should now refer back to Figure 5.3 and relate these results to (a) and (b) of that diagram.)

Optimal period 1 price and output are found by maximizing $B_1(q_1) - C_1$, yielding

$$p_1(q_1^*) = v + \beta, \tag{A.5.6}$$

the long-run marginal cost pricing solution.

2 Peak-load pricing

We can in this Appendix be quite general, and allow n 'demand periods', where n can be as large as we wish. Let q_i, $i = 1, \ldots n$ be demand in period i, $B_i(q_i)$ corresponding consumer benefit, and $\bar{q}$ capacity, in terms of the maximum output which can be produced in any period. Let the total cost function be

$$C = \sum_{i=1}^{n} vq_i + \beta\bar{q}, \tag{A.5.7}$$

where v represents the variable cost per unit of q_i (assumed independent of output), while β represents the cost of one unit of capacity over the entire demand period. For example if the demand period is the day, β would be the daily cost of one unit of capacity output; q_i could be demand in the ith minute of the day, so that $i = 1440$, and v is the cost of producing one unit of q_i.

The short-run problem, with p_i the price which is to be set in period i, and no restrictions on the possibility of price variation across periods, is to maximize $\sum_i B_i(q_i) - C$ subject to the capacity constraint:

$$q_i \leqslant \bar{q}_0 \qquad i = 1, \ldots, n \tag{A.5.8}$$

where $\bar{q}_0$ is the given capacity level. The necessary conditions are:

$$p_i^* - v - \lambda_i^* = 0 \quad i = 1, \ldots, n \tag{A.5.9}$$

$$q_i^* - \bar{q}^0 \leqslant 0 \quad \lambda_i^* \geqslant 0 \quad \lambda_i^*(q_i^* - \bar{q}^0) = 0 \quad i = 1, \ldots, n \tag{A.5.10}$$

implying that if in period i, $q_i^* < \bar{q}^0$, then $p_i^* = v$, while for any period in which $\lambda_i^* > 0$, $q_i^* = \bar{q}^0$ and price is at whatever level restrains demand to capacity. λ_i^* then measures $p_i^* - v$ at this constrained position, the net willingness of consumers in period i to pay for capacity.

The long-run problem allows $\bar{q}$ to become a choice variable, and so we obtain the conditions:

$$p_i^* - v - \lambda_i^* = 0 \tag{A.5.11}$$

$$\sum_i \lambda_i^* = \beta \tag{A.5.12}$$

$$q_i^* - \bar{q}^* \leqslant 0 \qquad \lambda_i^* \geqslant 0 \qquad \lambda_i^*(q_i^* - \bar{q}^*) = 0 \tag{A.5.13}$$

where $\bar{q}^*$ is now optimal capacity. (A.5.11) and (A.5.12) then imply the *optimal capacity rule*:

$$\sum_i (p_i^* - v) = \beta. \tag{A.5.14}$$

Thus, for any period in which $q_i^* < \bar{q}^*$, $p_i^* = v$, while across all those periods for which $\lambda_i^* > 0$, $q_i^* = \bar{q}^*$ and the sum of their willingness to pay for capacity equals the marginal capacity cost.

Setting $n = 2$, the reader should now relate these conditions to the discussion in section 5.2.

3 Uniform pricing

Suppose now that only one price, p, can prevail across the entire demand cycle. We let $q_i(p)$ denote the demand function for output in period i. Consider first the 'flexible output' case, where $C_0(q_i)$ denotes the short-run marginal cost. The problem is then to maximize $\sum_i B_i(q_i(p)) - \sum C_0(q_i(p))$ with respect to the uniform price p. This yields the necessary condition:

$$\sum_i (p^* - C_0'(q_i^*)) \frac{dq_i}{dp} = 0 \qquad (A.5.15)$$

which, in the case $n = 2$, gives condition (5.11) of this chapter.

Where capacity is rigid, we have to consider the problem of non-price rationing, and this means we have to define the objective function of the problem with some care. In any period i, the previous formulation of the consumer benefit function $B_i(q_i)$ only holds if $q_i \leqslant \bar{q}$, so that each consumer's demand can be met. If there is non-price rationing, then aggregate consumer benefit will depend on precisely how available output will be allocated under the rationing mechanism. Also we need to introduce the idea of non-price rationing costs.

Thus, let I denote the index set of time-periods in which, at the optimum, non-price rationing occurs. Then for $i \in I$ let $V_i(\bar{q})$ denote total consumer benefit from consumption and $R_i(q_i, \bar{q})$ total rationing cost. The argument of $V_i(\bar{q})$ is capacity $\bar{q}$ because of course for $i \in I$ this gives *actual* total consumption as opposed to desired demand. For $i \notin I$, $B_i(q_i)$ denotes total consumer benefit and no R_i function exists. Clearly, $i \in I$ if and only if, at the optimum, $q_i > \bar{q}$. The total cost function is, as before, $C = \sum_i vq_i + \beta\bar{q}$. Then optimal uniform price and capacity are found by maximizing:

$$\sum_{i \notin I} [B_i(q_i(p)) - vq_i(p)] + \sum_{i \in I} [V_i(\bar{q}) - v\bar{q} - R_i(q_i(p), \bar{q})] - \beta\bar{q}. \qquad (A.5.16)$$

Necessary conditions are given by:

$$\sum_{i \notin I} [p^* - v] \frac{dq_i}{dp} = \sum_{i \in I} \frac{\partial R_i}{\partial q_i} \frac{\partial q_i}{\partial p} \qquad (A.5.17)$$

$$\sum_{i \in I} \left[\frac{(dV_i - v)}{d\bar{q}} - \frac{\partial R_i}{\partial \bar{q}} \right] = \beta. \qquad (A.5.18)$$

These conditions then form the basis for (5.19) and (5.20) in this chapter, and are illustrated in Figure 5.10, to which the reader should refer at this point.

Note that this analysis brings out something which is easily overlooked in the case where $n = 2$. Conditions (A.5.17) and (A.5.18) require us to know, in advance of the solution to the problem, exactly which will be the periods when non-price rationing will take place and which not (i.e. the set I needs to be known *a priori*). In fact this would not in general be known, and is something which would have to be found out explicitly. This greatly complicates the problem, and it is doubtful if it would be worthwhile to pursue the question in general terms. Once the non-price rationing mechanism is specified in detail, the problem becomes more tractable. This is shown in chapter 10, where a specific type of rationing mechanism – that of random rationing – is considered.

4   Indivisibilities

For simplicity we ignore the peak-load pricing issue, and consider demand simply as growing steadily through time. It will also be convenient to regard time as continuous rather than discrete. Thus let $q(p(t), t)$ be demand at time t, with consumer benefit at t correspondingly given by $B(q(p, t))$. The situation is that at the present time, there is a given capacity output $\bar{q}^0$, and this can only be increased in discrete steps. Again for simplicity we assume capacity increments are all of the same size, $\bar{q}^0$, and also that the capital expenditure per unit of an increment of capacity is c. We let t_i, $i = 1, 2, \ldots, \infty$ be the points in time at which a capacity increment will be made, so that at t_1 capacity becomes $2\bar{q}^0$, at t_2 it becomes $3\bar{q}^0$, and in general at t_i capacity becomes $(i+1)\bar{q}^0$. It follows that we have the capacity constraints:

$$q(p(t), t) \leqslant i\bar{q}^0 \quad \text{when} \quad t_{i-1} \leqslant t \leqslant t_i \quad i = 1, \ldots \quad \text{(A.5.19)}$$

and $t_0 = 0$, the present. One part of the problem is of course to find the optimal values of t_i, i.e. the optimal points in time at which to make the capacity expansions. The other part of the problem is to find the optimal time-path of prices, $p(t)$. At any time t, total operating costs will be $v \cdot q(p, t)$. Hence, over any time-interval (t_{i-1}, t_i), the present value of the net benefit of consumption, discounted to time 0 at the given discount rate r, will be:

$$B_i = \int_{t_{i-1}}^{t_i} \{B(q(p, t)) - vq(p, t)\} e^{-rt} dt. \quad \text{(A.5.20)}$$

It follows that the maximand of the problem is the present value of net consumption benefits *minus* the present value of capital costs, which is given by

$$N = \sum_{i=1}^{\infty} [B_i - c\bar{q}^0]e^{-rt_i}. \tag{A.5.21}$$

N is to be maximized with respect to each $p(t)$ and t_i, and subject to the constraints in (A.5.19). Necessary conditions are:

$$[B(q(p^*, t_i^*)) - vq(p^*, t_i^*) - B(q(\hat{p}, t_i^*)) + vq(\hat{p}, t_i^*) + rc\bar{q}^0]e^{-rt_i} = 0 \tag{A.5.22}$$

$$[p(t) - v]e^{-rt} - \lambda^*(t) = 0 \tag{A.5.23}$$

$$q(p(t), t) - i\bar{q}^0 \leqslant 0 \qquad \lambda^*(t) \geqslant 0$$

$$\lambda^*(t)[q(p(t), t) - i\bar{q}^0] = 0 \qquad t_{i-1} \leqslant t \leqslant t_i \tag{A.5.24}$$

where $\lambda^*(t)$ is the optimal value at t of the dual variable associated with the capacity constraints, p^* is the price at t_i^* *without* the capacity expansion (the 'high' price) and $\hat{p}$ is the price at t_i^* *with* the expansion (the 'low' price). Rearranging condition (A.5.22) with an obvious change in notation gives:

$$\hat{B}(t_i^*) - B^*(t_i^*) - v(\hat{q} - q^*) = rc\bar{q}^0 \tag{A.5.25}$$

which is the condition on the optimal timing of capacity expansion. When the increase in consumer benefit made possible by the capacity expansion, net of increased operating costs, is just equal to the cost per unit of *capacity* output, the capacity expansion is warranted. The remaining two conditions then determine the optimal time-path of prices. If at any t demand is less than capacity, $\lambda^*(t) = 0$ and, in (A.5.2), price is equal to marginal operating cost. If, however, $\lambda^*(t) > 0$, demand is at capacity and price exceeds v to an extent required to restrain demand to capacity. Then, at each instant, $\lambda^*(t)$ is the present value of the marginal willingness to pay for capacity. Note, however, that this does not play a role in the determination of the optimal timing of a capacity increase. That decision is determined by the value of a discrete jump in output, rather than by a marginal calculation.

Chapter 6

Further applications of marginal cost pricing: the energy industries

6.1 Introduction

The problems considered in the previous chapter – rigid capacity, peak-loads, indivisibilities – arise in many public enterprises, and it is useful to have developed the analytical means of handling them. The treatment of these problems was quite general. We now take a step nearer reality by examining some aspects of the pricing and investment problems of the major public enterprises in the energy sector. We shall make good use of the analysis developed in chapter 5, but shall also find that we have to extend it in some respects if we are to capture the main elements of the real problems.

The energy industries which, in the UK, are operated as public enterprises are coal, gas and electricity, and so these are the subjects of this chapter. Coal and gas are similar to each other, and different to electricity, in three main economically relevant respects:

(1) gas and coal are both traded on world markets, unlike electricity;
(2) gas and coal are both exhaustible natural resources,[1] whereas electricity is a manufactured good which could be produced indefinitely into the future as long as the required inputs are still available;
(3) gas and coal are storable, which has important implications for peak-load pricing.

These economic characteristics of the gas and coal industries require us to modify the analysis of the last chapter when seeking to apply it to them. In the case of electricity, the main additional element is the 'plant-mix problem': the existence of a number of alternative technologies for producing electricity presents, first of all, the problem of determining the optimum combination of them in production and, secondly, leads to an interesting development of the analysis of peak-load pricing.

6.2 World markets

In keeping with the general approach of this book, we shall first of all take a simple case and then consider the light it may shed on the problems of the industries it is intended to model. Suppose a public enterprise produces an output which is freely tradeable on a perfectly competitive world market. It knows the current world price, p_0, and can forecast with certainty next year's world price, p_1. Then in the current period the economically efficient policy is to charge p_0 to consumers and produce up to the point at which short-run marginal cost is equal to this price. If the desired demand at p_0 exceeds this production level the difference is imported, if production exceeds demand the difference is exported. For next year, the economically efficient plan is to charge consumers p_1, and choose next year's capacity at the level which equates long-run marginal cost to this price. Again, any difference between production and consumption will take the form of exports or imports.

The argument underlying these propositions – which is in fact simply the standard argument for free trade, adapted to this particular context – can be made with the help of Figure 6.1. We again assume rigid capacity in the short run, so that MC_0 is the short-run 'marginal cost curve' with current capacity at $\bar{q}^0$. For $q_0 \leqslant \bar{q}^0$, short-run marginal cost is assumed to be increasing. The assumption of increasing long-run marginal cost, MC_1, is substantive: if it were constant (and below the $p_0 = p_1$ line) or decreasing, then there would be no determinate long-run equilibrium (we could conjecture that the enterprise would expand until the world market was no longer perfectly competitive). The line labelled $p_0 = p_1$ shows the level of the world price this year and next – purely for simplicity it is assumed constant over time. Finally, D_0 is the demand curve in the domestic market this year and D_1 is that next year.

Then the optimal policy is to charge consumers p_0 this year, implying domestic consumption q_0^*, and then to use the remaining capacity $\bar{q}^0 - q_0^*$ for exports. The principle underlying this policy is that the world price always measures the *opportunity cost* of domestic consumption and the *value* of domestic production. If one unit of domestic output is sold on the world market for, say, £1, this means that the value of domestic consumption of imported goods can increase by £1. There would therefore be a net loss of consumer benefits if the domestic output were diverted to domestic consumption at a price less than £1, since that would imply that it is less valuable to consumers than the £1 worth of imported goods forgone. Charging consumers p_0 ensures that the value to them of their marginal unit of consumption will just equal its opportunity cost.

This point can be reinforced by considering the (spurious) argument: short-run marginal cost pricing implies setting current price at $\hat{p}_0$ in Figure 6.1 and domestic consumption at $\hat{q}_0$, since short-run marginal cost is MC_0 and not p_0. This argument is false because clearly the output $\hat{q}_0 - q_0^*$ could be exported at price p_0, consumption of imports could increase by $p_0(\hat{q}_0 - q_0^*)$, and this exceeds the value to domestic consumers of the output $\hat{q}_0 - q_0^*$ by the (left-hand) shaded triangle in the figure.

98 *Public enterprise economics*

Turning now to the plan for year 1, the same principle implies charging price p_1 and so next year's demand will be q_1^*. The optimal capacity will now be $\bar{q}_1$, since that is the point at which $p_1 = MC_1$. Hence, the amount $q_1^* - \bar{q}_1$ will be imported. The reason capacity is set where world price equals domestic marginal cost is that a capacity greater than this would imply that, at the margin, more resources are being used to produce the good domestically than would be required to produce the exports which would pay for the imports of the good. This point can be reinforced by considering the welfare losses involved in a policy of 'self-sufficiency' or ignoring the world market. This would imply setting capacity at $\hat{q}_1$ and price at $\hat{p}_1$. The overall welfare loss created by this policy is shown by the shaded triangle *abc*. The triangle *abd* represents the net welfare loss to consumers arising out of having a lower consumption at a higher price: the triangle *acd* represents the net cost of producing output $\hat{q}_1 - \bar{q}_1$ domestically: the area $\bar{q}_1 ca\hat{q}_1$ represents the total cost of producing this extra output domestically, while the area $\bar{q}_1 cd\hat{q}_1$ represents the cost of the resources absorbed in producing the exports to pay for the imports of $\hat{q}_1 - \bar{q}_1$. Hence there is a net extra cost of producing this output domestically instead of importing it. The two net losses taken together, one on the consumption side and the other on production, give the total welfare loss implied by the policy of self-sufficiency, area *abc*.

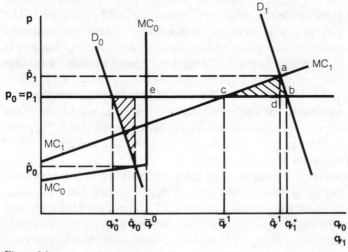

Figure 6.1

Two central principles then emerge from this analysis:

(a) *Consumption* is always determined by the world price in conjunction with domestic demand, and is independent of marginal costs.
(b) *Production* is always determined by the world price in conjunction with marginal costs, and is independent of the demand curve.

Whether the economy exports or imports the good then depends on the consumption and production levels which follow from these principles. Clearly the case shown in Figure 6.1 shows only one set of possibilities. If D_0 were to cut the world price line to the right of point e there would be imports in the current period, while if D_1 cut the line to the left of point c there would be exports next period.

Figure 6.1 shows the nice case of an expanding industry. Difficulties tend to arise in applying the logic of the 'world price' argument in cases, such as coal in the UK, where it implies imports and contraction of capacity. Figure 6.2 shows such a case. p_0 is the current world price, and this will rise next year to p_1. For simplicity, domestic demand is assumed to stay constant at D over both periods. The short- and long-run marginal cost curves for domestic production are again shown in the figure as MC_0 and MC_1 respectively. Then the efficient solution is to produce output $\hat{q}_0$ and import $q_0^* - \hat{q}_0$ this period, and reduce capacity to $\bar{q}^1$ by next period, increasing imports to $q_1^* - \bar{q}^1$. Allowing for the inevitable simplifications involved in the figure, this appears to be essentially the situation which confronts the UK coal industry. However, the coalminers' union has effectively been able, up to the time of writing, to prevent imports, and the industry has produced to capacity, stockpiling unsold coal (domestic price has been higher than the world price, implying demand below capacity by a larger margin than would exist if the world price were set). The union has also been resisting the closure of existing capacity: the attempt has been to maintain production and employment at capacity $\bar{q}^0$ (if not actually to expand it).

However, the implications of a diagram like Figure 6.2 should be drawn with some care. First, we should be sure that the marginal costs involved refer to real social opportunity costs and not simply accounting costs or money outlays. If coalminers' wages are, as a result of their union's monopoly power, held above their social opportunity cost – the real output elsewhere in the economy which is forgone by employing them as coalminers – then the costs of coal should be adjusted downward accordingly.[2] It is with respect to the social opportunity costs that output and capacity decisions should be made. Secondly, there are considerable uncertainties in forecasting the future world price of coal. If the long-run marginal cost curve for coal is relatively elastic, quite small changes in the forecast future world price could imply wide variations in desired capacity. Once coalmines are closed down they are prohibitively costly to reopen. Thus, in the light of the uncertainty over future world energy prices, it may be considered desirable to maintain a margin of capacity over and above that implied by the 'most probable' or 'best estimate' of the future world coal price. Both these questions could be subjected to further economic analysis,[3] but here we simply leave them as cautionary qualifications.

6.3 Pricing exhaustible resources

In the previous section, the marginal costs of gas and oil were not specifically defined, though the presumption would be that these would be the costs of 'production' – mining coal, bringing oil up from the ground or sea bed and transporting it ashore. We shall now refer to these costs as *extraction costs*. The question then is: can pricing policy of outputs such as coal and gas be based solely on marginal extraction costs, or are things more complex than that? It turns out that because coal and gas are exhaustible resources,[4] in general prices should be higher than marginal extraction costs. This is, however, only relevant in practical terms for gas. UK stocks of gas are due to be exhausted (at current consumption rates) over the next couple of decades, whereas UK stocks of coal are sufficient for at least 300 years or so. These exhaustion periods mean that the principles discussed in this section are important for gas but virtually irrelevant for coal.

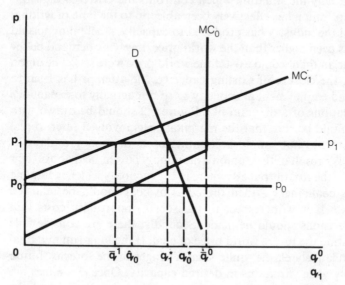

Figure 6.2

Suppose then that the economy has a fixed stock S of some resource, and that the production and sale of this are controlled by a public enterprise. The greater the rate of consumption or extraction of the resource per period, the sooner it will be exhausted. The problem of setting optimal price in each time-period – say, each year – and optimal production or extraction capacity is then equivalently the problem of choosing the optimal *rate of depletion* of the resource. The basic principle involved can be clearly brought out by a very simple example. We consider only two periods, 1 and 2 (at the end of period 2 we take it that the world will end). In each year there is a demand curve for output of the resource. Denote the amount of the resource extracted in years 1 and 2 by q_1 and q_2 respectively. Then we have immediately the resource constraint:

$$q_1 + q_2 \leqslant S. \tag{6.1}$$

This is graphed as the shaded area in Figure 6.3. Note that the line S^0, which defines the upper boundary of the feasible set of time-streams of extraction (q_1, q_2), has a slope of -1, since the equation of the line is $q_2 = S - q_1$. Thus any point on S^0 corresponds to an extraction time-stream which exactly exhausts the stock S. The point a, at which the 45° line OC intersects S^0, corresponds to an extraction time-stream in which $q_1 = q_2 = S/2$. Then the problem is to find the optimal point on S^0 or in the shaded area in Figure 6.3.

For simplicity let us assume the marginal cost of extraction or production is zero. Does this mean then that the price of the resource should be set at zero? Clearly not: at a zero price, demand in the first year could exceed the entire stock and leave nothing for the second year. Even if the first year's demand at zero price could be met out of the stock, the implied extraction time-stream might not be optimal, in a sense still to be defined. The appropriate prices to charge in each period must emerge out of the choice of an optimal extraction time-stream, and will be the means by which consumers are induced to take the quantities of the resource given by that time-stream. These prices will usually be positive, despite zero extraction costs, because the stock of the resource is finite and exhaustible.

Let the total benefits of consumption of the resource in year 1 be $B(q_1)$, and those in year 2, $B(q_2)$. These can be taken as corresponding to the areas under the market demand curves in each year. For simplicity, assume the demand curves are the same in each year, and so, if $q_1 = q_2$, $B(q_1) \equiv B(q_2)$. We want to choose a pair of values (q_1, q_2) in such a way as to maximize the present value of benefits:

$$V = B(q_1) + \frac{B(q_2)}{1+r} \tag{6.2}$$

where r is a given interest rate.[5] If we now fix a value for V, and allow q_1 and q_2 to vary in such a way that the right-hand side of (6.2) stays equal to this fixed value, then we define in effect an indifference curve, showing pairs of (q_1, q_2) values which yield the same present value of benefits. Some examples of such indifference curves are shown in Figure 6.3. Then the solution to the problem is straightforward. The optimal extraction time-stream (q_1^*, q_2^*) is found at the tangency point of the line S^0 with the indifference curve V^*, since this represents the highest level of present value of benefits it is possible to achieve while remaining within the feasible set.

It is no accident that the optimal pair (q_1^*, q_2^*) lie on S^0 to the right of point a, the equal consumption point. As long as the interest rate r is positive, the indifference curve passing through point a *must* be steeper there than S^0, as shown, and so the optimal point must be to the right of a. Hence a positive interest rate, with constant demand, implies a *falling* depletion time-path, with less extraction next year than this.

To see this, we first note that at any point on an indifference curve in Figure 6.3 the slope, or marginal rate of substitution of q_1 for q_2, is given by:

$$\frac{\Delta q_2}{\Delta q_1} = MRS_{12} \cdot = \frac{p_1}{p_2}(1+r) \tag{6.3}$$

where p_1 is the price or marginal benefit of consumption in year 1 and p_2 is the price

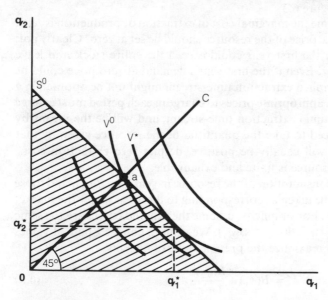

Figure 6.3

or marginal benefit of consumption in year 2.[6] Now at point a, $q_1 = q_2$ and, since the demand curve is the same in each period, $p_1 = p_2$. Thus the marginal rate of substitution at point a is $(1+r)$, which exceeds 1, the (absolute value of the) slope of S^0 as long as $r > 0$. Thus indifference curve V^0 must be steeper than S^0 at a.

Since the optimal point is a point of tangency, it also follows that at (q_1^*, q_2^*):

$$MRS_{12} = 1 \text{ implying } \frac{p_1}{p_2}(1+r) = 1 \quad \text{or} \quad \frac{p_2}{p_1} = (1+r). \qquad (6.4)$$

This tells us that over the two periods, price will be increasing, which of course we could have guessed since $q_2^* < q_1^*$. More importantly, since $p_2/p_1 = 1 + (p_2 - p_1)/p_1$, we have

$$\frac{p_2 - p_1}{p_1} \equiv \frac{\Delta p}{p_1} = r \qquad (6.5)$$

that is, the proportionate rate of increase of the price of the resource is exactly equal to the interest rate. This underlines the importance of the interest rate in determining the optimal depletion policy.

Note finally that (6.4) implies that

$$p_2 = (1+r)p_1. \qquad (6.6)$$

Since $r > -1$, either *both* prices are strictly positive, or *both* are zero (negative prices are of course ruled out). The case where both prices are zero could be thought of as 'superabundance' or 'bliss'. There is so much of the resource that the demands which would arise at zero prices in each period can be satisfied – the resource is in effect a free good. If there is not enough of the resource to make it a free good in one period, then (6.6) tells us it will not be a free good in the other. For example, if we extract enough of the resource to meet demand at zero price in period 1, but we cannot do this in period 2, then it will always be worthwhile to leave a little more in the ground by reducing extraction in year 1, since the marginal loss of benefit this year will be less than the marginal gain next year. Thus for any resource which is not a free good, its price will be positive in each year even though, as in this case, its marginal extraction cost is zero. Figure 6.4 completes this analysis by illustrating the way quantities and prices move along the demand curve over time.

In applying this analysis to a real resource such as natural gas or coal, the two obvious limitations are, first, the assumption of zero extraction costs and, secondly, the assumption of only two periods. It is, however, straightforward to generalize to positive extraction costs and any number of periods. Thus suppose in each of our two-year example total extraction costs are given by the cost function $C(q_1)$ and $C(q_2)$ respectively. Then the expression for the present value of (net) benefits now becomes:

$$V' = B(q_1) - C(q_1) + \frac{B(q_2) - C(q_2)}{1+r}.$$ (6.7)

The slope of an indifference curve in Figure 6.3, the marginal rate of substitution, is now:[7]

$$MRS_{12} = \frac{(p_1 - MC_1)}{(p_2 - MC_2)}(1+r)$$ (6.8)

where MC_1 and MC_2 are marginal extraction costs in each period. Hence, the optimality condition, the counterpart of (6.4), is now:

$$\frac{(p_2 - MC_2)}{(p_1 - MC_1)} = 1 + r.$$ (6.9)

We again have that if there is not enough of the resource to allow price to equal marginal extraction cost in each period, then price must exceed marginal cost in both. It is usual to call this excess of price over marginal cost a *royalty*, since it is a kind of profit or rent which accrues to the resource owner (in this case the public enterprise) because of the relative scarcity of the resource. If we denote this royalty by R_t in year t, so that $R_t = p_t - MC_t$, then the counterparts of (6.4) and (6.5) are:

$$\frac{R_2}{R_1} = (1+r), \quad \text{and} \quad \frac{R_2 - R_1}{R_1} \equiv \frac{\Delta R}{R_1} = r$$ (6.10)

so that it is now the *royalty* rather than the price which grows at a rate given by the interest rate. If marginal cost of extraction increases with the amount extracted in

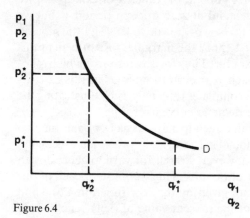

Figure 6.4

any year (which seems a reasonable assumption in the case of natural resources), then the growth in the royalty can be thought of as being due to the widening gap between price (increasing) and marginal cost (decreasing) as the quantity extracted falls. (The reader should draw the counterpart of Figure 6.4.) That the quantity extracted *does* fall can be shown by precisely the same argument as before: at $q_1 = q_2$, $p_1 = p_2$ and $MC_1 = MC_2$, while, assuming constant or increasing marginal cost, $p_2 - MC_2 > p_1 - MC_1$ (implied by (6.9) with $r > 0$) requires $q_1 > q_2$.

Generalization to any number of time-periods is also straightforward. Assuming the interest rate r is constant over time, the present value of net benefits is now given by:

$$V = B(q_1) - C(q_1) + \frac{B(q_2) - C(q_2)}{1+r} + \frac{B(q_3) - C(q_3)}{(1+r)^2} + \cdots + \frac{B(q_T) - C(q_T)}{(1+r)^{T-1}}$$

$$= \sum_{t=1}^{T} \frac{B(q_t) - C(q_t)}{(1+r)^{t-1}} \tag{6.11}$$

for any number of years T. The resource constraint is now:

$$\sum_{t=1}^{T} q_t \leqslant S. \tag{6.12}$$

Suppose we have some feasible time-stream $(q_1, q_2, \ldots, q_T)$, and it is possible to increase V by transferring one unit of output between periods 1 and $t > 1$. This can only be possible if

$$p_1 - MC_1 > \frac{p_t - MC_t}{(1+r)^{t-1}} \quad \text{or} \quad p_1 - MC_1 < \frac{p_t - MC_t}{(1+r)^{t-1}}. \tag{6.13}$$

In the first case, reducing period t output by 1 unit loses a present value of

$$\frac{p_t - MC_t}{(1+r)^{t-1}}$$

and increasing period 1 output by 1 unit gains a present value of $p_1 - MC_1$, a net gain. In the second case the opposite move brings a net gain. Such transfers of course would leave the total resource use unchanged and so are feasible. Thus maximization of V requires:

$$p_1 - MC_1 = \frac{p_t - MC_t}{(1+r)^{t-1}} \quad \text{for all } t, \tag{6.14}$$

implying in turn:

$$p_t - MC_t = \frac{p_{t+1} - MC_{t+1}}{1+r} \quad \text{for all } t. \tag{6.15}$$

Thus we have a straightforward generalization of (6.9). Using the 'royalty' concept, (6.14) implies:

$$R_t = R_1(1+r)^{t-1} \tag{6.16}$$

which tells us how the royalty, or gap between price and marginal extraction cost due to the relative scarcity of the resource stock, grows over time.

At the beginning of this section it was suggested that the excess of price over marginal cost resulting from the exhaustibility of the resource would be significant in the case of gas but not in that of coal, the reason being the relation between consumption and stock, or alternatively the period to exhaustion. We can use the above analysis to illustrate this. Thus suppose the interest rate $r = 0.05$, and the demand and marginal cost relationships in each period are given by:

$$p_t = 1 - \tfrac{1}{2}q_t \qquad MC_t = \tfrac{1}{2}q_t \qquad t = 1, 2, \ldots, T \tag{6.17}$$

Then the conditions in (6.14) become simply:

$$1 - q_1 = \frac{1 - q_t}{(1.05)^{t-1}} \qquad t = 2, 3, \ldots, T \tag{6.18}$$

We therefore have:

$$q_t = 1 - (1 - q_1)(1.05)^{t-1}. \tag{6.19}$$

Substituting for each q_t in the resource constraint then gives:

$$q_1 + \sum_{t=2}^{T} q_t = q_1 + (T-1) - (1-q_1) \sum_{t=2}^{T} (1.05)^{t-1} = S. \tag{6.20}$$

Given a value of T, say 100, we can calculate q_1 in (6.20) as a (linear) function of S. Table 6.1 shows values of output, the royalty, and the royalty as a proportion of price, all at period 1, for two assumed values of S.

Table 6.1

	q_1	$p_1 - MC_1 = R_1$	p_1	R_1/p_1
$S = 5$	0.9636	0.0364	0.5182	0.07
$S = 100$	0.9997	0.0003	0.5001	0.0006

Thus we see that when the resource is very scarce, at only about five times the first year's consumption, an initial royalty of about 7 per cent of the price is required, whereas when the resource is relatively abundant, the initial price and quantity are just about equal to the marginal cost pricing values (0.5 and 1 respectively) and the royalty is negligible. Of course, in both cases price and the royalty will rise, and the rate of output will fall over time, but the reader should confirm that in the case of $S = 100$, even after 80 years the royalty rate is less than 3 per cent of the price, while, when $S = 5$, after 4 years the royalty is about 9 per cent of the price.

We should now relate the analysis of this section to that of the previous one: here we have assumed the public enterprise had monopoly control of the resource, but what if there is also a perfectly competitive world market to which it has access? In this case the analysis becomes even simpler, provided the sequence of *given* world prices, $\bar{p}_1, \bar{p}_2, \ldots, \bar{p}_T$ can be accurately forecast. In that case, the enterprise seeks to maximize the present value of net benefits defined as:

$$V = \bar{p}_1 q_1 - C(q_1) + \frac{\bar{p}_2 q_2 - C(q_2)}{(1+r)} + \cdots + \frac{\bar{p}_T q_T - C(q_T)}{(1+r)^{T-1}} \qquad (6.21)$$

subject to the same resource constraint as before. The basic equilibrium condition is now:

$$\bar{p}_1 - MC_1 = \frac{\bar{p}_t - MC_t}{(1+r)^{t-1}} \qquad t = 2, \ldots, T \qquad (6.22)$$

Thus, we simply substitute the *given* world prices for the *derived* resource prices obtained in the previous analysis. Condition (6.22), in conjunction with the resource constraint, will of course determine domestic production in each period. The domestic consumption in each period will be determined by charging consumers the world price for that period, and the difference between production and consumption will be made up of exports or imports.

6.4 Peak-load pricing and storage

Both coal and gas demands have the type of peaked pattern discussed in chapter 5. In the case of coal, the main distinction is between summer and winter, while the demand pattern for gas is quite similar to that for electricity, with marked variations within the day as well as between parts of the week and seasons of the year. We shall assume here, however, that chapter 5's assumption of just two periods of equal duration continues to hold. An extension of the earlier analysis is required because of the possibility of storage – at a cost – which exists in the case of coal and gas. During the off-peak (lower-demand) period, output can be stored and then used to meet demand during the peak period. We are interested first in determining the optimal amount of output to store, and secondly in clarifying how the possibility of storage affects the peak-load pricing principles developed earlier.

We take the model of section 5.2, with costs exactly as specified in equations (5.4) to (5.6). We now introduce the variable $s \geq 0$, denoting the amount of output which is put into store in period 1 (low-demand) and brought out in period 2 (high-demand). The capacity of the storage facility is $\bar{s}$. For simplicity we make the same assumptions for storage costs as we do for output, in that storage costs $C(s)$ are given by:

$$C(s) = cs + \gamma \bar{s} \qquad s \leqslant \bar{s} \tag{6.23}$$

where c is the variable cost of putting one unit of output into storage *and* taking it out again, and γ is the cost of providing one unit of storage capacity. As before, 'in the short run', or current period 0, production capacity is fixed at $\bar{q}^0$ and storage capacity is fixed at $\bar{s}^0$, but 'in the long run', when planning for period 1, both $\bar{q}$ and $\bar{s}$ can be taken as variable.

Consider first the problem of optimal pricing and storage in period 0. Two types of solution are possible, one of which is shown in Figure 6.5, the other in Figure 6.6. In Figure 6.5, the unit cost of storage, c, is relatively high. Output capacity is fixed at $\bar{q}^0$, demands in periods 1 and 2 are shown by D_1 and D_2 respectively. Assuming for the moment that the storage-capacity constraint is not binding, the optimal peak price is: ·

$$p_2^* = v' + c \tag{6.24}$$

i.e. peak price is equal to the sum of marginal production and storage costs. The optimal storage is s^*, implying peak consumption of $q_2^* = \bar{q}^0 + s^*$. The optimal off-peak price is $p_1^* = v'$, with off-peak consumption at q_1^*. Hence off-peak production is $y_1^* = q_1^* + s^*$. Note that this is below capacity $\bar{q}^0$. Some capacity, of the amount $\bar{q}^0 - y_1^*$, is left lying idle off-peak, because the cost of producing an increment of output beyond y_1^*, *and* storing it, $c + v'$, exceeds the price peak consumers would be willing to pay for it. This then is a straightforward marginal cost pricing solution.

Suppose, however, that storage capacity $\bar{s} < s^*$. Then this capacity will be used to the full, while the peak price will have to be raised to ration demand to available capacity output *plus* stored capacity. If in the figure it is assumed that $\bar{s} = \hat{q}_2 - \bar{q}^0 < s^*$, then peak price must be set at $\hat{p}_2$, and off-peak production will be at $\hat{y}_1 = q_1^* + \bar{s}$. At this point, peak consumers are willing to pay a price greater than the cost of producing and storing an additional unit of period 1 output, but there is insufficient capacity.

In Figure 6.6, the unit storage cost is relatively low, and we have an interesting alternative solution possibility. If the previous principle of setting $p_2 = v' + c$ were adopted, and $p_1 = v'$, then it can be verified in the figure that the demand for stored output in period 2 would exceed the difference between capacity and consumption in period 1. However, if, at the level of s just equal to this difference, peak consumers value output sufficiently, they could induce off-peak consumers to *reduce* their consumption and put it into storage for consumption at peak (given that storage capacity exists). This will occur as long as $p_2 - c > p_1$, since then there is a net welfare gain from reducing consumption in period 1 by 1 unit (with a welfare loss of p_1), storing it at a cost of c, and then consuming it at peak (with a welfare gain of p_2). The optimal prices therefore now satisfy:

$$p_2^* - c = p_1^* \qquad (6.25)$$

or equivalently:

$$p_2^* - v' - c = p_1^* - v'. \qquad (6.26)$$

The solution shown in Figure 6.6, with peak consumption q_2^*, storage s^*, off-peak consumption q_1^*, and *both* off-peak *and* peak production at $\bar{q}^0$, clearly satisfies this condition. The peak solution is found at the point at which the kinked line *abc* cuts the demand curve D_2. The kink, at b, occurs at the same distance from the vertical line at capacity $\bar{q}^0$, as is point b'. The angle θ made by bc at b is the same as the angle θ made by the demand curve D_1 at b'. This ensures satisfaction of the condition in (6.26).

The significance of storage in this case is that it not only allows the utilization of spare capacity in period 1, but also allows output to be transferred from the period in which its marginal value is low, to that in which it is high. The existence of positive

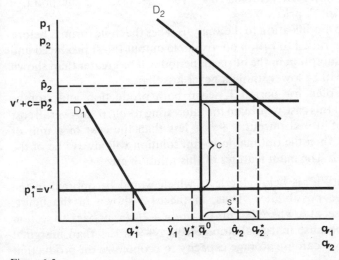

Figure 6.5

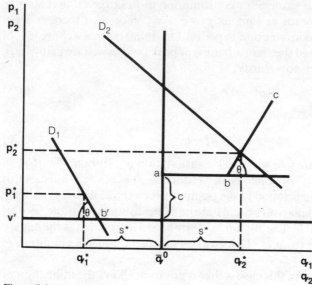

Figure 6.6

marginal storage costs, however, prevents this 'arbitrage' reaching the point of equality of peak and off-peak prices.

If of course $s^* > \bar{s}$, the modification to the analysis takes the same form as before, with the peak price being raised to ration off available output (both produced and stored). In that case consumption in the off-peak period will be greater than shown in the figure, and price will be lower, though never less than v'.

We now turn to the plan for period 1, when both production and storage capacities are variable. In this case we obtain the interesting result: if the overall cost of providing one unit of stored output, $c+\gamma$, is less than the cost of a unit of production capacity, 2β, then the optimal long-run solution will always be of the form shown in Figure 6.7. The main features of this solution are:

(1) Production capacity $\bar{q}^*$ is below the level which would be optimal in the absence of storage possibilities. Thus, in the case shown in the figure, capacity would be set at b, where D_2 cuts the line $v' + 2\beta'$ (refer back to section 5.2). Essentially, because marginal storage cost $c+\gamma$ is less than marginal capacity cost $2\beta'$, we can use storage capacity to economize on production capacity.

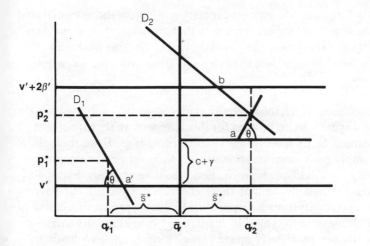

Figure 6.7

(2) The optimal peak-load pricing condition is:

$$p_2^* = p_1^* + c + \gamma \tag{6.27}$$

which has a straightforward interpretation. The marginal unit of peak consumption is provided by withdrawing the marginal unit of off-peak consumption and putting it into store. The cost of this is the value of that unit of consumption to off-peak consumers, p_1^*, plus the long-run marginal cost of capacity, $c + \gamma$. Thus (6.27) is a straightforward marginal cost pricing rule.

(3) Off-peak price will always exceed marginal operating cost, v', and off-peak consumption will always be below the level at which $p_1 = v'$, i.e. point a' in the figure. Thus, in the long run storage does not only use up spare capacity, but actually transfers consumption between periods. We shall return to this result when the remaining features of the solution have been given.

(4) Output is at capacity in both periods, so we have 100 per cent round-the-clock capacity utilization. We would expect this from the fact that both production and storage capacity are now variable. Storage capacity is also of course just right for the optimal amount of storage.

(5) Peak price is always less than long-run marginal cost, i.e. $p_2^* < v' + 2\beta'$, while we have a condition which looks just like the optimal-capacity condition in the absence of storage:

$$(p_1^* - v') + (p_2^* - v') = 2\beta' \tag{6.28}$$

i.e. the sum of willingnesses to pay for capacity must equal the marginal cost of capacity. The important difference is now that although $p_1^* > v'$, we *do not* have the same result for *consumptions* as in the earlier 'shifting peak' case. Off-peak consumption q_1^* must be less than capacity $\bar{q}^*$ in order for some output to be stored.

The features of the solution which most require explanation are 3 and 5, which are in fact closely related. Figure 6.8 can be used for this. Suppose we set capacity at $\bar{q}^1$ in the figure, which would be its level in the absence of storage. If we then allow storage, this would imply peak consumption at q_2^1, while off-peak consumption would be at q_1^2, where $p_1 = v'$. Off-peak production would be at q_1^1, so that $q_1^1 - q_1^2 = q_2^1 - \bar{q}^1 =$ the amount stored. Note that there is excess production capacity in period 1. We can, however, easily improve upon this. Reducing production capacity to $\bar{q}_2$, we can leave peak consumption at q_2^1 by increasing storage capacity to $\bar{q}^2 - q_1^1 = q_2^1 - \bar{q}^2$. This absorbs the previously spare capacity off-peak, and leads to a significant cost saving while leaving consumptions unaltered. The reduction in production capacity saves capacity costs of $2\beta'(\bar{q}^1 - \bar{q}^2)$. The increase in storage increases storage costs by $(c + \gamma)(\bar{q}^1 - \bar{q}_2)$. Thus there is a net cost reduction, shown by the area of the rectangle *abcd* in Figure 6.8. This is as far as we can go without cutting consumption in at least one of the periods.

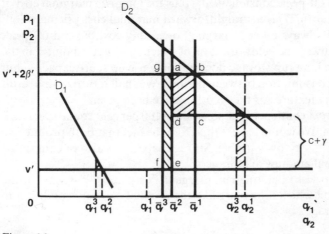

Figure 6.8

However, we can now show that there is a net gain in reducing capacity further. Suppose we make a small reduction in capacity, from $\bar{q}^2$ to $\bar{q}^3$ in the figure, holding the amount of storage fixed. This saves an amount of capacity cost shown by the shaded area *aefg*. If, given this capacity level, the amount of storage is unchanged, this will imply reductions in consumption in *both* periods by the amount of the reduction in capacity, to q_1^3 in period 1 and q_2^3 in period 2. This gives rise to net welfare losses shown by the shaded areas. Clearly the sum of these welfare losses is less than the saving in capacity costs, and so the capacity reduction should be made. Then, *given* the amount of storage, capacity should be reduced until the marginal saving in capacity cost, $2\beta'$, is just equal to the total marginal welfare loss, $(p_1 - v')$ $+ (p_2 - v')$. But this is precisely condition (6.28). It requires $p_1^* > v'$ because, if $p_1^* = v'$ we would have $p_2^* = v' + 2\beta'$, implying a level of consumption in the peak period which we know from the analysis just conducted cannot be optimal. The reader should confirm that in the optimal solution shown in Figure 6.7, a reduction in capacity from $\bar{q}^*$, with storage held constant, will imply a reduction in net consumption benefits in excess of the saving in capacity costs.

Thus we see that the existence of storage possibilities leads to an interesting extension of marginal cost-based pricing principles. In general storage permits a higher level of consumer benefit than in the case where it is prohibitively costly, not only because it permits utilization of off-peak capacity which might otherwise lie idle, but also because it enables a degree of arbitrage, transferring consumption from the period in which its value is lower to that in which it is higher, to an extent determined by the costs of storage. Consumers of coal and gas are to this extent in a better position than consumers of electricity, transport and communications services.

6.5 Multiple technologies

Throughout the analysis of chapter 5 and so far in this chapter we have assumed a single type of technology, with just one value of unit operating cost and one value of unit capacity cost. In one important case, that of electricity supply, this is obviously highly unrealistic. It is well known that electricity can be generated from power stations burning coal or oil, from power stations using nuclear fission as the heat source, from hydroelectrical installations and from gas turbine generators. At any one time there may well be several alternative *undominated* technologies, which may be defined as technologies whose operating and capital costs are not *both* higher than others. Thus at the present time in the electricity supply industry in England and Wales, nuclear and coal-fired power stations have high capital and low operating costs (the precise relation between them being a matter of some controversy), and the converse is true for gas turbine generators. Oil-fired power stations and hydroelectric installations appear to be dominated technologies. A large number of power stations are also already in existence, whose capital costs are largely sunk costs and so can be ignored; utilization decisions in their case depend only on operating costs, which tend to be relatively high.

Though electricity is the most striking example of multiple technologies, it is not unique. In the case of gas supply, for example, as natural gas reserves dwindle the various technologies of manufacturing gas from coal again become relevant. Similarly in various forms of transport there may be choice between technologies involving trade-offs between capital and operating costs, as in the case of aircraft size.

Two issues then arise out of this observation. Given the systematic fluctuation in demand which creates the peak-load problem, how are the principles of peak-load pricing affected by the existence of multiple technologies, and how is the optimal mix of plant types chosen? These questions are closely related because the solution to the 'optimal plant mix' problem determines the structure of marginal costs which feed into the solution of the peak-load pricing problem. We shall see that analysis of these questions leads to an interesting extension of the principle of peak-load pricing.

We analyse here the simplest possible case. The 'load curve' is as shown in Figure 5.5 of chapter 5. The day is again divided into two 12-hourly periods, in one of which demand is higher than the other. Output is non-storable, so we are concerned with electricity rather than gas or coal. We assume only two alternative technologies, and let v_1, β_1, be respectively the unit operating cost and unit capacity cost under the first technology, and v_2, β_2 the corresponding costs under the second. Clearly, if one technology is not to dominate the other we must have, say, that if $v_1 < v_2$, then $\beta_1 > \beta_2$.

Consider first the short-run pricing decision for the current year, 0. Capacity is given, and, to differentiate the analysis from that in chapter 5, we assume that the enterprise has both types of capacity in existence. The solution for optimal prices, shown in Figure 6.9, is then straightforward. Capacity output of plant type 1 is $\bar{q}^1$ per 12-hourly period, that of type 2 is $\bar{q}^2 - \bar{q}^1$ per 12-hourly period. The plants are placed in order of increasing marginal operating cost or, as it is phrased in the electricity industry, in *merit order*. Given the off-peak demand curve D_1, the optimal price is $p_1^* = v_1$, implying off-peak consumption q_1^*. This implies not only excess capacity of the first type of plant in period 1, but also that the type 2 plant lies idle. A number of possible demand curves, $D_2^0, D_2^1, D_2^2, D_2^3$, are shown for the peak period. If D_2^0 obtains, peak price is also at v_1; if D_2^1, peak price is p_2^1, which just rations demand to capacity of the first plant (note that it would not be optimal to allow consumption to expand beyond $\bar{q}^1$, even though plant 2 capacity exists – explain why); if D_2^2

obtains, peak price is set at v_2 and peak consumption is q_2^2, $\bar{q}^1$ of which is produced by plant 1 and $q_2^2 - \bar{q}^1$ by plant 2; finally, if the demand curve is D_2^3, then peak price is set at p_2^3 to ration demand to capacity overall, and both plants are used to capacity in the peak period. Note that this implies that plant 1 operates for 24 hours a day.

The underlying principle for year 0 (the 'short run') then is that price should be set at the unit operating cost of the *marginal* plant in each period, except when we are on a vertical portion of the relevant MC_0 curve, in which case price rations demand to capacity.

When we turn to the planned price and capacity for the future, year 1, we have to confront the 'optimal plant mix problem'. If capacities of both plants are now variable, we have to determine their relative amounts as well as total capacity. We approach the problem by first considering the conditions under which only one plant type would be installed. Thus suppose first that, given the demand curves, we install only plant 1 according to the marginal cost pricing principle of chapter 5. Then (assuming for convenience the firm-peak case), we shall have $p_1 = v_1$ and $p_2 = v_1 + \beta_1$. Under what conditions would it *not* now pay to introduce one unit of capacity of type 2? The answer is that we must have as a *necessary* (*though not sufficient*) condition for introducing plant 2:

$$v_2 + \beta_2 < v_1 + \beta_1 \quad \text{or} \quad v_2 - v_1 < \beta_1 - \beta_2 \tag{6.29}$$

so the reduction in capital costs from installing a unit of plant 2 must exceed the

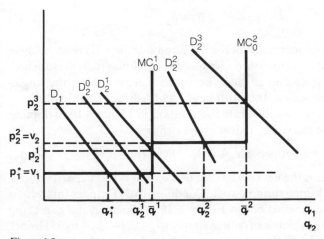

Figure 6.9

increase in operating cost or, equivalently, its long-run marginal cost must be less. The argument goes as follows. If we introduce a unit of plant 2, this would not be used in the off-peak period, because $v_2 > v_1$, and so there is no cost change in that period. By replacing a unit of type 1 capacity, we save $\beta_1 - \beta_2$ in capital cost, but have to replace the unit of output in period 2 by producing from the higher operating cost plant 2, and so incur a cost penalty of $v_2 - v_1$. Only if the capital cost saving exceeds the running cost penalty, should the substitution be made.

But if the condition in (6.29) is met, should not plant 1 be entirely replaced by plant 2? This would imply that the 'optimal plant mix problem' only has extreme solutions: only plant 2 if (6.29) is satisfied, and only plant 1 if it is not. We shall now see that this is not in fact the case: even if plant 2's long-run marginal cost is less than that of plant 1, we may still want both types of capacity, or indeed *only* plant 1. Thus suppose that capacity consists entirely of type 2 plant. If we now introduce a unit of type 1 plant, we shall certainly operate it in *both* periods, since $v_1 < v_2$. Thus we save $2(v_2 - v_1)$. We also reduce plant 2 capacity by one unit, and so save β_2 in capacity costs. Thus the *net* cost of the extra capacity is $\beta_1 - \beta_2$, and if this is less than the saving in operating costs then it is worth installing the type 1 capacity. Thus we have the condition:

$$\beta_1 - \beta_2 < 2(v_2 - v_1) \quad \text{or} \quad \frac{\beta_1 - \beta_2}{2} < v_2 - v_1 \qquad (6.30)$$

as the necessary condition for installing some type 1 plant. Thus, putting (6.29) and (6.30) together, we see that we will have both plant types *only if*:

$$\frac{\beta_1 - \beta_2}{2} < v_2 - v_1 < \beta_1 - \beta_2. \qquad (6.31)$$

Note that the 2 arises in the denominator of the left-hand side of (6.31) because there are just two demand periods. From now on we assume condition (6.31) is satisfied.

Turning to the optimal price and capacity decisions there are, as in the single-plant analysis, two possible cases: the 'firm-peak' and 'shifting-peak' solutions. Taking first the firm-peak case, we illustrate the solution in Figure 6.10. Adopting the terminology used in the electricity industry, we define:

$$\text{net effective cost, } nec \equiv v_1 + [(\beta_1 - \beta_2) - (v_2 - v_1)]. \qquad (6.32)$$

The term in square brackets is the net capital cost of a unit of type 1 capacity minus the offsetting saving in peak-time running cost. Condition (6.31) implies this term is positive, and hence the line labelled *nec* in Figure 6.10 is above v_1, the gap being equal to the term in brackets (which is of course simply $(\beta_1 + v_1) - (\beta_2 + v_2)$). The *nec* is the marginal cost of period 1 – off-peak – consumption. An increment of demand off-peak is met by increasing type 1 capacity, and so the marginal cost of meeting this increment of demand is the operating cost of this type of plant, together with the capital cost *net of* the capital and running cost savings implied by the reduction in type 2 capacity needed at peak time. Thus, as the figure shows, off-peak price is set equal to this *nec*, and capacity of type 1 plant is set equal to the off-peak demand which is forthcoming at this price. The peak price p_2^* is set at the marginal cost of type 2 plant, $v_2 + \beta_2$. Total peak capacity is $\bar{q}_2^*$, given by demand at p_2^*, and this implies an amount of type 2 capacity of $\bar{q}_2^* - \bar{q}^1$. Type 1 plant operates in both periods (it is often referred to as 'baseload plant'), while type 2 plant meets the peak (peaking capacity). The diagram emphasizes that, subject to condition (6.31) being met, the 'optimal plant mix' depends not only on relative costs but also on demands: for example, a growth in off-peak demand would increase type 1 capacity and, with peak demand constant, reduce that of type 2.

We now list and rationalize the main features of the solution in Figure 6.10.

(1) In the peak period, an increment of demand would be met only by type 2 capacity, since $v_2 + \beta_2 < v_1 + \beta_1$. This determines the marginal cost and therefore price at peak.
(2) Type 1 capacity is fully utilized in both periods because $v_1 < v_2$.
(3) Type 1 capacity is exactly equal to off-peak demand at $p_1^* = nec$. This has two implications:
    (a) It will not be *less* than off-peak demand, i.e. off-peak demand will not be met in part by type 2 capacity. In such a case, replacing a unit of type 2

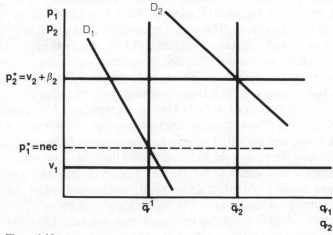

Figure 6.10

capacity with one of type 1 would yield the overall cost saving $2(v_2 - v_1)$ $-(\beta_1 - \beta_2)$ which from condition (6.30) we know is positive.

(b) It would not be *greater* than off-peak demand. In that case it would either be lying idle (a total waste), or be in existence *only* to meet peak demand. But then replacing one unit of type 1 plant by one unit of type 2 reduces costs by $(v_1 + \beta_1) - (v_2 + \beta_2)$ (recall condition (6.29)).

Hence baseload capacity equals off-peak demand.

The main overall modification to the peak-load pricing principles derived for the single-plant case is that off-peak price is no longer (even in this firm-peak case) equal *only* to unit operating cost. It now contains an element of capital cost, though properly adjusted for 'system cost savings'.

Suppose, however, that when the two pricing principles were applied, setting p_1^* $= nec$, and $p_2^* = v_2 + \beta_2$, we found that 'off-peak' demand exceeded 'peak demand'. In other words we now consider the 'shifting-peak case'. This is illustrated in Figure 6.11. With the demand curves as shown, an off-peak price at *nec* now generates off-peak demand at $\bar{q}^1$, and this exceeds the peak demand $\bar{q}^2$ at a peak price of $v_2 + \beta_2$. The solution for this case is also shown in the figure: we treat it as if type 2 capacity did not exist, and apply the standard shifting-peak solution with type 1 capacity. This implies, as before,

$$(p_1^* - v_1) + (p_2^* - v_1) = \beta_1$$

as shown in the figure. To justify this solution, we have to explain why type 2 capacity would not be introduced. The essential reason is that if it were, it would have to be operated for *both* periods and this makes it more costly than type 1 capacity. Thus, given the solution in Figure 6.11, suppose that we replaced 1 unit of type 1 capacity by 1 unit of type 2 capacity. The saving in capacity cost would be β_1 $-\beta_2$. However, this unit of type 2 capacity would have to be operated in both periods, if outputs are to remain unchanged. But this means that operating costs increase by $2(v_2 - v_1)$ which we know, from (6.30), exceeds the saving in capacity cost. Thus we could not reduce costs, leaving outputs unchanged, by introducing type 2 capacity. Moreover, it would not be justified to introduce type 2 capacity only to meet demand in one period, since *both* p_1^* and p_2^* are below $v_2 + \beta_2$, implying that consumers in one period would not be willing to pay for the capacity increment.

This shifting-peak solution is the reason for stressing earlier that the condition v_2 $-\beta_2 < v_1 + \beta_1$ is necessary but not sufficient for type 2 capacity to be used. The condition ensures that this is worthwhile *only if* that capacity will be used in just one period. This is true in the firm-peak case, but not in the shifting-peak case.

The analysis of this section is highly simplified in at least three respects. In reality there are more than two plant types, and many more demand periods than just two.

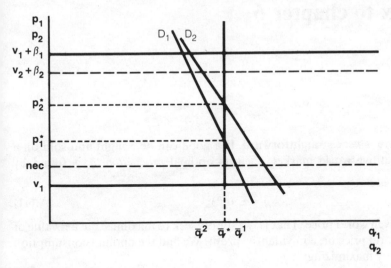

Figure 6.11

Moreover, the optimal plant mix problem requires calculation of the relative costs of different plant types over their entire lifetimes of thirty years or so, which in turn requires forecasts of load curves over this period. The rather simple analysis of this section has, however, served to bring out the main economic principles involved. The reader with an interest in the specific problem of the optimal plant mix in electricity supply should read Turvey (1968b). Crew and Kleindorfer (1979) also provide an exhaustive analysis of the case with any (finite) number of plant types and demand periods.

6.6 Conclusions

In this chapter we have extended the analysis of marginal cost pricing with fixed capacity and peak loads to the three major public enterprises in the energy sector – coal, gas and electricity. The analysis was still very much simplified. To obtain realistic pricing structures for these industries would require much more complex specifications of demands, technologies and costs. It is indeed doubtful if it is worth pursuing these complications with analytical models, since the real problems are more likely to be solved by extensive computer simulations using realistic data. Rather, the aim here has been to clarify the central economic principles which underlie the solutions, and for this the simple models are quite adequate.

Appendix to chapter 6

1 World markets

The analysis here is very straightforward. If a good can be bought and sold on a perfectly competitive world market, then its optimal *production*, q, is found by maximizing:

$$\bar{p} = C'(q^*) \tag{A.6.1}$$

where $\bar{p}$ is the given world price. That is, we simply seek to maximize the net value of output at the world price or, equivalently, profit. We find the optimal consumption of the good, x, by maximizing:

$$B(x) - \bar{p}x \tag{A.6.2}$$

where B is our usual benefit function. This reflects the fact that the social opportunity cost of a unit of consumption of the good is its world price. Given the optimal production q^* which satisfies:

$$\bar{p} = C'(q^*) \tag{A.6.3}$$

and the optimal consumption x^* which satisfies:

$$B'(x^*) = p(x^*) = \bar{p} \tag{A.6.4}$$

imports (exports) will be implied if $x^* - q^* > (<)0$.

2 Exhaustible resources

We can generalize the analysis in this chapter by allowing time, t, to extend to infinity. It is also convenient to treat time as continuous. If $C(q(t))$ is the extraction cost function, and $B(q(t))$ the benefit function, each at any t, then the maximand of the problem is:

$$V = \int_0^\infty [B(q(t)) - C(q(t))]e^{-rt}dt \tag{A.6.5}$$

where r is the given discount rate. The resource constraint is:

$$\int_0^\infty q(t)dt \leqslant S \tag{A.6.6}$$

with S again the fixed stock of the resource. Denoting the Lagrange multiplier associated with (A.6.6.) by λ, which, note, is *not* a function of time, we have as necessary conditions:

$$[p^*(t)-C']e^{-rt}-\lambda^* = 0 \tag{A.6.7}$$

$$\int_0^\infty q^*(t)dt - S \leqslant 0 \qquad \lambda^* \geqslant 0 \qquad \lambda^*\left[\int_0^\infty q^*(t)dt - S\right] = 0 \tag{A.6.8}$$

If the resource will never be exhausted, then from (A.6.8) $\lambda^* = 0$ and in (A.6.7) $p_t^* = C'$, or we have marginal cost pricing. If $\lambda^* > 0$, so that the resource *will* be exhausted, price exceeds marginal cost at every instant and, moreover, for $t_1 \neq t_2$,

$$[p^*(t_1)-C'(q^*(t_1))]e^{-rt_1} = [p^*(t_2)-C']e^{-rt_2} \tag{A.6.9}$$

or, in terms of the royalty $R(t) \equiv p^*(t)-C'(q^*(t))$:

$$R(t_1) = R(t_2)e^{-r(t_2-t_1)}. \tag{A.6.10}$$

Finally, differentiating through (A.6.7) with respect to t (recalling that λ^* is constant over time) gives:

$$\frac{\dot{R}(t)}{R(t)} = r \tag{A.6.11}$$

the instantaneous version of (6.10).

Note that since $\lambda^* = \partial V/\partial S$, it measures the marginal *present* value of increment of the resource stock. It would then be an important parameter in deciding whether to undertake exploration or research to increase the stock.

Much more complex models for exhaustible resources can of course be constructed. The literature is large and growing (perhaps faster than the resources are dwindling). The interested reader is referred to Dasgupta and Heal (1979) and the references cited there.

3 Feasible storage

First we derive the results extensively discussed in this chapter, for the two-period case. We then generalize to n periods.

The benefit function, $B_1(q_1)+B_2(q_2)$, is just as in the analysis of peak-load pricing in chapter 5. We now let q_i denote *consumption* in period $i = 1, 2$, and y_i denote *production* in that period. If $s \geqslant 0$ is the amount of output stored, we have simply:

$$q_1 = y_1 - s; \qquad q_2 = y_2 + s \tag{A.6.12}$$

where we simply take it for granted that output is stored in period 1 and consumed in period 2. Given production capacity $\bar{q}$, (A.6.12) implies the constraints:

$$q_1 + s \leqslant \bar{q} \qquad q_2 - s \leqslant \bar{q} \qquad \text{(A.6.13)}$$

and the cost function is now:

$$C = v(q_1 + s) + v(q_2 - s) + cs + \beta\bar{q} + \gamma\bar{s}$$
$$= v(q_1 + q_2) + cs + \beta\bar{q} + \gamma\bar{s} \qquad \text{(A.6.14)}$$

We then seek to maximize benefits less costs, taking account also of the constraints:

$$s \geqslant 0 \qquad \text{(A.6.15)}$$

$$s \leqslant \bar{s} \qquad \text{(A.6.16)}$$

In year 0, $\bar{q}$ and $\bar{s}$ are fixed, q_1, q_2 and s are the choice variables, and so necessary conditions are:

$$p_1^* - v - \lambda_1^* = 0 \qquad \text{(A.6.16)}$$

$$p_2^* - v - \lambda_2^* = 0 \qquad \text{(A.6.17)}$$

$$-\lambda_1^* + \lambda_2^* - c - \sigma^* \leqslant 0 \qquad s^* \geqslant 0 \qquad s^*[\lambda_2^* - \lambda_1^* - c - \sigma^*] = 0 \quad \text{(A.6.18)}$$

$$q_1^* + s^* - \bar{q} \leqslant 0 \qquad \lambda_1^* \geqslant 0 \qquad \lambda_1^*[q_1^* + s^* - \bar{q}] = 0 \quad \text{(A.6.19)}$$

$$q_2^* - s^* - \bar{q} \leqslant 0 \qquad \lambda_2^* \geqslant 0 \qquad \lambda_2^*[q_2^* - s^* - \bar{q}] = 0 \quad \text{(A.6.20)}$$

$$s^* - \bar{s} \leqslant 0 \qquad \sigma^* \geqslant 0 \qquad \sigma^*[s^* - \bar{s}] = 0 \quad \text{(A.6.21)}$$

Clearly a large number of cases are logically possible, but we confine ourselves to the most interesting. Suppose first that:

(a) $s^* < \bar{s}$, $\lambda_1^* > 0$, $\lambda_2^* > 0$.

In this case, the storage constraint is non-binding and the capacity constraints are binding in each period. Since $\sigma^* = 0$, the first three conditions yield:

$$p_2^* = p_1^* + c \qquad \text{(A.6.22)}$$

which is (6.25) in the chapter (refer to that for further discussion). Note further that $(p_1^* - v) > 0$, $(p_2^* - v) > 0$, the case analysed in Figure 6.6.

(b) $s^* < \bar{s}$, $q_1^* < \bar{q}$, $\lambda_2^* > 0$.

In this case, the capacity constraint is non-binding in period 1, as also is the storage constraint. Then we have:

$$p_2^* = v + c \qquad p_1^* = v \qquad \text{(A.6.23)}$$

as in Figure 6.5. The storage cost is sufficiently high, and there is enough spare capacity in period 1, that optimal storage is reached before consumption in period 1 has to be reduced below the level at which $p_1^* = v$.

(c) $\sigma^* > 0$, $q_1^* < \bar{q}$, $\lambda_2^* > 0$.

In this case the storage-capacity constraint is binding. Then we have:

$$p_2^* = v + c + \sigma^* \qquad p_1^* = v \qquad\qquad (\text{A}.6.24)$$

so that the storage-capacity constraint prevents the optimal storage in case (b) being achieved. p_2^* is then raised to the level which rations demand to capacity. Note that we can interpret $\sigma^* = p_2^* - (v + c)$ as a 'willingness to pay for storage capacity'.

(d) $-\lambda_1^* + \lambda_2^* - c < 0$, $\lambda_1^* > 0$, $\lambda_2^* > 0$.

In this case $s^* = 0$, while the capacity constraints bind in each period. From the first three conditions we must therefore have:

$$p_2^* < p_1^* + c \quad \text{or} \quad p_2^* - p_1^* < c \qquad\qquad (\text{A}.6.25)$$

The marginal value of consumption in period 2 is not sufficiently higher than that in period 1 to cover the cost of storage, and so none takes place.

(e) $-\lambda_1^* + \lambda_2^* - c < 0$, $q_1^* < \bar{q}$, $\lambda_2^* > 0$.

In this case again $s^* = 0$, even though consumption is below capacity in period 1 and at capacity in period 2. We then have:

$$p_2^* < v + c. \qquad\qquad (\text{A}.6.26)$$

The marginal value of consumption in period 2 is not high enough to cover the cost of producing and storing a unit of output.

Other cases are of course possible, but (a)–(e) seem to be the main ones of interest.

When planning for year 1, $\bar{q}$ and $\bar{s}$ both become variable. To save space, we simply note that the necessary conditions for this case can be expressed by adding to (A.6.16)–(A.6.21) the two further conditions:

$$\sigma^* \leqslant \gamma \qquad \bar{s}^* \geqslant 0 \qquad \bar{s}^*(\sigma^* - \gamma) = 0 \qquad\qquad (\text{A}.6.27)$$

$$\lambda_1^* + \lambda_2^* = \beta \qquad\qquad (\text{A}.6.28)$$

The cases now of interest are:

(a) $s^* > 0$, $\lambda_1^* > 0$, $\lambda_2^* > 0$

so that there *is* storage, $\sigma^* = \gamma$, and the production-capacity constraint binds in both periods. Then we have:

$$(p_1^* - v) + (p_2^* - v) = \beta \qquad\qquad (\text{A}.6.29)$$

$$p_1^* - p_2^* = c + \gamma \qquad\qquad (\text{A}.6.30)$$

The first of these two conditions relates to optimal production capacity and is familiar from the earlier analysis of peak-load pricing. The second relates to optimal storage capacity and was discussed in the context of Figure 6.7. Note that (A.6.29) implies:

$$p_1^* = \beta + 2v - p_2^* \qquad (A.6.31)$$

and so substituting into (A.6.30) gives:

$$\beta = c + \gamma + 2(p_2^* - v) > c + \gamma \qquad (A.6.32)$$

and so a necessary condition for this case is that marginal operating and capacity cost of storage is less than marginal capacity cost.

(b) $s^* > 0$, $q_1^* + s^* < \bar{q}^*$, $\lambda_2^* > 0$

so now there is excess capacity in period 1 and $\lambda_1^* = 0$. In that case we have

$$p_2^* - v = \beta = c + \gamma \qquad (A.6.33)$$

and so a necessary condition for this case to occur is the rather stringent one that production capacity and storage have the same unit cost.

(c) $\sigma^* < \gamma$, $q_1^* < \bar{q}^*$, $\lambda_2^* > 0$.

Here there is no storage, $s^* = \bar{s}^* = 0$, and excess production capacity in period 1, and so $\lambda_1^* = 0$. Conditions (A.6.16)–(A.6.18) and (A.6.28) then imply:

$$(p_2^* - v) = \beta \quad \text{and} \quad p_1^* = v \qquad (A.6.34)$$

$$(p_2^* - v) < c + \gamma \qquad (A.6.35)$$

which in turn imply $\beta < c + \gamma$. Thus a necessary condition for no investment in storage is that it is cheaper simply to provide production capacity. We thus obtain the standard peak-load pricing result as a special case of the present analysis.

These then are the three cases of interest. Note that we need not consider the possibility that $\bar{s}^* > 0$ and $\lambda_1^* > 0$, since this is a contradiction: $\lambda_1^* > 0 \Rightarrow q_1^* = \bar{q}^* \Rightarrow \bar{s}^* = 0$. From this, and the results in (A.6.32)–(A.6.35), we can conclude that a necessary *and* sufficient condition for case (a) to hold is that $c + \gamma < \beta$.

The multi-period generalization of this analysis is perfectly straightforward. We let q_i, $i = 1, \ldots, n$, be consumption in period i, $s_i \gtrless 0$ the amount put into (> 0) or taken out of (< 0) storage in period i, and simply impose the constraints:

$$s_i \leqslant \bar{s} \qquad \forall i = 1, \ldots, n$$

$$\sum_i s_i = 0$$

The analysis goes through in an obvious way, and the analysis of this section gives the economic rationale for the basic result: output is put into store in periods when there is spare capacity or when the marginal value of output is low relative to the marginal storage cost and its value in other periods, and taken out of store when the marginal value of output is high relative to storage costs and its value in other periods. Storage performs an arbitrage function. The interested reader can consult Crew and Kleindorfer (1979) for the detailed results for this case.

4 Multiple technologies

Here we shall simply give the derivation of the results for the two-period two-plant case discussed in this chapter. This case is quite adequate to bring out the main points of principle, and the generalization to any number of periods and plant types only creates notational complexities which tend to obscure understanding.[8]

We again denote consumptions by q_i, and benefits by $B_i(q_i)$, $i = 1, 2$. We denote output in period i from plant of type $j = 1, 2$ by y_{ij}, and production capacity of type j by $\bar{y}_j$. We can then formulate the problem as

$$\text{max. } V = B_1(q_1) + B_2(q_2) - v_1(y_{11} + y_{21}) - v_2(y_{12} + y_{22}) - \beta_1\bar{y}_1 - \beta_2\bar{y}_2 \quad \text{(A.6.36)}$$

subject to:

$$q_i = y_{i1} + y_{i2} \qquad i = 1, 2 \quad \text{(A.6.37)}$$

$$y_{ij} \leqslant \bar{y}_j \qquad i = 1, 2, j = 1, 2. \quad \text{(A.6.38)}$$

and $y_{ij} \geqslant 0 \quad \bar{y}_j \geqslant 0$.

Clearly the simplest procedure is to substitute from (A.6.37) for the q_i in (A.6.36). Then, associating the dual variables λ_{ij} with the four constraints in (A.6.38), we have as necessary conditions:

$$p_i^* - v_j - \lambda_{ij}^* \leqslant 0 \qquad y_{ij}^* \geqslant 0 \qquad y_{ij}^*[p_i^* - v_i - \lambda_{ij}^*] = 0 \quad \text{(A.6.39)}$$
$$i = 1, 2, j = 1, 2$$

$$\sum_i \lambda_{ij}^* - \beta_j \leqslant 0 \qquad \bar{y}_j^* \geqslant 0 \qquad \bar{y}_j^*\left[\sum_i \lambda_{ij}^* - \beta_j\right] = 0 \quad \text{(A.6.40)}$$
$$j = 1, 2$$

$$y_{ij}^* - \bar{y}_j^* \leqslant 0 \qquad \lambda_{ij}^* \geqslant 0 \qquad \lambda_{ij}^*[y_{ij}^* - \bar{y}_j^*] = 0 \quad \text{(A.6.41)}$$
$$i = 1, 2, j = 1, 2$$

To save space, these conditions relate to the long-run planning problem. Dropping (A.6.41) would give us the short-run problem, but detailed analysis of this (in conjunction with the discussion of Figure 6.9) will be left to the reader.

Recall that we assume $v_1 < v_2$ and $\beta_1 > \beta_2$. Now let us consider the interesting cases.

(a) $\bar{y}_1^* > 0, \bar{y}_2^* > 0, \lambda_{i1}^* > 0, i = 1, 2, \lambda_{22}^* > 0, y_{12}^* = 0.$
In this case, both plants are used, with plant 1 working at capacity in both periods ($\lambda_{i1}^* > 0$) while plant 2 does not operate in period 1 ($y_{12}^* = 0$). This is then the case considered in the context of Figure 6.10. Given $y_{12}^* = 0 < \bar{y}_2$, we have $\lambda_{12}^* = 0$. Substituting from (A.6.40) into (A.6.39) then gives:

$$p_1^* = v_1 + (\beta_1 - \beta_2) - (v_2 - v_1) = \text{n.e.c.} \qquad (A.6.42)$$

$$p_2^* = v_2 + \beta_2 \qquad (A.6.43)$$

while (A.6.41) of course implies:

$$y_{i1}^* = \bar{y}_1 \qquad i = 1, 2 \qquad (A.6.44)$$

$$y_{22}^* = \bar{y}_2 \qquad (A.6.45)$$

so that plant 1 is operated at capacity in both periods, plant 2 only in period 2.

(b) $\bar{y}_1^* = 0, \bar{y}_2^* > 0, \lambda_{22}^* > 0, \lambda_{12}^* \geqslant 0.$
In this case no type 1 capacity is installed. It then follows of course that $y_{i1}^* = 0, i = 1, 2$. The capacity constraint binds in period 2, but may or may not bind in period 1 – we allow either a firm or shifting peak. From (A.6.39) and (A.6.40) we then have:

$$p_1^* - v_1 + p_2^* - v_1 < \beta_1 \qquad (A.6.46)$$

$$p_1^* - v_2 + p_2^* - v_2 = \beta_2 \qquad (A.6.47)$$

and so:

$$p_1^* + p_2^* = 2v_2 + \beta_2 < 2v_1 + \beta_1 \qquad (A.6.48)$$

yielding:

$$2(v_2 - v_1) < \beta_1 - \beta_2. \qquad (A.6.49)$$

Thus we have (A.6.49) as a *necessary condition* for the case in which only type 2 capacity is used. It follows that type 2 capacity will not be the only one used when $\beta_1 - \beta_2 < 2(v_2 - v_1)$, which of course is condition (6.30) of this chapter.

(c) $\bar{y}_1^* > 0, \bar{y}_2^* = 0, \lambda_{21}^* > 0, \lambda_{11}^* > 0.$
In this case no type 2 capacity is installed, and so $y_{i2}^* = 0, i = 1, 2$. The capacity constraint binds in both periods, so that we have the 'shifting-peak case'. From (A.6.39) and (A.6.40) we have:

$$p_1^* - v_1 + p_2^* - v_1 = \beta_1 \qquad (A.6.50)$$

$$p_1^* - v_2 + p_2^* - v_2 < \beta_2 \tag{A.6.51}$$

yielding:

$$\beta_1 - \beta_2 < 2(v_2 - v_1). \tag{A.6.52}$$

This tells us that in the shifting-peak case, if the condition (A.6.49) for use of *only* plant 2 is *not* satisfied, then *only* plant 1 is installed. This was discussed in the context of Figure 6.11.

(d) $\bar{y}_1^* > 0$, $\bar{y}_2^* = 0$, $\lambda_{21}^* > 0$, $\lambda_{11}^* = 0$.

Again no type 2 capacity is installed, and we have the firm-peak case. Then (A.6.39) and (A.6.40) give:

$$p_1^* = v_1 \quad \text{and} \quad p_2^* = v_1 + \beta_1 \tag{A.6.53}$$

$$p_2^* - v_2 \leqslant \lambda_{22}^* < \beta_2 \tag{A.6.54}$$

implying:

$$v_1 + \beta_1 < v_2 + \beta_2. \tag{A.6.55}$$

Thus, in the firm-peak case, a necessary condition for only plant 1 to be used is given by (A.6.55), which we met earlier in this chapter as condition (6.29). Of course we cannot conclude that reversal of the inequality in (A.6.55) implies that type 2 plant *will* be used (we have already seen that it will not be in the shifting-peak case), only that we could not then rule it out automatically.

Chapter 7

Some problems of the second best

Recall from chapter 3 that a second-best economy is one in which the market system is incapable of achieving unaided a Pareto-optimal resource allocation. One or more of the assumptions defining a first-best economy is not fulfilled, and we find in general that the market equilibrium resource allocation yields a lower level of welfare for everybody, than some resource allocations which are attainable with the resources and technological possibilities available to the economy. The analysis of second-best economies has had two sets of implications for public enterprise economics, one negative and the other positive and constructive. The former consists mainly of the undermining of the rationale for marginal cost pricing as a general optimality rule. The so-called[1] 'general theorem of the second best' can be interpreted as follows. In a second-best economy there are certain 'deviant sectors' (monopolies, oligopolies, generators of external effects) whose behaviour cannot be directly modified by a central planner. In trying to achieve a Pareto optimum in this second-best economy, the planner will find that the necessary conditions (pricing rules) which must be satisfied in the sectors he does control may differ in general from those which would obtain in a first-best economy. If these sectors are public enterprises, it immediately follows that marginal cost pricing (the first-best condition) may no longer be optimal. As a result of subsequent analysis,[2] rather more than this can be said. Where the equilibrium position of each deviant sector (for example, a monopolist's output) is unaffected by the choices made by a decision-taker in some other sector, then the first-best condition for the latter continues to apply. In other words, account need only be taken of changes which actually cause deviants to vary outputs, prices, etc. It is very doubtful if this qualification can rescue marginal cost pricing, however, since several important public enterprises are closely related economically to 'deviant' sectors in one way or another. Thus, the general theorem of the second best makes the position of general advocacy of the marginal cost pricing rule untenable.

The constructive aspect of the theory of the second best is that it suggests how we may set about developing pricing 'rules' which are more relevant to the real economy. Since the optimal conditions for any one sector will depend on the nature of its interdependence with the deviant sectors, actual pricing policies may have to be developed on a case-by-case basis. However, it is still possible to conduct analysis at the general level, to show what the broad outlines of such policies should be. This analysis is carried out with models which explicitly embody the main features of the second-best economy. In this chapter we shall adopt this positive approach and shall examine the nature of optimal pricing policies in a number of second-best situations.

Before following up this apparently quite reasonable approach, however, we ought to discuss a rather odd implication of it. In the course of the analysis, we find that we are implicitly making the assumption that public enterprise policies are the sole instruments of the economic policy by which the 'central planner' tries to achieve a Pareto optimum in a second-best economy. This in spite of the fact that in many circumstances they do not appear to be the best instrument. In chapter 3, for example, we saw that direct price regulation of monopolies was a more effective instrument than indirect manipulation of their outputs through the price of their public enterprise competitor. Faced with monopolistic price–output policies of the private operators of cross-channel ferries, consumer welfare would appear to be better served by price regulation than by having British Rail join the cartel.[3] The point which then occurs to logical minds is: why does the planner not adopt policies which influence deviants directly, rather than confining himself to public enterprise policies as the sole policy instruments?[4] From this it is a short step to the belief that the economy can be treated as if more rational policies could indeed be implemented, which ultimately brings us back to marginal cost pricing policies for public enterprises. But then we have turned a full circle and again confront the proposition: implementation of marginal cost pricing rules cannot be justified because the appropriate policies are not in fact adopted.

A way out of the impasse is provided by the distinction between what is and what ought to be. To meet the case of what is, we should develop the theory on the assumption that the policy-maker constrains himself to use as instruments only public enterprise policies. This is rather like writing tunes for a pianist to play only with the left hand, when we know that if he also used the right hand we could write much better tunes. However, there are good reasons for developing the theory in this way. First, it allows us to evaluate the policies which are actually being carried out in the second-best world, or those which are proposed for implementation in it. It also helps us to understand why policies derived from first-best models tend to become incoherent when modified in the light of reality. Secondly, many might argue that since more general policies aimed directly at achieving allocative efficiency stand no strong chance of being adopted, whereas (the presumption is) optimal public enterprise policies would be, the 'piecemeal' second-best approach is actually most relevant. This argument must rest on some view of the policy-making machine as fragmented, imperfectly co-ordinated, and internally inconsistent. In terms of our earlier metaphor, the right hand does not know, does not care or is too busy to notice what the left hand is doing, and is playing some other kind of tune altogether.

To take care of what ought to be requires an expansion in scope of the entire analysis. We would have to consider the entire set of aims of economic policy, and the entire set of instruments which can be designed to achieve them. This would involve analysis of the properties of taxes, subsidies, price regulation, and any other kind of policy instrument, as well as public enterprise pricing. In designing an optimal set of policies, comparisons would have to be made of the differential impacts of the instruments on the objectives, and the costs associated with each type of instrument. Any constraints which exist on the set of available instruments would have to be taken into account. Thus, acceptance of the logic of the arguments against 'piecemeal' second-best policy leads to a complete analysis of optimal economic policy in the course of which optimal public enterprise policies would be determined, rather than to a reversion to first-best assumptions.

To embark on the second stage of this programme would lead us well beyond the scope of this book. In this chapter and the next two, we shall be mainly concerned with some aspects of the first stage. In accepting the limitations of the piecemeal approach, we can console ourselves with the thought that at worst it is realistic, and at best it is provisional.

7.1   Public enterprise pricing and monopoly[5]

We take the following situation first of all: in an otherwise competitive economy there is a single public enterprise, producing a good which is a close substitute to that produced by a single monopoly. We assume that the behaviour of the monopolist cannot be controlled directly, and that the only policy open to the 'central planner' is the choice of output for the public enterprise.[6] He wishes to maximize social welfare, which we take to mean that he seeks a Pareto optimum. The key element in the problem is the relationship between the output chosen by the monopolist, and that chosen for the public enterprise. Assume that this relation can be exactly specified (this assumption is further discussed later), and can be written quite simply as

$$q_1 = \beta_1(q_2), \tag{7.1}$$

where q_1 is the monopolist's *chosen* output, q_2 is public enterprise output, and β_1 is a *reaction function*. Then, we can show[7] that the optimal public enterprise price p_2^*

must satisfy the condition

$$p_2^* - MC_2 = -[p_1^* - MC_1]\beta_1'$$ (7.2)

where MC_1 and MC_2 are the respective marginal costs, and β_1' gives the effect on the monopolist's chosen output of a small change in output of the public enterprise. To interpret this condition: since q_1 is produced by a monopolist, $p_1^* > MC_1$, and so the term in square brackets is positive. If the two goods are substitutes, β_1' is likely to be negative. Hence (because of the sign in front of the brackets) the term as a whole is positive. This tells us that in this case the public enterprise price should optimally exceed marginal cost, by an amount which is greater, other things being equal, the greater is the price–marginal cost divergence in the monopoly sector. If the two goods had been complements, then this result would have been reversed since then $\beta_1' > 0$. We see also that $\beta_1' = 0$ implies that price equals marginal cost in the public sector. The result can also readily be generalized beyond monopoly. If $p_1^* \neq MC_1$ for any reason, then equation (7.2) implies $p_2^* \neq MC_2$ (as long as $\beta_1' \neq 0$ of course). If a tax is imposed on good 1, for example, we have $p_1^* > MC_1$ and (7.2) applies;[8] alternatively, if a subsidy is paid, then $p_1^* < MC_1$, and a similar divergence is implied for good 2 (assuming the goods are substitutes). Thus (7.2) gives the basic qualitative result for the case of a public enterprise interdependent with a single, uncorrected 'deviant sector'.

To interpret further the condition in (7.2), first recall that the marginal net social benefit of output of a good is measured by price *minus* marginal cost. However, in the present case we have that the marginal net social benefit of the public enterprise good q_2 depends not only on its own price and marginal cost, but also *on the changes it induces* in the output of the monopoly. Thus, rewriting (7.2) as

$$[p_2^* - MC_2] + [p_1^* - MC_1]\beta_1' = 0$$ (7.3)

we can interpret the first term as the *partial* marginal net social benefit of q_2 in market 2, and the second as the *partial* marginal net social benefit of q_2 in market 1, so that the sum of these could be called the *total* marginal net social benefit of q_2. This condition then says that welfare is maximized when a small variation in q_2 cannot increase total welfare.

A further explanation of the condition can be given with the help of Figure 7.1. On the horizontal axis, we measure output q_2 *leftward*, beginning at the value $\bar{q}_2$, which is defined to be the output at which $p_2 = MC_2$. It is therefore the public enterprise output which would obtain if the first-best rule were implemented. Curve A shows the value of the difference $p_2 - MC_2$ as q_2 is reduced (and its price raised) from that initial point.[9] Thus, it shows the relation between the first *partial* marginal net social benefit and q_2. Given the usual assumptions about slopes of demand and marginal cost curves, it is reasonable to expect the difference $p_2 - MC_2$ to increase as q_2 is reduced. Curve B shows how the second partial marginal net social benefit varies with q_2. Thus, it shows $-[p_1 - MC_1]\beta_1'$ as a function of q_2. We *assume* that the curve falls with reduced q_2, which may be due to one or both of the following: as q_2 falls (and p_2 rises) each successive reduction leads to a smaller increase in monopoly output q_1; and as q_1 increases, the difference $p_1 - MC_1$, which is the marginal net social benefit with respect to q_1, becomes smaller. This assumption, which is made essentially as a stability or second-order condition, will be discussed later. Taking it as given, we see that optimal output is at q_2^*, where A and B intersect. This is the point at which the two *partial* marginal net social benefits of q_2 are equal, thus satisfying equation (7.2). We can rationalize this as follows: at output $\bar{q}_2$, the loss of welfare in market 2 arising from a small reduction in q_2, is measured approximately by $p_2 - MC_2$ and is therefore zero. The gain in welfare in market 1, on the other hand, is measured at $\bar{q}_2$ approximately by $-[p_1 - MC_1]\beta_1'$, represented by point b in the figure. Hence the gain in welfare in market 1 from a reduction in q_2 exceeds the loss in market 2, and there is scope for Pareto improvement. Consumers in market 1 can bribe those in market 2 to accept the reduction in output

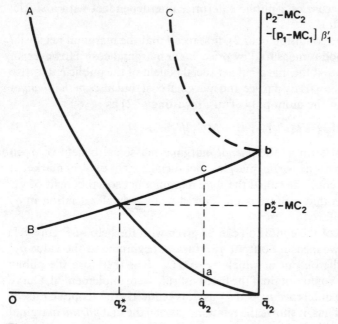

Figure 7.1

and diversion of resources, and still be better off. This holds true at any value of q_2 between $\bar{q}_2$ and q_2^*. For example, at $\hat{q}_2$, the welfare loss to q_2 consumers of a further small reduction is shown by point a, while the welfare gain in market 1 is shown by point c, and so again there is a possibility of making everyone better off. Only at output q_2^* is there no such possibility, and so this is the Pareto-optimal point.

This illustration helps to make clear the nature of the second-best argument: in the initial situation, because of the monopoly in good 1, consumers in that market value their consumption at the margin sufficiently to be able to pay consumers of good 2 to reduce their consumption and release resources into production of good 1. The market fails to organize this mutually beneficial exchange. By adopting an appropriate pricing policy, the planner is able to bring about the required resource reallocation and, given the continued existence of the monopoly, to exhaust all possibilities for such exchange.[10]

The illustration also forces us to consider an important point which could easily be overlooked. We have to assume that the relationships are such that an intersection does take place. For example, if curve B in Figure 7.1 were replaced by C, then no optimal second-best policy for the public enterprise exists. Alternatively, we might have a curve which intersected A at several points, implying several local optima, among which we would have to find in some way the global optimum. There is, therefore, scope for further analysis of the more fundamental restrictions which have to be placed on cost and demand functions to ensure a 'well-behaved' result, and this is further discussed in the Appendix to this chapter.

We can now generalize the condition in (7.2) by extending it first to the case of a single public enterprise with two monopolies.

Let q_0 and q_1 be the monopoly outputs, and q_2 the public enterprise output. Again, the crucial elements in the analysis are the functions relating the monopoly output choices to public enterprise price, $\beta_i(q_2)$, $i = 0, 1$. Given these, we can write the necessary condition[11] for optimal public enterprise price and output as

$$p_2^* - MC_2 = -\{[p_0^* - MC_0]\beta_0' + [p_1^* - MC_1]\beta_1'\}, \tag{7.4}$$

or alternatively as

$$p_2^* - MC_2 + [p_0^* - MC_0]\beta_0' + [p_1^* - MC_1]\beta_1' = 0. \tag{7.5}$$

Here, we have three *partial* marginal net social benefits of q_2, and condition (7.5) simply states that the sum of these must equal zero, this sum being the *total* marginal net social benefit of q_2. The chief point to note is that condition (7.4) implies a price–marginal cost divergence for the public enterprise which is a weighted *sum* of those in the monopolized markets, rather than an average, as is sometimes suggested. An intuitive explanation of this is as follows: the marginal welfare gains, net of the cost of the increased resources, accruing to consumers of q_0 and q_1 are $p_0 - MC_0$ and $p_1 - MC_1$, respectively, so that the *total* net welfare gain from a diversion of resources away from q_2 is the sum of these, weighted by the increases in their outputs which actually result. As long as this sum exceeds the welfare loss sustained by consumers of good 2, the possibility of a mutually beneficial exchange exists, and so a Pareto optimum has not been achieved. Only when the amount consumers of good 2 would require to compensate them for a marginal reduction in consumption is just equal to the total net welfare gain to the consumers of good 0 *and* 1, is a Pareto optimum achieved.

We can again work variations on the interpretation of condition (7.4). Thus, if goods 1 and 2 are substitutes, and 0 and 2 complements, the two terms on the right-hand side of (7.4) would be offsetting: consumers of good 1 would be prepared to bribe consumers of good 2 to reduce their consumption, while consumers of good 0 would be prepared to bribe them not to. Indeed, we could interpret the condition as implying in this case that consumers of goods 0 and 2 all have to be compensated for a reduction in q_2 by consumers of good 1. Whether p_2 ends up above or below MC_2 depends entirely on the price–marginal cost divergences in the two monopolized markets, and the relative values of β'_0 and β'_1, which measure the effects of the public enterprise price on the respective monopolized outputs. We have no reason for assuming, of course, that in general these all cancel out.

Similarly, if a tax existed in market 0 and a subsidy in market 1, while both 0 and 1 are substitutes for 2 (or both complements), then the terms would again be offsetting, and the price–marginal cost divergence for the public enterprise depends on their relative magnitudes.

7.2   Some problems of strategic interdependence

The analysis of the previous section can be used to illustrate both negative and positive aspects of the theory of second best. The conditions in (7.2) and (7.4) show quite clearly that marginal cost pricing is not a necessary condition for a Pareto optimum in the second-best economy. They also give us quite useful insights into the general qualitative nature of the appropriate second-best policies. However, we now have to consider the difficulties of actually implementing such policies. It will in general be necessary to know the relevant demand and cost functions, and, most importantly, the functions which relate monopolists' output choices to public enterprise outputs. In the latter case, there is a conceptual problem which goes beyond the usual difficulties of econometric estimation. It is usually assumed that the monopolist maximizes profit with respect to the cost and demand functions which he perceives to exist. He takes the public enterprise output as a parameter in the perceived demand function, and adapts to a change in it by recomputing his profit-maximizing output with respect to the new demand function. The β function then traces out the path of such output choices as the public enterprise output varies continuously.

However, this account misses an important point. The situation we have been analysing is essentially one of oligopoly,[12] and the basic term in condition (7.3), β'_1, is what has been called in the literature of oligopoly theory a 'conjectural variation'. It is not simply derivable from a measured cross elasticity of demand, but rather must represent the planner's conjecture of the way in which the monopolist will vary his output when the public enterprise varies its own output. In the analysis, we assumed in effect that the monopolist acted as envisaged in the Cournot duopoly model, where a firm maximizes its profit, taking the other's output as given. This assumption may or may not hold in particular areas of the economy to which the above analysis may be relevant, but in any case it is important to be aware of its existence. This also suggests that there may be a class of cases in which second-best policies should be derived by examining explicitly the oligopolistic nature of the situation, i.e. by regarding it as one in which all participants recognize their strategic interdependence. We now consider two examples of such cases.

Suppose first that we have two enterprises, one private, one public, producing undifferentiated outputs, and supplying an entire market. This is a simplification of the kind of situation which, for example, faces British Rail in its cross-channel ferry and hotel operations, and the British Gas Corporation in the sale of gas to the industrial bulk fuel market (where all that matters is heat content per £, and so gas is effectively homogeneous with oil when both are measured in thermal units). The situation is shown in Figure 7.2, where D is the market demand curve, and MC_1 and MC_2 are the marginal cost curves of the private and public enterprises respectively. The curve MC_T is the horizontal sum of MC_1 and MC_2, and so shows 'industry' marginal costs on the assumption that total output, q, is divided between private and public enterprise outputs, q_1 and q_2 respectively, in such a way as to equalize marginal costs. The 'competitive' or first-best solution in the market is at price p^*, with total output q^*, and individual enterprise outputs q_1^* and q_2^*. In this solution, price equals marginal cost and outputs are allocated in a cost-minimizing way (the rest of the economy is assumed perfectly competitive). Suppose now that the private enterprise, in a desire to increase profit, announces that it intends to set the price at p_0. The public enterprise may fall in with this, perhaps on the basis of the following argument: because outputs are homogeneous, only one price can prevail in the market. If the public enterprise maintains price at p^*, it captures the entire market, putting the private firm (which will no doubt claim unfair competition from a heavily subsidized public enterprise) out of business. If the public enterprise continues to set price at p^*, it will itself produce q^* at a marginal (and possibly average) cost well in excess of this price. If it raises price to equal marginal cost at a in the figure, then we have a price–output situation almost the same as that proposed by its private-sector competitor.[13] Hence, the best policy is to accept the suggested price increase.[14] The private enterprise may gamble on its competitor's acceptance of this reasoning. On the other hand (assuming output q_1^* yielded at least normal profit for the private enterprise), if the public enterprise threatened to maintain price at p^* and if need be let the private enterprise go out of business, this would act as an effective constraint on the latter, and could forestall the price rise. Thus, given the nature of the situation, the optimal strategy for the public enterprise is to threaten, or, if the need arises, actually to adopt, maintenance of the price at p^*, by expanding its output to whatever level is required to maintain market output at q^*.

The second case of strategic interdependence which we shall consider is that of bilateral monopoly, with the public enterprise as the sole buyer of a good, and the private enterprise as the sole seller. Again we assume that the rest of the economy is competitive. This is a simplification of the kind of situation in which the British Gas Council buys North Sea gas, the electricity industry buys generating equipment, and

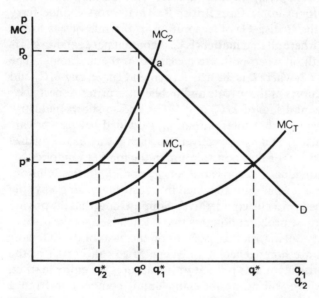

Figure 7.2

British Telecom buys telephone exchange equipment. In Figure 7.3, D is the demand curve of the public enterprise, for the good to be exchanged, MC is the marginal cost curve of the private enterprise producing the good, and MR is the marginal revenue curve corresponding to D. We take it that D shows, at each level of output q, the marginal value product of the good, which in an otherwise first-best economy measures its marginal social value. The optimal quantity of the good which should be produced by the monopolist and bought by the public enterprise is q^*; at any other quantity, its marginal cost differs from its marginal value product, and so welfare could be improved by an output change. If the public enterprise can negotiate this quantity, therefore, it will actually be achieving the first-best solution for this second-best economy. There are two bargaining strategies it may adopt to achieve this solution, the first of which would require it effectively to have complete control of the situation, while the second takes a more realistic view of the bargaining process.

First, suppose that the public enterprise announced that it would accept any quantity, but would pay at most the price p^* in the figure. In effect, p^* *becomes the marginal revenue of the monopolist* – he can sell as much as he likes at that price. It follows that his profit-maximizing quantity is q^*, so this is the amount he will offer. Thus, if the public enterprise determines price, while the private enterprise determines quantity, the first-best solution can be achieved by this strategy.

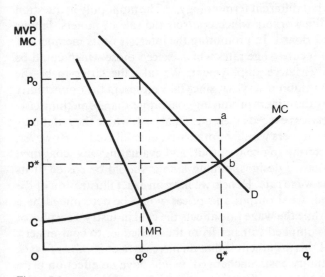

Figure 7.3

However, that solution may yield the monopolist a smaller profit than he thinks he should get, and, given the realities of the bargaining situation, may not be possible. Suppose that instead, therefore, the public enterprise announces that it will buy an amount q^*, and is prepared to negotiate over the price. It is then possible to ensure that the monopolist can have his profit goals at least to some extent satisfied by deciding on a price greater than p^*, say p' in the figure. In that case, the monopolists' total revenue is $Op'aq^*$, his total costs are given by the area $OCbq^*$ under his MC curve, and so total profit is the area $Cp'ab$. It is obviously possible to find some price greater than p^* at which the monopolist's profit is as great as if he were able to exercise his monopoly power in full.

In order for this second strategy actually to lead to a first-best optimum, it is necessary that the public enterprise use, in its determination of input mix, output level and final price, the 'shadow price' p^* rather than the actual price p'. This is because p^* measures the marginal cost of the good. The significance of p' is that it determines the monetary deficit or surplus of the enterprise, and so the result of paying a price p' instead of p^* can be viewed as essentially a transfer payment from the exchequer to the monopolist. Hence (given that there are no welfare effects associated with the deficit or surplus) the value of p' determines the distribution of income in the economy, rather than the allocation of resources.

In case this second strategy should appear fanciful, note that it is essentially the procedure which has been advocated for price and output policies in the coal industry, although in somewhat different terminology.[15] The monopoly in question is the National Union of Mineworkers which controls the sale of miners' labour services to the National Coal Board. In promoting the interests of its members, it uses its bargaining power to secure wage rates which exceed those which could be earned by coal-miners in alternative employment. We take the latter to be the 'marginal social cost' of mining labour services, since they represent the opportunity cost to the economy of having the miners producing coal rather than something else. Hence, the price of labour services exceeds their marginal cost, where the latter may even be regarded as zero if the miners would be otherwise unemployed.[16] However, it has been argued that in determining coal output, and evaluating, say, coal-fired power stations against alternative designs, mining labour should be costed at its opportunity cost, and not the wage rate. Hence, we have an exact illustration of the second strategy just analysed. Coal output and prices would be determined by a 'shadow price' calculation, while the wage rate affects the coal industry's surplus or deficit, and so determines the implied transfer from the exchequer to coal-miners. An interesting implication of this argument is that an increase in coal-miners' wage rates, with their true opportunity costs unchanged, would have no effect on price and output of coal, at least on resource allocation grounds. It would increase the size of transfer from the exchequer to coal-miners, and so require an increase in taxation, in government borrowing, or a reduction in other forms of public expenditure. The question of whether coal prices should then rise must therefore be discussed in terms of tax-expenditure policy, viewing the increase in coal prices essentially as a form of indirect taxation. Similarly, the question of how large the rise in wage rates should be relates primarily to considerations of income distribution and tax-expenditure policy, which explains why it is inevitable that a government would become involved in the bargaining process.

To summarize the analysis of this section and the last: we have been considering second-best situations in which a public enterprise is economically interdependent with a private monopoly. We derived and interpreted some results for optimal pricing rules in such cases, suggesting in a qualitative way the kinds of departures from marginal cost pricing which would be required. In applying this approach, a major problem would be the estimation of the 'conjectural variation', defining the change in the monopolist's choice of output in response to a change in public enterprise price. This suggested that it may often be important to examine explicitly the oligopolistic nature of the markets concerned, taking into account the types of strategic interdependence perceived by the private and public sector participants. Some examples were analysed, where this analysis was intended to be suggestive rather than exhaustive. In the rest of this chapter, we shall look at a somewhat different second-best situation.

7.3 Uncorrected externalities

The existence of external effects implies that the market mechanism will not achieve, unaided, a Pareto optimum, and so also implies existence of a second-best economy. It is in principle possible to design a set of policies which would 'correct for' all externalities, and bring about a first-best Pareto optimum, but it seems impossible to argue that the policies towards externalities which actually exist have this effect, and there are certainly many examples of uncorrected externalities.

Where a public enterprise generates external effects, we can envisage that appropriate corrections would be made, so that it makes choices on the basis of social rather than private costs. Here, we shall not be concerned with the problem of determining the corrections,[17] since nothing there is specific to public enterprise. Rather, we shall take the case of a public enterprise which does not itself generate externalities, but which is interdependent with a sector in which uncorrected externalities exist. The analysis will be conducted in terms of an example: there are two towns, Alpha and Omega, which are connected by a road and a railway line. The only form of road transport is the motorcar (this could be generalized with no real gain in insight). Private motorists are assumed to reckon as the cost of a journey from Alpha to Omega, the cost of petrol, vehicle wear and tear and the value of their time (assumed always positive). Given the details of road conditions and of the characteristics of the cars driven by the motorists, we assume that it is possible to estimate the aggregate cost incurred by a given number of motorists q_m wishing to make the trip from Alpha to Omega within a specified time-period. The relationship between this total cost C_m and q_m is graphed as the curve OC_m in Figure 7.4(a). Its shape reflects the assumption that as traffic builds up average speed declines, thus (after some point) increasing the petrol consumption, wear and tear on the car and journey time of each motorist. Hence, after some point, total costs rise more than proportionately with the number of motorists, as shown by the curvature of OC_m. In Figure 7.4(b), MC_m and AC_m are the marginal and average cost curves derived from OC_m in the usual way. From the curvature of OC_m, we know that MC_m lies above AC_m and has a steeper slope at every point. The important point to note for the subsequent analysis is that each motorist will take, as the cost to himself of the road trip, the *average* cost AC_m, at any given total number of road trips q_m. That is, assuming that each motorist is identical in terms of time value and car characteristics, the cost of making the trip is the same for each motorist and corresponds to the average cost AC_m. The nature of the situation, as one involving external effects, results from the fact that the *marginal* cost of a road journey is above the *average* cost. For example, at $\bar{q}_m$ in the figure, each motorist reckons the cost of the trip as the

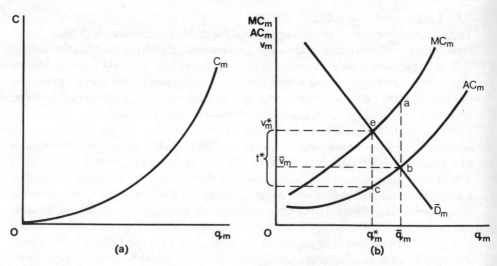

(a)   (b)

Figure 7.4

average cost at point b on AC_m, but the decision of the marginal motorist to take the trip has a cost given by point a on MC_m, since this represents the *increase in total costs* to all users, arising from his taking the trip. The distance ab then measures the divergence between the social cost and the private cost of the marginal road trip. The increment in total cost resulting from the marginal trip exceeds the average cost, on which the motorist bases his decision, by an amount which can be interpreted as the increase in cost to all motorists following from the marginal trip undertaken.

Denote the price of a rail trip from Alpha to Omega by p_r, and assume that it is fixed throughout the following analysis at the value $\bar{p}_r$. Now suppose that a price v_m were to be set for road trips from Alpha to Omega, which would be *inclusive of costs* incurred by each motorist. Effectively, therefore, v_m consists of the average cost of a road trip AC_m plus some *toll*, t, which the motorist pays. Given $\bar{p}_r$, by varying v_m we would trace out a demand curve for road trips, which is drawn as D_m in Figure 7.4(b). We take the situation to be that in which no toll is actually levied on road trips, so that the 'price' of a road trip v_m is equal to the average cost, AC_m. It follows that the equilibrium number of road trips is given by $\bar{q}_m$ in the figure, since that is the number of motorists who will want to make the trip at the price $\bar{v}_m = AC_m$. We can give this position our usual welfare interpretation: the market price measures the value of the marginal unit of consumption. In this case, the value of the marginal trip is just equal to the private cost of undertaking it, AC_m, whereas the social cost of that marginal trip is the value of MC_m at point a in the figure, and so we have an 'uncorrected external diseconomy' in the amount $MC_m - AC_m$ at $\bar{q}_m$.

A first-best solution[18] would be to levy a toll such that the value of the marginal trip is equal to its social cost. In the figure, we see that the optimal toll is given by t^*: with this toll, the 'price' of a road trip is v_m^*, resulting in the total number of trips q_m^*, and a market equilibrium[19] at e, where $v_m^* = MC_m$.

The second-best situation is created by the impossibility, for some reason, of imposing the optimal, or indeed any, toll on road users. The problem becomes that of determining the optimal price of rail trips, given the dependence on it of the demand for road trips. Thus, the rail price p_r becomes the only instrument with which to optimize the 'modal split', to use the jargon of transport economists, in the market for trips from Alpha to Omega.

In Figure 7.5(a) we show the marginal cost and demand curves for rail trips MC_r and $\bar{D}_r$, respectively. The position of the rail demand curve will in general depend on the 'price' of a road trip, AC_m, and so we assume that $\bar{D}_r$ corresponds to the value of AC_m at the number of road trips $\bar{q}_m$. Figure 7.5 therefore represents initial, mutually consistent equilibrium positions in the two markets, with $\bar{D}_m$ corresponding to a marginal cost price for rail, $\bar{p}_r$, and $\bar{D}_r$ corresponding to the average cost of a road trip at $\bar{q}_m$.

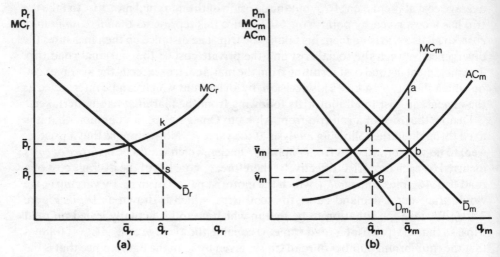

Figure 7.5

In this initial situation, there is a divergence between the marginal value of a road trip, and its marginal cost, of the amount $MC_m - AC_m$ at $\bar{q}_m$. Hence, a small reduction in the number of road trips would generate a welfare gain of approximately this amount. In the rail market, the marginal value of a rail trip p_r is equal to its marginal cost MC_r and so the welfare loss from a small increment in rail trips is approximately zero. By reducing the rail price from $\bar{p}_r$, we achieve the reduction in road trips and increase in rail trips, and hence generate a net welfare gain. In the figure, we illustrate this by reducing the rail price to $\hat{p}_r$, which expands rail trips to $\hat{q}_r$, causes the road demand to shift to D_m, and hence causes an initial fall in road trips to $\hat{q}_m$, thus reducing the marginal welfare loss $MC_m - AC_m$ to that at $\hat{q}_m$ (shown by the distance hg). However, the figure does not show the end of the story, since the fall in AC_m will cause a downward shift in $\bar{D}_r$, so that if $\hat{p}_r$ is held, there will be a smaller increase in rail trips than $\hat{q}_r - \bar{q}_r$. Because of the demand interactions, the figure is not well suited to find the final solution, but it indicates the general nature of the argument. The necessary condition which must be satisfied by the optimal rail price is

$$p_r^* - MC_r = [MC_m - AC_m]\frac{\Delta q_m}{\Delta q_r} \qquad (7.6)$$

which is clearly similar to the sorts of conditions we derived in the earlier sections of this chapter. Here $\Delta q_m / \Delta q_r$ is the effect of a small increase in rail traffic on the number of road trips. The term in square brackets is effectively the marginal welfare loss of road trips, since, in the absence of a toll, the value of the marginal road trip is always equal to AC_m. Moreover, this term is always positive, while $\Delta q_m/\Delta q_r$ is negative, and so a rail price below marginal cost is called for. Finally, we emphasize that this 'correction' to the marginal cost price of the public enterprise good is made, not because it itself generates externalities, but because it is closely related in demand to a sector in which uncorrected externalities exist. If this demand relation did not exist, marginal cost pricing would be optimal.

7.4 Conclusions

In this chapter we have considered second-best situations in which a public enterprise is interdependent with a 'deviant sector', which may be a monopoly, or a market in which non-optimal taxes or uncorrected externalities exist. The initial assumption is that the public enterprise price is the sole instrument of second-best policy, even though better ones can clearly be designed. To pursue the full implications of this assumption would require a more general analysis of the cost, effectiveness and feasibility of a wide set of policy instruments, which would be an important though large undertaking. We have here adopted the assumption provisionally, as being the most useful way to begin the analysis of what appear to be the real problems. We find that in general marginal cost pricing is not justified on the Paretian grounds from which it usually derives its support. If the public enterprise price is set equal to marginal cost, there is in general a way of reallocating resources so as to make everyone better off, and using the public enterprise price as a means of exhausting such possibilities will imply in the end a non-marginal cost pricing condition. There is a strong similarity among the forms of such conditions for the various cases analysed, and they can usually be rationalized in an intuitively appealing way. To implement pricing policies based on such conditions will in general require more information than that needed by any pricing rule which does not take into account interactions between sectors. Moreover, a particular problem arises in the class of cases in which the public enterprise is closely related to a 'monopoly', since here in effect we have a situation of oligopoly. In such a case, it may be difficult to measure the 'conjectural variation', which is a crucial element of the second-best pricing condition, and it has been suggested that the appropriate approach may be to set up a model of the situation which explicitly incorporates the types of strategic interdependence which exist. The overall conclusion of the analysis, which cannot possibly be exhaustive, is that actual pricing policies must be developed on a case-by-case basis, since the particular nature of the second-best situation may differ from enterprise to enterprise. However, the kind of analysis carried out here is useful in indicating the general forms such policies would take.

Appendix to chapter 7

1 Public enterprise pricing and monopoly

With q_1 as the monopoly output and q_2 the public enterprise output, the total consumer benefit function is $B(q_1, q_2)$ with $\partial B/\partial 1_i = p_i$, $i = 1, 2$. Given the cost functions $C_i(q_i)$, $i = 1, 2$, we seek to maximize net social benefit $B - \sum_i C_i$, *given* the relationship $q_1 = \beta_1(q_2)$. We can use this relationship to eliminate q_1 from the problem, and the conditions for a maximum with respect to q_2 are:

$$[p_1 - C_1']\beta_1' + p_2 - C_2' = 0 \tag{A.7.1}$$

$$[p_1' - C_1'']\beta_1' + [p_1 - C_1']\beta_1'' + p_2' - C_2'' < 0. \tag{A.7.2}$$

The necessary condition in (A.7.1) was discussed at some length in section 7.1 of this chapter, and so let us consider the second-order condition (A.7.2). We cannot in general be sure this will be satisfied. We normally expect $p_i' - C_i'' < 0$, $i = 1, 2$. The sign of β_1' depends on the reaction the monopoly would adopt to an expansion in public enterprise output, induced by a cut in its price. If the goods are substitutes and the monopoly adopts Cournot-type behaviour, $\beta_1' < 0$. Hence the first term in (A.7.2) has the opposite sign to the third term, and satisfaction of the condition is not guaranteed. If on the other hand the monopoly responded aggressively by cutting its own price and expanding its output, $\beta_1' > 0$ and the first and third terms have the same sign. However, the sign of the second term is also relevant. If β_1 is linear, $\beta_1'' = 0$ and the term vanishes. Otherwise, since in general $p_1 - C_1' > 0$, the term is negative (positive) as β_1'' is negative (positive). Unfortunately, we cannot in general place restrictions on the sign of β_1''. Thus we cannot in general be sure that an output q_2^* which satisfies (A.7.1) is indeed a second-best welfare optimum.

For the case in which we have $n > 1$ monopolies, the analysis extends readily. Given the n reaction functions $q_i = \beta_i(q_0)$, $i = 1, \ldots, n$, where q_0 now denotes the public enterprise output, the problem becomes that of maximizing $B(q_0, \beta_1(q_0), \ldots, \beta_n(q_0)) - C_0(q_0) - \sum_{i=1}^{n} C_i(\beta_i(q_0))$, yielding conditions:

$$p_0 - C_0' + \sum_{i=1}^{n} [p_i - C_1']\beta_1' = 0. \tag{A.7.3}$$

This assumes of course that each β_i depends only on q_0, and not on outputs of other private monopolies, although to allow this would simply complicate the analysis with no real gain in insight. The problem of sufficiency, however, still remains: there is nothing in general to guarantee that an output which satisfies (A.7.3) is in fact second-best optimal.

In the case where the private and public enterprises are essentially duopolists producing undifferentiated outputs, the optimal solution is perfectly straightforward. Optimal market output is found from the condition for first-best optimality:

$$p(q_0^* + q_1^*) = C_0'(q_0^*) + C_1'(q_1^*) \qquad (A.7.4)$$

where public enterprise output is q_0 and private output is q_1. Then, the public enterprise threatens, and if necessary carries out the threat, to produce $\hat{q}_0 = q_0^* + q_1^* - q_1$ for any output $q_1 < q_1^*$ the private enterprise may produce. This maintains the first-best optimum.

Note, however, that this assumes that capacity is not rigid – it is feasible for the public enterprise to expand output by any required amount. (This point is made by R. Harris (1981)). Thus in cases where capacity is rigid in the short run we can best think of this as a long-run strategy, to be enforced by varying capacity as well as output. In the short run, the private enterprise may be able to raise price and restrict its own output, if $\hat{q}_0 > \bar{q}_0$, the public enterprise capacity output.

2 The road-rail problem

The total cost function for road trips is $C_m(q_m)$. Writing this as $q_m \cdot AC_m(q_m)$, where $AC_m = C_m/q_m$ is average cost, we see that:

$$MC_m = \frac{dC_m}{dq_m} = AC_m + q_m \frac{dAC_m}{dq_m} \qquad (A.7.5)$$

where MC_m is marginal cost. The excess of marginal over average cost, $q_m(dAC_m/dq_m)$, is interpreted as the sum of the effects on the costs to all motorists, of the entry of the marginal motorist onto the system. The externality exists because each motorist considers AC_m as the 'price' of a trip, whereas the marginal social cost of a trip is MC_m.

If it is impossible to set a toll on road trips, the second-best problem is to set price p_r and output q_r of rail trips to maximize net social benefits $B(q_m, q_r) - C_m(q_m) - C_r(q_r)$. We have to define the relationship $q_m = m(q_r)$, which specifies exactly how many road trips will be taken at each level of rail output (and price). Note that, since the 'road market' is essentially 'competitive', this function does not involve conjectural variations. Given this relationship we can eliminate q_m from the problem and maximize net social benefits with respect only to q_r. Necessary and sufficient conditions are:

$$p_r - C'_r + [AC_m - C'_m]m' = 0 \qquad (A.7.6)$$

$$p'_r - C''_r + [AC_m - C''_m]m' + [AC_m - C'_m]m'' < 0 \qquad (A.7.7)$$

where, it should be recalled, AC_m measures the effective price, and therefore the marginal benefit, of road trips. Since $m' < 0$ and $AC_m - C'_m < 0$, we have that $p_r < C'_r$ at the optimum. Again, however, we cannot be certain the second-order condition is satisfied. The first term in (A.7.7) is negative. The second term is most probably positive, since $m' < 0$ and it is reasonable to suppose $AC'_m < C''_m$ (the marginal cost curve is steeper than the average cost curve). Finally, the third term could be positive or negative, depending on the sign of m'', on which no restrictions can in general be placed. Again therefore we cannot be sure that the rail price and output satisfying (A.7.6) are the true second-best optimum.

Chapter 8
Profitability, taxation and income distribution

In the previous five chapters, we have been concerned with the characterization of pricing and investment policies which achieve allocative efficiency. The purpose was always to find necessary conditions under which the public enterprise resource allocation was Pareto optimal, and then to use these conditions to determine the appropriate policy. Implicit in this, therefore, is the assumption either that our 'policy-maker' is indifferent to the distribution of welfare, or that he is able to achieve any desired distribution by making lump-sum transfers which leave the marginal conditions unaffected (recall the discussion of chapter 3). Also implicit was the assumption that the profit or loss of the enterprise was a matter of indifference, presumably for a similar reason: that any deficit could be financed in a lump-sum way, and any surplus distributed in a similar fashion. Finally, although economic efficiency is a matter of both allocative efficiency and technological efficiency, the latter received no explicit attention: it was implicitly assumed that public enterprise managers would choose the technologically most efficient set of input combinations for each output, and then the cost-minimizing combinations within this set, so that the cost of producing each given level of output was at a minimum.

As we saw in chapters 1 and 2, however, a great deal of attention is paid by policy-makers to precisely these issues – profitability, income distribution and technological efficiency – to the extent that allocative efficiency may well be sacrificed in pursuit of them. Therefore, any attempt to formulate decentralized pricing and investment policies is incomplete unless it extends to these. It is worth while to recapitulate the reasons for the explicit attention which must be paid to these goals. Of prime importance is the impossibility of devising lump-sum taxes which would achieve distributional objectives, and provide finance for public enterprise deficits and other forms of public expenditures whose revenues do not cover costs. Thus, taxes are imposed on incomes and outputs. These taxes are not only a means of raising revenue, but are also instruments of income redistribution. Public enterprise prices relate directly to the government's fiscal concerns, since gross trading surpluses are an important source of government revenue, and public enterprise investment constitutes a heavy claim on public expenditure. Thus, the surpluses of public enterprises can be looked upon as a form of indirect taxation. In addition, the nature of most public enterprise outputs, as 'public utilities', raises important distributional issues, as does the fact that inputs, especially labour services, may be supplied by households whose real income it is desired to increase, for one reason or another. Clearly, therefore, public enterprise prices are likely to be seen as useful instruments in taxation and income redistribution policies.

Profitability has a further significance: the self-interest which is at the root of profit maximization leads an entrepreneur to seek to minimize costs at each level of output, and hence to pursue technological efficiency. Once the connection between efficiency and self-interest is removed, managers may pursue the 'quiet life', and adopt 'satisficing' goals, which may well imply technological and managerial inefficiency.[1] The problem as policy-makers see it is to find a way of stimulating managers to technological efficiency, by reintroducing profit as a goal but not as a maximand. The problem is compounded when income-distributional goals exist, the pursuit of which appears in turn to imply technological inefficiency. This is a fine example of the policy conflict discussed in chapter 1.

In the rest of this chapter, we shall try to answer the question: how may pricing policies be defined, which meet profit and income-distributional objectives with the minimum loss of economic efficiency?

8.1 Profit targets

The way in which both profitability and efficiency goals have been brought to bear upon public enterprises is through the device of a 'financial target', described in chapter 3. For present purposes, we take this to be a specified value[2] of the gross trading surplus, or excess of revenue over direct operating costs. Thus, the surplus includes provision for those costs which can be taken as fixed with capacity. The value of the surplus reflects the contribution to the exchequer which it is desired that the enterprise should make. The precise way in which technological and managerial efficiency is supposed to be stimulated by the profit target is somewhat unclear, as is the relation between the strength of this stimulus and size of the target. We shall discuss this question later in this section. For the moment, we concern ourselves only with the question: how should prices and outputs be chosen, in a way which meets the profit target with a minimum loss of allocative efficiency?[3]

First, note that if the public enterprise produces only a single product then the problem is relatively trivial. Figure 8.1 illustrates. In the figure, p^* is the allocatively optimal price (assuming there are no other second-best problems) but, at the corresponding output q^*, average total cost AC exceeds price, and so the enterprise makes a loss. Suppose it is required to 'break even', i.e. to cover total costs including fixed costs (in which case the required surplus is effectively equal to fixed cost): then this requires price to equal average total cost, AC. There are two outputs at which this occurs in the figure, namely q^0 and q^1, corresponding to the points a and b at which AC intersects the demand curve D. Clearly there is a smaller welfare loss at a, and this is the optimal output. Thus, in the case of a single output, the set of output levels which satisfy the profit target will typically contain at most two values (or one if the target is for *maximum* profit) and so the problem of choice is very straightforward.[4]

In general, however, public enterprises produce more than one output, and so we have the important problem of the *allocation* of the profit target among different outputs. We shall, as is our usual practice, begin with the simplest possible case, in which the public enterprise produces two outputs, which in addition are unrelated in demand and cost: the cross-elasticities of demand are zero, and variations in production of one output do not affect costs of the other. We then have the problem of determining the optimal prices.

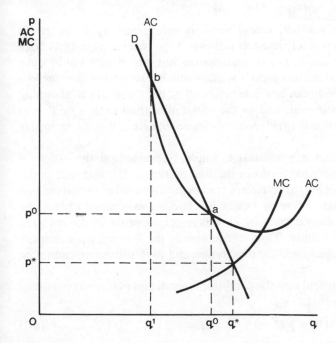

Figure 8.1

The argument underlying derivation of these can be described as follows: suppose that the two outputs, q_1 and q_2, are initially at the level at which their respective prices are equal to marginal cost. A small reduction in q_1 will reduce consumer welfare by its price p_1, since this is the marginal value of output to consumers; it will, however, release resources which can be used elsewhere, the value of this being measured by marginal cost, MC_1. Hence, the marginal net welfare loss corresponding to a reduction in q_1 is measured by $p_1 - MC_1$. Likewise, $p_2 - MC_2$ measures that of good 2. The effect of the change in output of good 1 on the profit it generates is given by the difference between marginal revenue, MR_1, and marginal cost. That is, the *marginal profit* of output 1 is $MR_1 - MC_1$, and that of good 2 is $MR_2 - MC_2$ (note that if outputs are *greater* than their profit-maximizing levels, which we take to be the case, these marginal profits are negative: a reduction in output increases profit, because $MC > MR$).

It can be shown[5] that the optimal outputs of the two goods must satisfy the condition:

$$\frac{p_1 - MC_1}{MR_1 - MC_1} = \frac{p_2 - MC_2}{MR_2 - MC_2} = \lambda < 0, \tag{8.1}$$

where λ is some negative number, whose value is determined by S, the profit constraint. This condition is interpreted as follows: if the two ratios in (8.1) were unequal, we could always find a way of reallocating outputs, which would leave profit unchanged ($= S$), but lead to a greater welfare gain in one market than the loss in the other. Hence, everybody can be made better off by the reallocation, assuming appropriate compensation is paid, and so the initial allocation cannot be Pareto optimal. A necessary condition for such possibilities not to exist is that the ratios are equal.

To illustrate this, consider a numerical example. Suppose that the ratio[6] of marginal welfare loss to marginal profit in the first market is 3/1, and that in the second is 2/1. Then, by choosing to increase output in the first market so that the loss of profit is 1, we can increase welfare by 3 units; by choosing to reduce output in the second market so that profit increases by 1, thus restoring profit to the required level, we lose two units of welfare. Thus, consumers in the first market can more than compensate those in the second for the change, and so this situation cannot be Pareto optimal.

To obtain some further insight into the conditions, recall that marginal revenue of each good can always be written as

$$MR_i = p_i(1 - 1/e_i), \qquad i = 1, 2 \tag{8.2}$$

where e_i is the price elasticity of demand for good i, given by

$$e_i = -\frac{p_i \, dq_i}{q_i \, dp_i}, \qquad i = 1, 2. \tag{8.3}$$

Now, from equation (8.1), we have that

$$p_1 - MC_1 = \lambda[MR_1 - MC_1] > 0 \tag{8.4}$$

and so, by using equation (8.2) and rearranging, we obtain

$$p_1(1 - 1/\hat{e}_1) = MC_1, \tag{8.5}$$

where

$$\hat{e}_1 = -\frac{(1-\lambda)e_1}{\lambda} \tag{8.6}$$

and similarly we can show for good 2 that

$$p_2(1 - 1/\hat{e}_2) = MC_2, \tag{8.7}$$

where

$$\hat{e}_2 = -\frac{(1-\lambda)e_2}{\lambda}. \tag{8.8}$$

The term $-[(1-\lambda)/\lambda]$ must be greater than 1, since λ is negative. The conditions in (8.5) and (8.7) then have the interesting interpretation: the public enterprise is, in effect, constrained to act like a 'quasi-monopolist', who must maximize profit, but with respect to a demand curve whose elasticity is increased by the factor $-[(1-\lambda)]/\lambda$, the value of which depends on the profit constraint S. As S tends to maximum profit, so this term tends to unity,[7] as we would expect. Since the 'correction factor' to the two demand elasticities is the same, we have the result that the relative deviations of price from marginal cost of the two goods are entirely determined by their elasticities. Each deviation varies inversely with the elasticity of demand of the good: goods with less elastic demands have higher divergences of price from marginal cost.

An illustration of these results is given in Figure 8.2. For simplicity, it is assumed that marginal costs are constant and equal for the two goods. The optimal outputs are q_1^* and q_2^* respectively, it having been assumed that the value of S is such as to imply a value of λ of -1. Thus, condition (8.1) is clearly satisfied in the figure, since the relevant divergences are given by ab, bc, ef and fg, and we have that $ab/bc = ef/fg = -1$. The price–marginal cost divergence is clearly greater in market 2, which has the less elastic demand, and that market also makes the greater profit contribution, shown by the area $p_2^* abk$, as compared to that in the first market, area $p_1^* efh$. The lines $\widehat{MR}_1$ and $\widehat{MR}_2$ are the *adjusted* marginal revenue curves, corresponding respectively to the elasticities $\hat{e}_1$ and $\hat{e}_2$ rather than the true elasticities. Thus, the profit constraints induce the public enterprise to act as a 'modified' profit-maximizer, restricting output, raising price, and 'charging what the market will bear' to an overall degree determined by the profit constraint.

Before going on to generalize these results, we can note a feature of them which is interesting from the viewpoint of empirical application. In practice, public enterprise prices are often set on the basis of 'what the market will bear'. Profit margins are higher in 'captive markets', or, in the terminology of economics, markets with low demand elasticity, than in competitive markets. The pricing rule just derived would therefore make a lot of sense to those who currently set pricing policy. Moreover, this suggests that the existing pattern of outputs may lie closer to the optimum than would the one which follows from making all prices bear the same proportionate relationship to marginal costs.

We can now generalize our earlier result by assuming that the two goods are interdependent in demand. It is then possible to show[8] that the optimal prices and quantities must now satisfy the relationship

$$\frac{p_1 - MC_1}{MR_{11} + MR_{12} - MC_1} = \frac{p_2 - MC_2}{MR_{22} + MR_{21} - MC_2} = \lambda, \qquad (8.9)$$

where MR_{ij}, $i,j = 1, 2$, is the effect of the ith output on the revenue of the jth. We can regard the sum $MR_{11} + MR_{12}$ as the *total* effect on the revenue of the enterprise, of a change in output 1, via the effects on both its own demand, and that of good 2. And likewise for the sum $MR_{22} + MR_{21}$. For example, if the two goods are substitutes, so that an increase in q_1, accompanied by a fall in its price, decreases demand and revenue of good 2, then MR_{12} will be negative. The basic rationalization of this condition is essentially as before: the only difference is that now the *total* effect of each output on the overall revenue of the enterprise must be taken into account. It follows that the price–marginal cost divergences will now depend not only on own-price elasticities of demand, but cross-price elasticities also. This of course increases the informational requirements for implementation of these conditions.

Similar conclusions follow when we consider the case of several public enterprises, each producing several outputs, many of which are interdependent in demand. This is the case in the energy and transport sectors, for example, where electricity and gas are close substitutes in the domestic space-heating market, coal and gas compete in the industrial bulk energy market, rail and air compete in long-distance interurban travel, and so on. Given that each enterprise is subject to a different profit constraint, the optimality condition for goods 1 and 2 now becomes[9]

$$\frac{p_1 - MC_1 - \sum_{i=2}^{n} \lambda_i MR_{1i}}{MR_{11} + MR_{12} - MC_1} = \frac{p_2 - MC_2 - \sum_{i=2}^{n} \lambda_i MR_{2i}}{MR_{21} + MR_{22} - MC_2} = \lambda_1, \qquad (8.10)$$

where λ_1 is determined by the profit constraint imposed on the first public enterprise. The condition clearly differs only by the subtraction from each numerator of the term $\sum_{i=2}^{n} \lambda_i MR_{ji}$, $j = 1, 2$, which is the sum of the effects of a change in q_j, on the revenues of all other profit-constrained public enterprises, weighted by *their* values of λ, the λ_i, $i = 2, 3, \ldots, n$. The significance of λ lies in its interpretation as the marginal welfare cost of the profit constraint; i.e. its value measures the reduction in consumer welfare which would result from a small increase in the required profit. Thus, the term $\lambda_i MR_1$ is the indirect effect on consumer welfare of a change in q_1, via its effect on the revenues (and therefore profits) of the other enterprise. Now since λ_i is negative, if MR_1 is negative (the goods are substitutes) this term is positive, and therefore, in (8.10), plays the part of a 'social cost': by reducing the profits of the other enterprise, an increase in q_1 causes them to make up for this by raising their prices and thus reducing welfare in their own markets. Such effects have to be taken into account in determining the output level of every good produced in the public enterprise sector. To do so is simply to recognize the common-sense argument that it is pointless to make one enterprise achieve its profit target, while ignoring the fact that this makes it harder for another

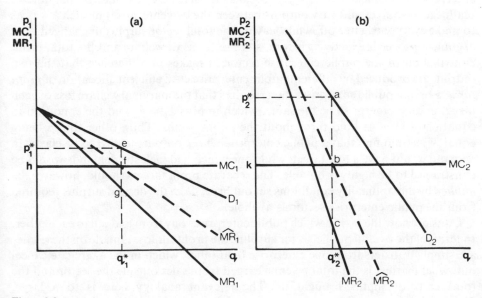

Figure 8.2

to do so, and in the end leads to a greater welfare loss over all. The condition in (8.10) essentially imposes the requirement for a *co-ordinated* public enterprise policy.

This suggests two further points of interest. First, how should we determine the *relative* profit targets of different public enterprises? And second, what should be the approach towards sales of intermediate goods *within* the public sector? We consider each of these in turn.

To examine the first question, let us return to the simple case of two goods and no demand interdependence, but assume that they are produced by different public enterprises (which produce other outputs as well). The optimum conditions relating to each good will now be

$$\frac{p_1 - MC_1}{MR_1 - MC_1} = \lambda_1 \quad \text{and} \quad \frac{p_2 - MC_2}{MR_2 - MC_2} = \lambda_2, \tag{8.11}$$

where λ_1 and λ_2 are determined by the target surpluses in the two industries. Recall that they are interpreted as the marginal welfare loss arising from the profit constraint on each enterprise. Now presumably, the subject of concern to the policy-maker is the *total* surplus generated by all enterprises, since this is the effective inflow into the exchequer. It follows that the allocation of this surplus among enterprises is inefficient if $\lambda_1 \neq \lambda_2$, because in that case it would be possible to reallocate resources and vary outputs between the two enterprises in such a way as to make everyone better off, while leaving the total *sector* surplus unchanged. The argument proceeds exactly as before, since in terms of welfare and the total profit contribution of the public enterprise sector, it makes no difference that the two outputs are produced by different public enterprises. An efficient allocation of *profit targets* among public enterprises then requires that the marginal welfare loss of each target in each enterprise be the same, which implies $\lambda_1 = \lambda_2$ and the condition in equation (8.1) must hold throughout the public sector. Thus, other things being equal, we would find that a public enterprise whose outputs tended to be elastic in demand would have a low target, while one which had inelastic demands would be constrained to be highly profitable. The separate profit targets should, however, be *implied* by the optimality conditions set out here, *given* the desired surplus required from the public enterprise sector as a whole.

Consider now the case in which public enterprises buy from and sell to each other. In terms of the overall public-sector surplus, the profits or losses made on these sales are simply transfers from one enterprise to another, which in the aggregate cancel out: what matters is the total revenue earned from sales outside the sector and the total costs of inputs brought in. The relevant analogy here is to a large, divisionalized, vertically integrated firm, and the problem is essentially to determine the correct set of *transfer prices*, i.e. the prices which co-ordinate and optimize transfers of intermediate goods between divisions in a decentralized way.[10]

Given a set of profit targets which are separately imposed on public enterprises, each enterprise will be constrained to make some profit on its sales to other public enterprises, even though this leads to distortions and welfare losses. This is more clearly seen if we take the case of a single public enterprise, E, which produces two outputs, one of which it sells to public enterprise A, the other to public enterprise B. E is the sole producer of these outputs. The rest of the economy is assumed perfectly competitive. Given the profit constraint which is imposed upon it, E will have to set its prices above marginal cost, and the relative profit contribution from sales A and B will depend on the elasticities of their demands for E's output, as we have already seen.[11] These elasticities depend partly on the technological possibilities of input substitution in A and B, and partly on the price elasticities of demand for their final outputs. Given that A and B must meet *their* profit targets, they will substitute other inputs for the public enterprise input, thus buying in from outside the public sector, and will also raise their own prices. But since E's profit simply represents higher costs to A and B, the *total* surplus of the three enterprises must be derived from the revenues of A and B in their sales to final consumers. Suppose instead that this total surplus were allocated only to A and B, and that the third enterprise is instructed to sell to them at marginal cost, i.e. no financial target is imposed upon it. There is an efficiency gain, because the input combinations chosen by A and B would then be based on a minimization of social costs. Given that the prices of inputs supplied by the private sector equal their marginal costs (i.e. we are in an otherwise first-best economy), a price of the public enterprise input above *its* marginal cost would distort the relative input prices which A and B face, and lead them to choose input combinations which do not minimize social cost.[12] Thus, the conclusion is that transfers within the public enterprise sector should be made at marginal cost, given that such transfers do not involve interdependence with 'deviant' markets in the private sector. The overall surplus required by the public sector should be generated by profits on sales to non-public enterprise buyers. Thus for example coal would be sold to the electricity and steel industries at a price equal to marginal cost, while coal sold to outside buyers would make a positive contribution (over and above that which is anyway implied by pricing at marginal cost in an increasing-cost industry) to profit.[13]

The argument so far has led to the conclusion that given the total required surplus from the public enterprise sector, which is determined by the government on revenue-raising grounds, the objective of minimizing the loss of allocative efficiency determines the way in which it can be allocated among all public enterprise outputs. The total surplus generated by any one enterprise is then a *derived* value: it will be the sum of the individual surpluses on the outputs the enterprise produces. By examining the converse case, in which targets are separately allocated to enterprises and then the effects on price–marginal cost divergences of specific outputs determined, we were able to show that the former is a better second best. This means that a public enterprise which sells most of its output to other public enterprises, and which in outside markets faces elastic demands, would be relatively 'unprofitable' (recalling that the 'surplus' includes interest and depreciation).

This conclusion cannot be left to stand, however, without a discussion of the second reason for the existence of 'financial targets', as stimuli to managerial and technological efficiency, and a yardstick of performance.[14] Clearly, there is no direct connection between profit targets and efficiency, since they can be achieved by price increases. There must exist some system by which price increases are monitored, so that the profit target is made to exert pressure on costs. Since this must be done by government agencies, we immediately lose many of the advantages which a decentralized system would bring. If the monitoring is to be effective, it would require exploration of the reasons for cost increases, analysis of productivity levels, and so on – price control alone cannot suffice. Often, price increases have been refused or scaled down in the (presumed) interests of counter-inflationary policy, with no monitoring of cost levels. Thus, public enterprises have been able to point to this as a reason for non-fulfilment of profit targets, and it has been *impossible to determine* whether or not this is true, whatever dark suspicions may be held.

This suggests, to the writer at least, that the pursuit of technological and managerial efficiency should be divorced from the question of profitability, and should be undertaken directly, rather than indirectly through pricing policy. The appropriate instrument would be the 'efficiency audit' suggested by Professor Robson.[15] An 'efficiency audit commission' would be exclusively concerned with producing analyses of the efficiency of all parts of the public enterprise sector, choosing its own areas of investigation, and having full rights to information. The gains in decentralization would come about because this commission would not be involved in the process of formulating decisions, but rather in appraising and monitoring the outcomes of decisions and operational and decision-taking procedures. In this way, the attempt to stimulate managerial and technological efficiency could be made consistent with greater decentralization of pricing and investment decisions. Profit targets would then simply reflect the government's desire for revenue.

To conclude this discussion of public enterprise profitability, we can note one further generalization. Recall the demonstration that to allocate surpluses to public enterprises, which must then be allocated to each group of outputs, leads to a worse second-best outcome than to allocate the total desired surplus optimally across all public enterprise outputs, so that the 'profit target' of each enterprise becomes derived rather than predetermined. This argument can be extended to the whole economy: given the overall tax revenue required by the government, this could be allocated optimally across all goods in the economy, and thus the total surplus to be generated by the public enterprise sector is derived from the tax revenue accruing from public enterprise outputs rather than being pre-determined.

The determination of 'optimal taxation' has a long history of study in economics, and given the nature of the problem, it is not surprising to find that the conditions for the optimal tax on goods in general are precisely those given earlier in equations (8.1), (8.5) or (8.9).[16] λ would now be determined by the total tax revenue requirement, and is interpreted as the marginal welfare loss, through the entire economy, of a change in the government's 'budget constraint', i.e. the relation between revenue and expenditure. Thus, if we define the specific tax on the ith good t_i as the difference between price and marginal cost of the ith good,

$$t_i \equiv p_i - MC_i, \tag{8.12}$$

then it can be shown that the optimal *rate* of tax, t_i/p_i, is given (in the demand independence case) by

$$t_i/p_i = 1/\hat{e}_i, \tag{8.13}$$

where, as before, $\hat{e}_i = -[(1-\lambda)/\lambda]e_i$, and e_i is own-price elasticity of demand for good i. It can be shown[17] that this is exactly equivalent to condition (8.1), assuming that the values of λ are in each case the same, which in turn requires that the 'target surplus' which is allocated to the public enterprise producing good i, is precisely that implied by the set of optimal taxes on all the outputs it produces. Thus, if an optimal taxation policy is applied throughout the economy, public enterprise prices are determined as part of this, and there is no separate public enterprise pricing problem.[18]

In reality, optimal taxation policies do not seem to be generally pursued. Again, we are led to the implication of the present analysis: we are searching for optimal policies in one part of the public sector, presuming they would be implemented, while assuming that policies in other parts of the public sector are non-optimal. In that case, the aggregate surplus required from public enterprises is not determined on a globally optimal basis, and public enterprise pricing policy (now in a world of 'deviant sectors' if taxes in the rest of the economy are non-optimal) becomes a separate problem.

There is one important result of this generalization, however: we can express optimal public enterprise prices in terms of a tax rate applied to marginal cost,[19] which may be useful from the point of view of decentralization.

8.2 Pricing policy and income distribution

The foregoing analysis has been concerned with pricing policies which meet profit targets with minimal losses in allocative efficiency, and so continued to assume that income distribution was a matter of indifference. We now assume that the 'policy-maker' has explicit objectives toward income distribution, which cannot be pursued through lump-sum taxation: he must achieve them through taxing goods and services. In particular, income distributional considerations will be brought to bear on public enterprise prices.

In actual practice, income-distributional aims are pursued by direct *ad hoc* intervention: proposed price increases may be rejected, loss-making services perpetuated, and manpower policies, whose purpose is to eliminate over-manning, may be refused implementation (examples were discussed in chapter 2). Our purpose here is to examine whether income-distributional aims can be incorporated into pricing policies in a systematic way, so that they become consistent with decentralized control, and do not require *ad hoc* intervention.

We take the case of a public enterprise producing two goods,[20] q_1 and q_2, subject to a profit constraint of the kind considered earlier. We shall be interested in formulating pricing policies which take into account the policy-maker's income-distributional preferences, as well as generating the required surplus. To simplify the analysis, we again assume that outputs are independent in demand; in addition, we assume there are only two consumers in the economy. This latter assumption generalizes easily;[21] the reader may like to think of them as in fact two *groups*, say 'poor' and 'rich'. Although there are other goods in the economy, we suppose that the policy-maker operates only on the prices of the public enterprise.

An important analytical device we use for this problem is the *indirect utility function*. Thus suppose, as in standard demand analysis, a consumer maximizes a utility function:

$$u = u(q_1 q_2, \ldots, q_n) \tag{8.14}$$

where $q_1, \ldots, q_n$ are quantities of the goods he may consume, subject to a budget constraint:

$$\sum_{j=1}^{n} p_j q_j = y \tag{8.15}$$

where the p_j are the goods' prices and y is the consumer's income. This results in standard demand functions which show how the consumer's optimal choices, q_j^*, depend on the prices and income, so that we have:

$$q_j^* = D_j(p_1, \ldots, p_n, y). \tag{8.16}$$

It follows that the value of the consumer's utility at the optimum is given by:

$$u = u(q_1^*, \ldots, q_n^*) = u(D_1(p_1, \ldots, p_n, y), \ldots, D_n(p_1, \ldots, p_n, y))$$
$$= v(p_1, \ldots, p_n, y). \qquad (8.17)$$

That is, the consumer's *maximized* utility can be expressed as a function of prices and income, since a change in one of these will change his chosen quantities and hence his maximized utility. The function v is called the consumer's indirect utility function, since it shows how utility depends indirectly on prices and income, rather than directly on quantities of goods consumed.

In the present analysis we have two consumers and two goods. Let us suppose that prices of all goods other than the first two – the public enterprise outputs – stay constant, so we can suppress them, and write consumer i's indirect utility function as:

$$u_i = v_i(p_1, p_2, y_i) \qquad i = 1, 2. \qquad (8.18)$$

If the policy-maker were neutral in respect of income distribution, he would look for Pareto-optimal prices by maximizing one consumer's utility while holding the other fixed (recall chapter 3). Alternatively, if he had specific preferences concerning the distribution of welfare between the individuals, *and* could redistribute income between them, then he could choose marginal cost prices (necessary for a Pareto optimum in the absence of a profit target) and redistribute income to achieve that one of the Pareto optima he prefers on distributional grounds (again recall chapter 3). The essence of the present problem is that such income redistribution is impossible and so prices have to carry the burden of income redistribution. They are, however, very imperfect instruments, if, as we assume, they cannot be given different values for different consumers. To hold down the price of a good because it is consumed by 'the poor' also benefits 'the rich' who consume it. As we shall see, therefore, an important determinant of the extent to which a price will be used as an instrument of income redistribution is the proportion of its output which is consumed by 'the poor' as opposed to 'the rich'.

The effect of a small increment of income on the utility of consumer i is his marginal utility of income and will be denoted λ_i. This represents the consumer's *own* valuation of the increment in income. Now suppose that we can represent the planner's evaluation of consumer i's utility gain by a weight, α_i, which he attaches to it. Then we can define i's marginal *social* utility of income as:

$$\sigma_i = \alpha_i \lambda_i \qquad i = 1, 2. \qquad (8.19)$$

If the planner *could* carry out lump-sum redistributions of income, it is easy to show that he would redistribute income in such a way as to equalize the σ_i. But in the present problem he cannot do so. Let us therefore suppose that $\sigma_1 > \sigma_2$, and we could think of consumer 1 as the 'poor' consumer, i.e. $y_1 < y_2$.

Now consider the planner's valuation of a price change, say for good 1. We can show this to be equal to:

$$w_1 = -\sigma_1 q_{11} - \sigma_2 q_{12} \qquad (8.20)$$

where q_{1i} is i's consumption of good 1. This can be explained as follows. Suppose consumer 1 currently buys 10 units of good 1, and its price rises by 1p. Then we can say that his real income has fallen by the equivalent of 10p; that is, it is just as if his money income had been cut by 10p with prices unchanged. Thus q_{11}, his consumption, gives a measure of the income reduction equivalent to the price rise. If the consumer's marginal utility of income is, say, 2, then the 1p rise in price causes a fall in utility of $2 \times 10 = 20$ units. Finally, if the weight, α_1, the planner gives to the utility of consumer 1 is, say, 3, then the effect of the 1p price rise is to reduce social welfare by $3 \times 2 \times 10 = 60$ units in respect of consumer 1 alone. But that is $-\alpha_1 \lambda_1 q_{11} = -\sigma_1 q_{11}$.

A similar argument in respect of consumer 2 gives the *total* loss of social welfare resulting from an increase in price of good 1 as w_1 in (8.20). Similarly we will have for the welfare effect of a rise in good 2's price:

$$w_2 = -\sigma_1 q_{21} - \sigma_2 q_{22} \qquad (8.21)$$

where the weights σ_1 and σ_2 are the same as in (8.20). We can then express w_1 and w_2 as:

$$w_1 = -(\sigma_1 \theta_1 + \sigma_2(1-\theta_1))q_1 = -d_1 q_1 \qquad (8.22)$$

$$w_2 = -(\sigma_1 \theta_2 + \sigma_2(1-\theta_2))q_2 = -d_2 q_2 \qquad (8.23)$$

where $\theta_1 = q_{11}/q_1$, and $\theta_2 = q_{21}/q_2$ are the proportions of the two outputs bought by consumer 1. We call[22] d_1 and d_2 the *distributional characteristics* of goods 1 and 2 respectively: they summarize the effects of a price rise of a good on social welfare by weighting the marginal social utilities of the consumers' incomes by the proportions of the outputs they consume. Figure 8.3 shows how we can compare distributional characteristics diagrammatically. The line $d = \theta \sigma_1 + (1-\theta)\sigma_2$ shows all possible d-values, since any point on the line is given by the expression $\theta \sigma_1 + (1-\theta)\sigma_2$ for some θ between 0 and 1. It has been assumed that $\theta_1 > \theta_2$, i.e. that a larger proportion of good 1 is consumed by the 'poor' consumer than is good 2. If, for good j, $\theta_j = 1$, then $d_j = \sigma_1$, while if $\theta_j = 0$, $d_j = \sigma_2$. Thus, for given values of θ_1 and θ_2, the line shows the spectrum of distributional characteristics.

We are now in a position to consider the solution to the problem of choosing optimal prices subject to a budget constraint in the absence of lump-sum redistribution. These prices must satisfy the conditions:[23]

$$\tau_i \equiv \frac{p_i - MC_i}{p_i} = \frac{1}{\lambda e_i}(\lambda - d_i) \qquad i = 1, 2 \tag{8.24}$$

The value of τ_i shows, for good i, the divergence between price and marginal cost as a proportion of the price. It could therefore be interpreted as a tax *rate* (recall (8.13) earlier). λ is the shadow price associated with the profit constraint (now defined in such a way as to be positive), and e_i is again the elasticity of demand for good i. Earlier we saw that τ_i would be greater, the lower was e_i, but now the good's distributional characteristic must be taken into account. The precise effect of this can be seen if we take the ratio of the two τ_i-values:

$$\frac{\tau_1}{\tau_2} = \frac{e_2(\lambda - d_1)}{e_1(\lambda - d_2)}. \tag{8.25}$$

Suppose, for example, the goods had equal demand elasticities. Then whereas, in the absence of distributional considerations, they would have the same proportionate 'mark-ups' of price over marginal cost, now that good with the higher distributional characteristic, here d_1, will have the lower mark-up. More generally, a high distributional characteristic would tend to offset the influence of a low demand elasticity in determining the relative contribution a good must make to the profit target.

Condition (8.24) shows that the mark-up is lower the higher is d. Indeed it is possible to have $d_1 > \lambda$, if the profit target is sufficiently low and θ_1 sufficiently high.

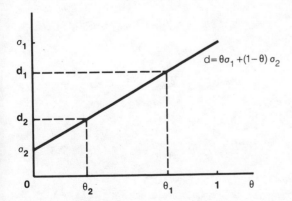

Figure 8.3

In that case $\tau_1 < 0$, and good 1's price would be below marginal cost. However, the profit constraint must always be met, and if, as we suppose, it requires an amount of profit greater than could be yielded by marginal cost pricing, we must have $\tau_2 > 0$ –at least one mark-up must always be above marginal cost.

This analysis has shown therefore how the pattern of a public enterprise's prices would be affected if distributional issues were taken into account. In implementing the pricing policy, the main difficulty would be that of assigning marginal social utilities to the consumption shares of the various income groups. The problems of estimating the demand elasticities and consumption shares are small compared to the difficulty of obtaining from policy-makers well-defined trade-offs between the welfares of different groups of consumers.

Appendix to chapter 8

1 Profit constraints

We proceed by solving the problem for the most general case and then make simplifications to generate the other cases considered in section 8.1. We wish to maximize $W = \sum_i B_i(q_i) - \sum_i C_i(q_i)$, subject to the profit constraint:

$$\sum_i (p_i q_i - C_i(q_i)) \geqslant S \qquad (A.8.1)$$

where we take it that S is always a larger profit than could be generated by marginal cost pricing of all outputs. Then necessary conditions are:

$$p_i - C_i' + \lambda \left[p_i + \sum_k q_k \frac{\partial p_k}{\partial q_i} - C_i' \right] = 0 \qquad i = 1, \ldots, n \qquad (A.8.2)$$

$$\sum_i (p_i q_i - C_i(q_i)) - S \geqslant 0 \qquad \lambda \geqslant 0 \qquad \lambda \left[\sum_i p_i q_i - C_i(q_i) \right] = 0 \qquad (A.8.3)$$

where we have used the inverse demand functions $p_i = p_i(q_1, \ldots, q_n)$. Since $\lambda = 0$ implies $p_i = C_i'$ in (A.8.2), which is ruled out by definition, we must have $\lambda > 0$, and so the constraint is satisfied as an equality. It can be shown in the usual way that:

$$\frac{\partial W}{\partial S} = -\lambda \qquad (A.8.4)$$

and so $-\lambda$ gives the marginal welfare cost of a tightening of the profit constraint. Rearranging (A.8.2) gives:

$$p_i - C_i' = \frac{-\lambda}{1+\lambda} \sum_k q_k \frac{\partial p_k}{\partial q_i}. \qquad (A.8.5)$$

Now assume demand independence, so that $\partial p_k/\partial q_i = 0$, $i \neq k$. Then we have simply:

$$\tau_i = \frac{p_i - C_i'}{p_i} = \frac{-\lambda}{1+\lambda} \frac{q_i}{p_i} \frac{dp_i}{dq_i} = \frac{1}{\hat{e}_i} \qquad (A.8.6)$$

where $\hat{e}_i$ is the price elasticity of demand $-(p_i/q_i)(dq_i/dp_i)$ 'inflated' by a factor

$(1+\lambda)/\lambda$. Simply by rearranging (A.8.6) we can write:

$$p_i\left(1-\frac{1}{\hat{e}_i}\right) = C_i' \qquad\qquad (A.8.7)$$

which is the 'adjusted marginal revenue' form of the rule. Alternatively, we could observe that the bracketed term in (A.8.2) is simply

$$p_i + q_i\frac{\partial p_i}{\partial q_i} + \sum_{k\neq i} q_k\frac{\partial p_k}{\partial q_i} - C_i' \qquad\qquad (A.8.8)$$

which, with $\partial p_k/\partial q_i = 0$, $i \neq k$, is simply $MR_i - MC_i$, where $MR_i \equiv p_i(1 - (1/e_i))$ and $MC_i = C_i'$. Moreoever, if we define $q_k(\partial p_k/\partial q_i)$ as MR_{ik}, and allow these to be non-zero, we obtain the condition in (8.9) of this chapter. Finally, if we partition the n goods into non-empty subsets $I_1, I_2, \ldots, I_m$, and replace (A.8.1) with the m profit constraints:

$$\sum_{i\in I_1} [p_iq_i - C_i(q_i)] \geqslant S_1 \qquad\qquad (A.8.9)$$

- - - - - - - - - - - -

$$\sum_{i\in I_m} [p_iq_i| C_i(q_i)] \geqslant S_m$$

then we obtain the general form of the condition given in (8.10) of this chapter.

2   Income distribution

Suppose we have n goods indexed $i = 1, \ldots, n$, and m consumers indexed $k = 1, \ldots, m$. The kth consumer's indirect utility function is:

$$u_k = v_k(p_1, \ldots, p_n, y_k) \qquad\qquad (A.8.10)$$

and the social welfare function is:

$$W = W(v_1, \ldots, v_m). \qquad\qquad (A.8.11)$$

We make use of *Roy's Identity*:

$$\frac{\partial v_k}{\partial p_i} = -\lambda_k q_{ik} \qquad\qquad (A.8.12)$$

where $\lambda_k \equiv \partial v_k/\partial y_k$ is k's marginal utility of income. The profit constraint is exactly as in (A.8.1), though we shall now regard quantities as functions of prices rather than *vice versa*. For simplicity, we again assume demand independence – the generalization is obvious from the previous section. We first maximize W on the assumption that lump-sum redistributions are feasible. Thus we introduce the m variables $h_k \gtrless 0$, one for each consumer, define consumers' incomes now as $y_k + h_k$, and introduce the constraint

$$\sum_k h_k = 0. \tag{A.8.13}$$

We then maximize W subject to the constraints (A.8.1) and (A.8.1), by choosing the p_i and h_k. Necessary conditions are:

$$-\sum_k \frac{\partial W}{\partial v_k} \lambda_k q_{ik} + \beta \left[q_i + p_i \frac{dq_i}{dp_i} - C_i' \frac{dq_i}{dp_i} \right] = 0 \qquad i = 1, \ldots, n \tag{A.8.14}$$

$$\frac{\partial W}{\partial v_k} \frac{\partial v_k}{\partial h_k} - \mu = 0 \qquad k = 1, \ldots, m \tag{A.8.15}$$

together with the constraints. Now

$$\frac{\partial W}{\partial v_k} \frac{\partial v_k}{\partial h_k}$$

is the marginal social utility of income of consumer k, and so (A.8.15) tells us that these are all equalized (μ is the dual variable associated with (A.8.13)). Call this common value σ. Then (A.8.14) becomes:

$$-\sigma \sum_k q_{ik} + \beta q_i + \beta [p_i - C_i'] \frac{dq_i}{dp_i} = 0 \tag{A.8.16}$$

But since $\sum_k q_{ik} = q_i$, this becomes simply:

$$\tau_i = \frac{p_i - C_i'}{p_i} = \left(\frac{\sigma - 1}{\beta} \right) \frac{1}{e_i} \tag{A.8.17}$$

implying:

$$\frac{\tau_i}{\tau_j} = \frac{e_j}{e_i} \tag{A.8.18}$$

which is what we would also have obtained from (A.8.6). Thus the pattern of tax rates depends only on relative demand elasticities.

Suppose now, however, that lump-sum redistribution is ruled out, so that the h_k do not exist. Then clearly we will have only condition (A.8.14). Defining:

$$\sigma_k = \frac{\partial W}{\partial v_k} \lambda_k \qquad \theta_{ik} = \frac{q_{ik}}{q_i} \tag{A.8.19}$$

we express the condition, in terms of the 'distributional characteristic', $d_i = \sum_k \sigma_k \theta_{ik}$, as:

$$-d_i q_i + \beta \left[q_i + p_i \frac{dq_i}{dp_i} - C_i' \frac{dq_i}{dp_i} \right] = 0 \qquad i = 1, \ldots, m \tag{A.8.20}$$

which yields directly the condition in (8.24) above.

Chapter 9

The public enterprise cost of capital

The analyses of optimal pricing policies in the previous five chapters have all presupposed the existence of an interest rate, r, which determines the cost of capital to a public enterprise. It is possible to discuss, quite adequately, pricing problems involving fixed capacity, without concern for this cost of capital, but once we treat capacity as variable it becomes an important parameter of the analysis. In this chapter we shall discuss theories of the determination of the public enterprise cost of capital.

Recall that the cost of capital enters into the analysis in two ways. First, in choosing the cost-minimizing way to produce any given output level, it will, in relation to the prices of all other inputs, determine the least-cost input combination or production process. Secondly, since it thereby partly determines the relation between total costs and output, it is an important component of marginal cost, and so will influence the planned price and output, and the current investment programme. This second role of the cost of capital can be described somewhat differently, using the results of the Appendix of chapter 14. The cost of capital is the rate used in discounting net social benefits of future consumption, so as to determine that level of investment which maximizes their net present value. Sophisticated pricing rules are unlikely to achieve economic efficiency, therefore, if the value of the cost of capital is non-optimally chosen, given its pervasive influence on the solution.

The question of the optimal public-sector cost of capital has a wider relevance than to public enterprises only. Much of the investment made by the state will provide future outputs of 'non-marketed goods' – education, health services, defence, police services, roads – and appraisal of these investments will also require a cost of capital. The analysis we shall set out is quite capable of application to these (and indeed much of it originated in this way), but for present purposes we shall proceed as if public-sector investment took place entirely in public enterprises. It should also be noted that the literature on this topic is large and growing, and at some points quite controversial. No attempt can be made here to survey this. Instead, we shall provide an introductory exposition of what seem to be the most fruitful lines of recent research.[1] As we shall see, the problem of determining the optimal public-sector cost of capital is essentially one in the second best, and so falls logically in sequence with the last two chapters. To begin with, however, we examine the problem in the context of the first-best economy.

9.1 The cost of capital in a first-best economy

The first-best economy to be defined here is a little different to that considered earlier, in that we assume there exists only a single good. This is a very useful simplifying assumption, the relaxation of which would make no essential difference to the results as long as we assume complete certainty, which we do. A simplifying, but not so innocuous,[2] assumption which we shall also make is that there are only two periods, year 0 and year 1, to be considered. The economy works as follows: each consumer in year 0 owns a given endowment of the good which he may divide between consumption and saving. Alternatively, he can augment his consumption in year 0 by borrowing against the amount of the good he will have in year 1. Saving is effected by buying bonds; borrowing by selling them. There are two firms in the economy, one public the other private. The public firm acquires, by selling bonds, some quantity of the good in year 0, which it invests to produce a corresponding output of the good in year 1. This output will then be distributed to consumers. The private firm invests some amount of the good in year 0, and this will determine the amount of the good it has available for distribution to shareholders in year 1. The total amount of the good which will be available for consumption in year 1 will be the sum of public and private outputs. The only market which exists in this economy is the bond market, on which individuals and the private firm may borrow and lend and the public firm borrows, all at the same interest rate r.

We first consider briefly the nature of the market equilibrium in this economy.[3] The ith consumer's budget constraints in years 0 and 1 are respectively,

$$x_0^i + b_i = \bar{x}_0^i \tag{9.1}$$

$$x_1^i = (1+r)b_i + g_i + s_i x_p. \tag{9.2}$$

Here x_0^i and x_1^i are i's consumptions in years 0 and 1 respectively, b_i is the amount of his bond purchases or sales, with $b_i > 0$ if he buys bonds (i.e. lends) and $b_i < 0$ if he sells bonds (i.e. borrows),[4] $\bar{x}_0^i$ is his current initial endowment of income, g_i is the income he will receive from government in year 1, and s_i is his share in the output, x_p, of the private firm in year 1. Thus (9.1) says simply that current consumption must equal current income plus (minus) borrowing (lending), while (9.2) says that next period's consumption will equal income from government and private shareholdings minus (plus) repayments (receipts) of interest and capital due on borrowing (lending) carried out in year 0. Note that we must assume the consumer knows for certain the values of his period 1 incomes from public and private production.

By solving for b_i in (9.2) and substituting into (9.1), we obtain the *wealth constraint*,

$$x_0^i + \frac{x_1^i}{1+r} = \bar{x}_0^i + \frac{g_i + s_i x_p}{1+r} = \bar{w}_i \qquad (9.3)$$

which reflects the fundamental insight: a perfect capital market allows a consumer to vary his actual consumption time-stream, (x_0^i, x_1^i) away from his endowed income time-stream, provided that the present value of the consumption time-stream equals that of his initial endowment. The latter present value we call his *wealth*, and this is denoted by $\bar{w}_i$ in (9.3).

Since r is a constant, the wealth constraint is a straight line analogous to the budget constraint in the single-period consumer model, and this is illustrated by the line $\bar{w}_i$ in Figure 9.1(a). The slope of the wealth line, $\Delta x_1^i / \Delta x_0^i$, is equal to $-(1+r)$ (to see this, rearrange (9.3) to express x_1^i as a function of x_0^i). If we now assume the consumer has a well-defined preference ordering of the usual kind over consumption time-streams (x_0^i, x_1^i), we can find an optimal solution to his problem of choosing such a time-stream (or, equivalently, deciding how much to lend or borrow this year) by superimposing the indifference curves onto the diagram. Figure 9.1(a) shows the solution, which is perfectly standard: the optimal time-stream $(\hat{x}_0^i, \hat{x}_1^i)$ occurs at a point of tangency of an indifference curve with the budget line. Thus, the optimal choice equates the consumer's marginal rate of substitution of consumption now for consumption next year, MRS^i with the (absolute value of the) slope of the wealth line, $(1+r)$.

In intertemporal consumer choice problems it is usual to express this MRS in a particular way, to match the way in which the price of consumption now relative to that next year is expressed. This latter is expressed in terms of an interest rate: if the interest rate is 10 per cent, this tells us that one unit of current consumption exchanges for 1.1 units of consumption in a year's time, so the price ratio is 1:1.1. In a similar way, we define:

$$MRS^i \equiv 1 + \rho_i \qquad (9.4)$$

where ρ_i is called i's *rate of time preference*. It can be thought of as the rate of interest just sufficient to induce i to give up one unit of current consumption for consumption next year, i.e. we have to give i $1 + \rho_i$ units of consumption next year to leave him no better and no worse off for giving up one unit of consumption now. Since MRS^i simply measures the (absolute value of the) slope of an indifference curve at a point, ρ_i is determined entirely by this slope. So, for example, around the indifference curve $\bar{u}_i$ in Figure 9.1(a), ρ_i increases steadily as we move from right to left, reducing current consumption and increasing next period consumption. The equality of slopes at the optimum then must imply:

$$1 + \rho_i = 1 + r, \text{ or simply } \rho_i = r. \tag{9.5}$$

This leads to two very important propositions about the equilibrium interest rate in a perfect capital market:

(1) it measures a consumer's equilibrium rate of time-preference, or subjective valuation of future consumption relative to current consumption;
(2) since all consumers face the same interest rate, in equilibrium their rates of time-preference are all equal.

These propositions are of course simply translations into the terminology of capital markets, of the standard propositions on the Pareto optimality of a competitive market and the welfare property of the equilibrium price on such a market (cf. the discussion in chapter 4).

Turning now to the production side of the economy, let y_g be the amount of the good devoted to public investment and y_p that to private investment. Then we have the 'investment production functions':

$$x_g = g(y_g) \qquad x_p = p(y_p) \tag{9.6}$$

which show how output of the good next period, x_g in the public and x_p in the private sector, vary with investment in the sector. Figure 9.1(b) shows a typical shape of the $g(y_g)$ relationship, and 9.1(c) shows $p(y_p)$. The amount of investment is measured *leftward* from the origin on the horizontal axis. Thus each curve reflects the assumption that next period output increases but at a diminishing rate as investment increases.

The slope of the $p(y_p)$ curve can be written $\Delta x_p / \Delta y_p$, and shows the increment in output next period resulting from a small increase in investment this period. We can then write:

$$\frac{\Delta x_p}{\Delta y_p} = 1 + \frac{\Delta x_p - \Delta y_p}{\Delta y_p} = 1 + m_p \tag{9.7}$$

where m_p is called the marginal rate of return to private investment. Clearly, the shape of $p(y_p)$ in Figure 9.1(c) implies that m_p falls as private investment increases. In the same way we can define m_g, the marginal rate of return to public investment, and this also diminishes with y_g. m_p and m_g simply express the marginal productivities of private and public investment in the form of an interest rate.

We define the *net present value* of private investment as:

$$v_p = \frac{x_p}{1+r} - y_p \tag{9.8}$$

where r is the given market interest rate. If we set v_p at some particular value, say $\bar{v}_p$, this equation defines a linear relationship between x_p and y_p of the form:

$$x_p = \bar{v}_p(1+r) + (1+r)y_p. \tag{9.9}$$

The line marked $\bar{v}_p^*$ in Figure 9.1(c) is one example of this relationship. The value of r determines the slope of the line, while increasing $\bar{v}_p$ with r fixed shifts the line upward to the right.

If the private firm seeks to act in the best interests of its shareholders, then its optimal policy is to choose y_p in such a way as to *maximize* the net present value of investment,[5] v_p. In the diagram, this means that it wants to find the point on the curve $p(y_p)$ which is on the highest possible $\bar{v}_p$ line. This will then be a point of tangency such as that shown in Figure 9.1(c), with y_p^* the optimal investment level and $x_p^* = p(v_p^*)$ the corresponding next period output. The equality of slopes of the $\bar{v}_p^*$ line and $p(y_p)$ curve at this point implies that the optimal private investment satisfies the condition:

$$1 + m_p' = 1 + r, \text{ or simply } m_p' = r. \tag{9.10}$$

Thus, the private sector invests up to the point at which the marginal rate of return

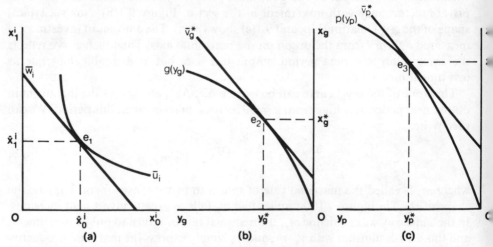

Figure 9.1

just equals the market interest rate. If it stopped short of this point it would be depriving its shareholders of profitable investment opportunities, since investment would yield more than shareholders could earn if they lent the money on the market, or, alternatively, they could replace the consumption forgone by borrowing at a lower interest rate than the return to that forgone consumption. If it went beyond that point, marginal investment would be yielding less than shareholders could earn on the market, or would not cover the cost of borrowing to replace the forgone consumption.

The analysis so far then yields an important conclusion. Ignoring for the moment the public sector, in an economy with a perfect capital market, and in which the private firm acts in the best interests of its shareholders, we have that at an equilibrium (putting together (9.5) and (9.10)),

$$m_p = r = \rho_i, \text{ all } i. \tag{9.11}$$

Thus the equilibrium market interest rate measures the marginal rate of return to private investment *and* the time-preference rate of every consumer.

Now we turn to the principal question of this section: what is the optimal allocation of resources between consumption and public and private investment for the economy as a whole? We put ourselves once again in the place of a central planner who wishes to find a Pareto optimum. Ignoring the details of bond markets, ownership of the private firm, etc., we have that the economy is constrained by the equations

$$\sum_i x_0^i + y_g + y_p = \sum_i \bar{x}_0^i \tag{9.12}$$

and

$$\sum_i x_1^i = g(y_g) + p(y_p). \tag{9.13}$$

The first says that the total consumption plus total investment in year 0 must equal the total endowment of the good available to the economy, and the second that total consumption in year 1 must equal output. This implies that consumption in year 1 can only be increased by reducing consumption in year 0, and investing in the two firms. The resource allocation problem can then be divided into three sub-problems:

(a) how should the reductions in year 0 consumption, and increases in year 1 consumption, be allocated among consumers?
(b) how should the total investment be allocated between public and private enterprises?
(c) how should the total investment be determined?

We shall give the solutions to these sub-problems in that order. First, if a Pareto optimum is sought, then the allocation of consumptions among consumers must satisfy the condition that the time-preference rates of all consumers be equal. To see this, suppose that any two, say ρ_1 and ρ_2, were not, and in particular that $\rho_1 > \rho_2$. Then consumer 1 could take one unit of consumption in year 0 from consumer 2, and would be prepared to give him more year 1 consumption in return, than 2 requires in order to be left just as well off. Hence, both can gain from the exchange, and this cannot be a Pareto-optimal situation.[6] If no such possibilities exist, we must have $\rho_1 = \rho_2$.

To solve the second problem, suppose that there is some given total amount of investment in the economy, $\bar{y}$, which must be divided between private and public enterprises. Given this total, we would expect that it is optimally allocated when the resulting total output in year 1 is maximized, which in turn implies the necessary condition

$$m_p = m_g, \tag{9.14}$$

which has the straightforward interpretation that investment is allocated between the two sectors in such a way as to equate marginal rates of return. If this were not so, investment could be diverted from the low rate of return enterprise to that with the higher rate, and so we could increase year 1 output (which makes everyone better off).

The solution to the third problem then follows immediately. The optimal total investment will be found when

$$\rho_i = m_p = m_g, \qquad i = 1, 2, \ldots, n, \tag{9.15}$$

i.e. when the time-preference rate of each consumer is equal to the marginal rate of return on investment in each sector. Again, the reasoning is straightforward: if $m_p = m_g > \rho_i$, for all i, then by reducing consumption in year 0 (in a way which keeps the ρ_i all equal) and investing it (in a way which maintains $m_p = m_g$), consumers can be more than compensated for this sacrifice. If $\rho_i > m_p = m_g$, on the other hand, the increase in year 0 consumption following from a reduction in investment would more than compensate consumers for the loss of year 1 consumption. If such improvements are not possible, we must have the equality in (9.15). Thus, we have three sets of conditions which characterize a Pareto-optimal resource allocation in this two-period economy.

In fact, of course, there is no central planner in control of the entire economy. Consumers in our model take their own consumption and bondholding decisions, the private enterprise invests on behalf of its shareholders, and the planner has only to determine the optimal investment policy for the public enterprise. Putting together all the steps in the analysis so far enables us to see what this policy requires.

Since all consumers confront the same interest rate, we know that the ρ_i will all be equal in an equilibrium. In addition, since the private enterprise acts in the best interests of its shareholders, we have that $m_p = r = \rho_i$. Thus, to satisfy the necessary conditions for a Pareto optimum, the investment of the public enterprise must satisfy the condition

$$m_g = r = m_p = \rho_i. \tag{9.16}$$

An obvious way in which this would be achieved is by the adoption of an investment appraisal rule similar to that used by the private enterprise: the public enterprise should maximize the net present value of its investment,

$$v_g = \frac{x_g}{1+r} - y_g, \tag{9.17}$$

using the market interest rate in discounting.

In Figure 9.1(b) we show the equilibrium position of the public enterprise. Its investment, y_g, is measured leftward from the origin, and the curve $g(y_g)$ shows how output in year 1 varies with y_g. It clearly embodies the assumption of positive but diminishing marginal productivity of investment, and its slope at any point is given by $1+m_g$. The problem of *maximizing* v_g can then be expressed as the problem of choosing values of y_g and x_g which are on the highest possible $\bar{v}_g$ line, given the set of technological possibilities defined by $g(y_g)$. The solution is of course a point of tangency. The line $\bar{v}_g^*$ is the highest which can be attained with a feasible pair (y_g, x_g), and the values which generate it are $(y_g^* x_g^*)$. At the point of tangency, the slope of the line, $1+r$, equals the slope of the curve, $1+m_g$, and so we have the necessary condition given earlier, $r = m_g$.

This completes the analysis of the equilibrium position for the first-best economy. Its conclusion is that the public enterprise should choose its investment by maximizing net present value, using the market interest rate in discounting. However, the real economy is not first-best, and so it is important to examine the validity of this result in a model which captures at least some features of the second-best reality.

9.2 The cost of capital in a second-best economy
A crucial assumption underlying the first-best model is that the capital market is perfect: there is a single interest rate, which is the same for all buyers and sellers of bonds, and whose value measures two things, from the point of view of the public-sector planner. First, it measures the time-preference rate of every consumer, and hence provides information on the value of current versus future consumption; and secondly, it measures the marginal rate of return on investment in the private sector,

and so provides information on the opportunity cost of resources devoted to public rather than private investment. The essential feature of most second-best models is that, because of market imperfections, the market rate of interest no longer measures *both* these values and, at best, is equal only to one of them. The problem then is to determine the appropriate public-sector cost of capital, taking explicit account of the failure of the market interest rate to provide all the necessary information.

There are several reasons for suspecting that real capital markets are imperfect. The existence of uncertainty leads to devices such as credit rationing, which place a limit on an individual's ability to borrow or 'issue bonds', and to different interest rates for different borrowers. Transactions in capital markets are effected through financial intermediaries, and there is the possibility that non-competitive conditions lead the spread between borrowing and lending interest rates to exceed the marginal costs of organizing these transactions. Taxation of various kinds exists, which, as we shall see, drives a wedge between time-preference rates and the marginal rate of return on investment. There are, therefore, several ways in which we could characterize a second-best economy. Here, on grounds of simplicity, we adopt the following assumption: the second-best economy differs from that of the previous section *only* in the existence of a tax, t, which is levied on the profits of the private enterprise. This tax is a parameter of the problem, rather than a variable of optimization. The proceeds of the tax are distributed, along with the profit of the public enterprise, among consumers in year 1.

Thus, we wish to determine the optimal investment plan for the public enterprise, given that a tax is levied on private enterprise profit. First we examine the effects of the profits tax. For the purpose of the tax, profit is defined as $x_p - y_p$: the value of output in year 1 *minus* the investment required to generate it.[7] Hence, the after-tax income available for distribution to shareholders in year 1 will be $x_p - t(x_p - y_p)$. If it is acting in the best interests of its shareholders, the firm will maximize net present value *after tax*, and so it will wish to maximize:

$$v_p^1 = \frac{x_p - t(x_p - y_p)}{1+r} - y_p.$$
(9.18)

This gives the necessary condition

$$1 + m_p = 1 + \frac{r}{1-t} = 1 + r',$$
(9.19)

where we again define m_p as the marginal rate of return on investment in the private enterprise (given $x_p = p(y_p)$). This condition implies that the private enterprise invests up to the point at which the marginal rate of return is just equal to the *tax-*

adjusted interest rate, r', which must exceed the actual interest rate, r, since t is defined on the interval $0 < t < 1$. Effectively, the private enterprise responds to taxation by acting as if it faced a higher market interest rate. An equivalent and intuitively more obvious way of expressing this is as follows: from (9.19) we see that the condition requires that

$$m_p = r' = \frac{r}{1-t}, \tag{9.20}$$

thus implying that

$$m_p(1-t) = r, \tag{9.21}$$

where the term on the left-hand side is the after-tax marginal rate of return on investment. The enterprise then equates this to the actual market interest rate.

The effect on the investment of the private enterprise is shown in Figure 9.2, where (a) reproduces (c) of Figure 9.1, with the addition of the line $\hat{v}_p^*$. This line is derived from equation (9.18) in the same way as $\bar{v}_p^*$ was derived earlier, and so relates to *after-tax* net present value. Its slope is equal to $1 + r'$, which is why it is steeper than $\bar{v}_p^*$. The solution to the investment decision is now at y_p' and not y_p^*, so we conclude that the imposition of the profits tax reduces investment in the private enterprise. Figure

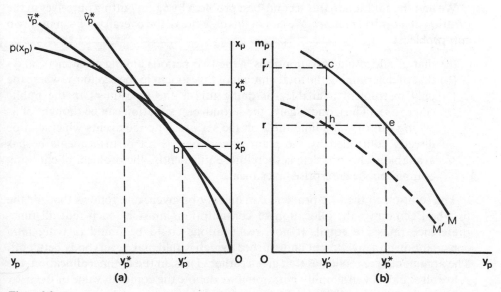

Figure 9.2

9.2(b) shows this result in somewhat different form. Given the function $x_p = p(y_p)$, we can graph the marginal rate of return m_p against the amount of investment y_p. This is shown as the curve M. Its negative slope follows from the curvature of $p(y_p)$. In an economy without tax, the private enterprise is in equilibrium when $m_p = r$, and this is shown at point e in the figure. We can represent the after-tax equilibrium in either of two ways: the tax can be viewed as increasing the interest rate to r', giving the equilibrium at c; or as reducing the marginal rate of return as shown by the curve M', thus giving the equilibrium at h. In each case, of course, the investment level is at y_p'.

The tax, since it is levied on private enterprise profits, does not directly affect the rate of interest at which consumers borrow and lend. Hence, as in the previous section, the ith consumer will be in equilibrium where $\rho_i = r$, which immediately gives us the result that $m_p > \rho_i$. Thus, the result of the profits tax is that investment is too low in the private enterprise: at the margin, a little more investment would yield more than enough output in year 1 to compensate shareholders for their current sacrifice, but because of the tax the shareholders would not in fact be compensated, and so the investment is not made. The non-optimality of private enterprise investment is the central feature of the second-best solution.

The second-best optimization problem can be described as follows: the central planner must choose a Pareto-optimal allocation of resources in the economy, taking the distortion in the private sector as given.

We find the solution to this second-best problem by again putting ourselves in the position of a central planner. We can in this case break the overall problem into two sub-problems:

(a) that of allocating consumptions in the two periods among consumers, and
(b) that of determining the total amount of investment in the economy, where the only instrument available for doing this is the investment in the public enterprise. (Thus, once again, the second-best situation can be thought of as arising out of some limitation on the set of economic agents which can be directly controlled by the planner, and on the set of instruments he has available.) This problem is therefore, equivalently, the problem of choosing optimal public enterprise investment.

The solution to the first problem can quickly be given, and follows that for the first-best economy: the allocation of consumptions must be such that all time-preference rates are equal. If not, reallocations could be found (leaving *total* consumption and investment undisturbed) which would make everybody better off. The argument here replicates that given earlier. Thus, in the optimal allocation, the ρ_i are all equal. It will simplify notation if we denote the common value of the ρ_i by ρ, and refer to this as *the* rate of time preference.

The problem of choosing the optimal second-best level of public investment can be tackled with the help of Figures 9.3 and 9.4. In 9.3 we again have the curve $g(y_g)$ showing the relationship between public investment and next period output, with the first-best optimal point (y_g^*, x_g^*) shown as before. Thus the slope of the line v_r is $-(1+r) = -(1+\rho)$, and reflects the time-preference rate. The line $v_{r'}$ has the slope $-(1+r') = -(1+m_p')$, and so reflects the marginal private rate of return at the equilibrium (y', x_p') of the private enterprise. Hence we could interpret point a in Figure 9.3 as the solution the public enterprise would reach if it *again* maximized the net present value of investment using the marginal private-sector rate of return m_p' as a discount rate, i.e. it adopted the first-best investment appraisal procedure, but using the actual achieved marginal private-sector rate of return rather than the market interest rate ($=$ consumer time-preference rates) to discount future output.

Much of the controversy over public-sector investment appraisal can then be put rather simply in terms of Figure 9.3 – is the correct policy in fact:

(a) to set public investment at y_g^*, by discounting future output at the consumer time-preference rate, as measured in this model by r?

(b) to set public investment at y_g', by discounting at the marginal private-sector rate of return or, as it is often called, the *social opportunity cost* rate?

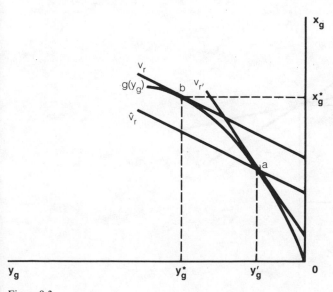

Figure 9.3

(c) to adopt some intermediate solution, which would involve discounting at some rate between the consumer time-preference rate and the social opportunity cost rate?

We shall answer the question by first assuming that public investment has been set at y'_g and then considering circumstances under which a change in public investment may or may not increase welfare. As we shall see, the crucial issue is that of the *displacement effect* of the public investment, defined as the precise way in which a marginal change in public investment affects the allocation of resources to current consumption and to private investment.

Thus in Figure 9.3 suppose we are initially at point a. The line $\hat{v}_r$ through a is parallel to v_r and so has a slope equal to $-(1+r) = -(1+\rho)$. Assume that we are considering sufficiently small changes in y_p that both the marginal private-sector rate of return, m'_p, and the market interest rate remain unchanged. To help us analyse, the position at a is 'blown up' into a much larger scale, as shown in Figure 9.4, where $\hat{v}_r$ and $v_{r'}$ are reproduced from Figure 9.3. Now consider a change in y_g equal to Δy_g, or the distance ba in Figure 9.4. Because, at a, the marginal rate of return on public investment is the same as that on private investment, the resulting increase in output next period is $\Delta x_g = (1+m'_p)\Delta y_g$, the distance bc in the figure.

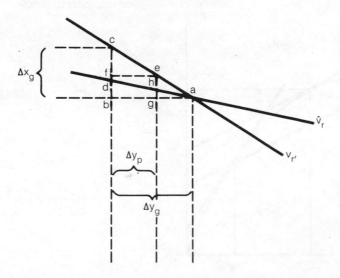

Figure 9.4

Now suppose this increase in public investment is *entirely* at the expense of current consumption: current consumption falls by $\Delta y_g = ba$. In order to compensate consumers for this loss, we have to give them an amount of consumption next period equal to the distance bd in Figure 9.4, since the slope of $\hat{v}_r$ measures each consumer's time-preference rate, i.e. $bd = (1+r)\Delta y_g = (1+\rho)\Delta y_g$. Clearly, the diagram shows that we can do this and more: if the public investment is undertaken there can be an increase in future consumption of dc, over and above what is required to compensate consumers. Hence, on *this* assumption about the displacement effect, point a is not an optimal solution for public investment, but rather represents *under*-investment in the public sector. The first-best rule of equalizing marginal rates of return in public and private sectors is not second-best optimal, not only because the marginal private-sector rate of return (the social opportunity cost rate) is 'too high', but more fundamentally because it is *not* in this case the real opportunity cost of the public investment. Note also that on this assumption of the displacement effect, the optimal point for public investment is b in Figure 9.3, since public investment should be increased as long as its rate of return exceeds the time-preference rate.

Let us now change the assumption on the displacement effect, and assume the increase in public investment is *entirely* at the expense of private investment, so that $\Delta y_p = -\Delta y_g$ (we have what is often called 'full crowding-out' of private by public investment). In that case, the net effect of the expansion of public investment is clearly zero. Again, the increase $\Delta y_g = ba$ would increase next period output by $\Delta x_g = bd$, but then the fall in private investment, also equal to ba, brings about an exactly compensating fall in next period private-sector output, and so we are back where we started. In other words, on this assumption about the displacement effect, neither an increase nor a decrease in public investment around point a can change total output next period, and so point a is the second-best optimum for the public sector. Thus we would continue to adopt the rule of equalizing marginal rates of return across the private and public sectors.

Take now an intermediate case, in which the fall in private investment is half the increase in public investment, the remainder being a fall in current consumption. Then, in Figure 9.4, the move from a to c along v_r, which results from the increase in public investment Δy_g, is partially offset by the move back from c to e, which results from the induced reduction in private investment $\Delta y_p = bg = fe$. Thus the expansion of public investment results in a *net* increase in next period output shown by $ge = fb = bc - fc$ in the figure. Given the fall in current consumption of ga, consumers require an increase in next period consumption of hg to compensate them for this. Since $eg > hg$, there is more than enough future output to do this and so the expansion in public investment is warranted. Thus, on this assumption of the displacement effect (what could be called 'partial crowding-out'), a is not the optimal point for public investment, and again we would not seek to equalize marginal rates of return across the two sectors. On the other hand, the final optimum position – and therefore the slope of the v-line which would define a discount rate at this point – will not be at b in Figure 9.3, but somewhere before it.

The question then arises: if we allow the full range of displacement effects to be possible, how can we characterize the optimal level of public investment and what does this imply for the *procedure* we adopt for appraising public investment? We answer this question by restating the above diagrammatic analysis. The optimal public investment level will have been found when a small increase in that level cannot more than compensate consumers for any loss in current consumption *after* the induced effect on private investment is taken into account. That is:

$$\Delta x_g - \Delta x_p = \Delta x_R \qquad (9.22)$$

where Δx_p is the loss of next period private output and Δx_R is the increase in next period output required to compensate consumers for loss of current consumption. Now for small changes:

$$\Delta x_p = (1+m'_p)\Delta y_p \qquad (9.23)$$

$$\Delta x_R = (1+r)\Delta x_0 = (1+\rho)\Delta x_0 \qquad (9.24)$$

where Δx_0 is the fall in current consumption. We can define the displacement effects as:

$$\Delta y_p = \theta_1 \Delta y_g \qquad \Delta x_0 = \theta_2 \Delta y_g. \qquad (9.25)$$

We would normally regard θ_1 as being a positive fraction, i.e. $0 \leqslant \theta_1 \leqslant 1$, and $\theta_2 = 1 - \theta_1$, so that θ_1 would simply represent the proportion of the increased public investment which displaces private investment (we might call θ_1 the 'coefficient of crowding-out'), but, as will be suggested below, we could envisage cases in which $\theta_1 > 1$ or $\theta_1 < 0$. Substituting from (9.25) into (9.24) and (9.23), then into (9.22) and rearranging, gives the *basic optimality condition*:

$$\Delta x_g = (1+m'_p)\theta_1 \Delta y_g + (1+\rho)\theta_2 \Delta y_g. \qquad (9.26)$$

If this equation were not satisfied, it must be possible to make a small change in public investment which makes consumers better off, in the sense of more than compensating them with consumption in one period for any loss of consumption in the other.

We can use the basic optimality condition (9.26) to define two possible procedures for finding the optimal level of public investment. By dividing through by Δy_g we would have

$$\frac{\Delta x_g}{\Delta y_g} = (1 + m_g) = (\theta_1 + \theta_2) + \theta_1 m'_p + \theta_2 \rho \tag{9.27}$$

so that if $\theta_1 + \theta_2 = 1$, we have simply

$$m_g = R \equiv \theta_1 m'_p + \theta_2 \rho. \tag{9.28}$$

We could define R as the 'required rate of return' on public investment, since any increment in y_g which yielded more than R would be accepted, and any increment which yielded less than R would be rejected. This procedure would then say: compute the appropriate weighted average of the social time-preference rate ($=$ market interest rate) and social opportunity cost rate ($=$ marginal private rate of return), and use this to define the net present value of public investment, $(x_g)/(1 + R) - y_g$. Then choose that investment total which maximizes this net present value, thus yielding the condition (9.28).

An alternative but, on the face of it, equivalent procedure is to divide through (9.26) by $(1 + \rho)$ to get,

$$\frac{\Delta x_g}{1 + \rho} = \frac{(1 + m'_p)}{1 + \rho} \{\theta_1 \Delta y_g + \theta_2 \Delta y_g\} = k \Delta y_g \tag{9.29}$$

where $k = (1 + m'_p)/(1 + \rho)\{\theta_1 + \theta_2\}$ would be called the *social opportunity cost of public investment*. In effect, this second procedure defines the net present value of investment as $(x_g)/(1 + \rho) - k y_g$, and then seeks to choose y_g so as to maximize this.

The key difference between the two procedures, therefore, is that the first discounts at a 'weighted average rate of return' R and counts the cost of £1 of public investment as £1, while the second discounts at the 'time-preference rate' ρ and counts the cost of £1 of public investment as £k. However, since these are simply different versions of the basic optimality condition the two procedures are equivalent *in the present case*. Note also that they require exactly the same information for implementation, namely the values of θ_1, θ_2, m'_p and ρ.

This fairly simple analysis of the second-best problem gives valuable insights, but has important limitations which we shall shortly consider. Before doing this, let us examine the question of the values of θ_1 and θ_2, and in particular whether they should add up to 1. The displacement effect of an increment of public investment will very much depend on how it is financed. In the discussion so far, we have assumed this would be by government borrowing on the capital market (the proceeds of the tax on private enterprise profits could be thought of as being used to finance redistributive transfers to households, rather than to finance investment). Additional public borrowing would then push up interest rates, and the relative displacement of current consumption and private investment would depend on the interest elasticities of saving and investment respectively. In this case, estimates of the θ-values would require estimates of these interest elasticities. However, additional public investment need not be financed by borrowing, but instead by additional taxation, money creation or cuts in other forms of public expenditure. In the category of 'additional taxation' would also be included public enterprise 'self-financing' – generation of surpluses explicitly to finance investment. A wide range of effects is possible. For example, investment financed by increases in public enterprise prices, reductions in social security benefits or increases in direct taxes would tend to reduce consumption rather more than private investment. On the other hand increased taxes on corporate profits or on dividend payments to shareholders would tend to have a relatively greater effect on private investment. The effect of financing by money creation would be hard to evaluate, since it would depend first on the extent to which this increased the rate of inflation, and secondly on the precise impact of higher inflation on real consumption and investment in the economy.

Moreover, it should be emphasized that it is the displacement effect at *the margin* of public investment which is relevant, and so to estimate θ_1 and θ_2 we would have to determine how this marginal investment is financed; it would not be enough to look at the average contribution of the various sources of government revenue to public expenditure as a whole.

This leads us to the question of whether θ_1 and θ_2 must sum to one. In general we might expect that an increment of public investment requires resources which must be diverted out of their other uses, current consumption and private investment, and so, since the value of resources absorbed equals the value of resources diverted, θ_1 and θ_2 must sum to one. However, other cases are possible. Suppose for example that there are unemployed resources in the economy and there is no macroeconomic constraint imposed by government on the general level of economic activity. In that case increased public investment may absorb, at least in part, some unemployed resources, the resources diverted from current consumption and private investment will be less than those absorbed by the public investment, and $\theta_1 + \theta_2 < 1$ as a result. Alternatively, suppose that an increment of public investment is financed by increasing the profit tax, which, as we saw earlier, is equivalent to raising the tax-adjusted interest rate r' to the private sector. Although the increase in tax will be designed to generate enough *revenue* to cover the cost of the public investment, the interest-elasticity of the private investment might be such that the value of this investment choked off by the increase in r' exceeds the value of the extra public investment. In that case, $\theta_1 > 1$, so that as long as $\theta_2 \geqslant 0$, $\theta_1 + \theta_2 > 1$.

The implication of the possibility that $\theta_1 + \theta_2 \gtrless 1$ is that the weighted average required rate of return R in equation (9.28) above need not lie between the time-preference rate ρ and the marginal opportunity cost rate m'_p. Thus we will have:

$$R < \rho \text{ if } \frac{\theta_1}{1-\theta_2} < \frac{\rho}{m'_p}, \text{ requiring } \theta_1 + \theta_2 < 1 \qquad (9.30)$$

$$R > m'_p \text{ if } \frac{\theta_2}{1-\theta_1} > \frac{m'_p}{\rho}, \text{ requiring } \theta_1 + \theta_2 > 1. \qquad (9.31)$$

Moreover, note that the inequalities in (9.30) and (9.31) could hold even if $\rho = m'_p$, with no second-best distortion in the capital market. The reason in each case is that the value of the public investment does not measure its opportunity cost in terms of the value of current consumption and private investment displaced.

The two-period assumption
Usually, in economics, an assumption of 'two-ness' – two goods, two consumers, two time-periods – is purely simplifying, and is intended to allow the analysis to proceed in terms of two-dimensional diagrams rather than algebra. In the present case, however, the results obtained so far do *not* carry over without modification when more than two periods are considered. The two most important issues that arise are:

(a) the equivalence between the procedure based on the weighted average required rate of return in (9.28), and that based on the time-preference rate and shadow price of capital in (9.29), no longer holds. We then have to decide which is appropriate.

(b) We have to consider the possibility that the future returns to private investment will be reinvested to generate consumption in later periods, and the effect this will have on the opportunity cost of the public investment.

We consider these points in turn. To keep matters simple, we assume that there are just *three* periods; this is enough to bring out the main points. We suppose that public investment y_g in year 0 yields output x_{g1} in year 1 and x_{g2} in year 2, while private investment y_p yields x_{p1} and x_{p2} respectively. We proceed as before, and suppose we have an allocation of current resources among consumption, private and public investment, which determines the time-preference rates for consumers and rates of return on private investment. Also as before, we assume an allocation among consumers which equalizes their time-preference rates, so we can still talk about 'the' time-preference rate. The displacement effects of the public investment on current consumption and private investment are still given by (9.25), but the effects on future consumption now have to be extended to the third period. To do this, we have to specify what is meant by the 'marginal private-sector of return' in this case. Clearly, with *two* future periods, the nice simplicity of the expression in (9.23) is lost. We now define m'_p as the value which satisfies the following expression:

$$\frac{\Delta x_{p2}}{(1+m'_p)^2}+\frac{\Delta x_{p1}}{(1+m'_p)}-\Delta y_p = 0 \qquad (9.32)$$

where Δy_p is the marginal private-sector investment, and Δx_{p1} and Δx_{p2} are its returns in years 1 and 2 respectively. Thus the marginal private-sector rate of return is the rate of discount which equates the present value of the output stream of the marginal private investment with the cost of that investment. It is therefore the *internal rate of return* on the marginal private-sector investment.

It is straightforward to define the 'weighted average required rate of return' procedure in this case. We simply take the value of R as in (9.28), and maximize the net present value of public investment, defined as:

$$\frac{x_{g2}}{(1+R)^2}+\frac{x_{g1}}{(1+R)}-y_g \qquad (9.33)$$

implying that the *marginal* public investment must satisfy the condition:

$$\frac{\Delta x_{g2}}{(1+R)^2}+\frac{\Delta x_{g1}}{(1+R)}-\Delta y_g = 0. \qquad (9.34)$$

However, as we shall see, this apparently straightforward procedure will not in general yield the correct answer. This will be clear once we have described the second procedure, involving discounting at the time-preference rate ρ and applying a shadow price of public investment, k (recall (9.29)). First assume that the allocation of resources is such that ρ is constant over time. Then the only problem is to define the opportunity cost of public investment to arrive at an expression for k. The argument proceeds as follows. If the marginal private investment is displaced, consumers will lose the time-stream of output this would have generated. The present value of this *to them* is:

$$\frac{\Delta x_{p2}}{(1+\rho)^2}+\frac{\Delta x_{p1}}{(1+\rho)} = v_p. \qquad (9.35)$$

Note that discounting is carried out at the *time-preference rate*, because we wish to know *consumers'* valuation of the forgone output stream. Since, in a second-best world, $\rho < m'_p$, it follows from (9.32) that $v_p > \Delta y_p$, i.e. the present value to consumers of the output stream forgone by the displacement of the private investment exceeds the amount of that investment. Thus let $v_p = \lambda \Delta y_p$, where $\lambda > 1$. Then the opportunity cost of the public investment is v_p, the present value of private output forgone, plus Δx_0, the current consumption displaced. Then using the definitions in (9.25) we have:

$$v_p + \Delta x_0 = (\lambda\theta_1 + \theta_2)\Delta y_g \equiv k\Delta y_g \qquad (9.36)$$

with $k \equiv (\lambda\theta_1 + \theta_2)$ as the shadow price of public investment. The net present value of public investment is now defined as:

$$\frac{x_{g2}}{(1+\rho)^2} + \frac{x_{g1}}{(1+\rho)} - ky_g. \qquad (9.37)$$

Maximization of this yields the condition:

$$\frac{\Delta x_{g2}}{(1+\rho)^2} + \frac{\Delta x_{g1}}{(1+\rho)} - k\Delta y_g = 0 \qquad (9.38)$$

i.e. the marginal public investment has zero net present value when discounted at the time-preference ρ, and when the cost of the investment is reckoned *not* as Δy_g, but rather as $k\Delta y_g$. The logic of this rule is straightforward: consumers require a future output stream from the public investment which compensates them for the loss of consumption required to undertake it. Hence *their* time-preference rate should be used in discounting the future public-sector outputs, and $k\Delta y_g$ is the appropriate present value of the forgone consumption. The nature of the comparison being made in this procedure can be further brought out by replacing $k\Delta y_g$ in (9.38) with $v_p + \Delta x_0$, using the definition of v_p in (9.35), and rearranging, to get:

$$\frac{(\Delta x_{g2} - \Delta x_{p2})}{(1+\rho)^2} + \frac{(\Delta x_{g1} - \Delta x_{p1})}{(1+\rho)} - \Delta x_0 = 0. \qquad (9.39)$$

This says that a public investment should only be undertaken if the excess of the output stream it generates over the private-sector output stream it displaces is enough to compensate consumers for the sacrifice of the current consumption it requires.

It is easy to show that the first procedure, based on the net present values defined in (9.33) and (9.34), need not in general yield the same results as the second, based on the net present values defined in (9.37) and (9.38). Consider the following numerical example. Let:

$\Delta y_g = £1\text{m}$	$\Delta y_g = £0.5\text{m}$	$\Delta x_0 = £0.5\text{m}$
$\Delta x_{g1} = £0.5\text{m}$	$\Delta x_{p1} = £0.28\text{m}$	$\rho = 0.02$
$\Delta x_{g2} = £0.594\text{m}$	$\Delta x_{p2} = £0.3\text{m}$	$m'_p = 0.1$

We then have:

$$\theta_1 = \theta_2 = 0.5 \qquad R = 0.5(0.1) + 0.5(0.02) = 0.06 \qquad v_p = £0.563m$$

$$\lambda = \frac{0.563}{0.5} = 1.126 \qquad k = 0.5(1.126) + 0.5 = 1.063.$$

Hence, under the first procedure we would calculate:

$$\frac{£0.594m}{(1.06)^2} + \frac{£0.5m}{(1.06)} - £1m = £1000 > 0$$

and under the second:

$$\frac{£0.594m}{(1.02)^2} + \frac{£0.5m}{(1.02)} - £1.063m = -£2000 < 0.$$

Thus, we can construct an example in which not only are the two net present values different, but the two procedures give opposing recommendations!

This example is clearly somewhat contrived: the difference between the two net present values is very small relative to the total scale of the investment. This is, however, due to the assumption of only two future periods, so that we are still 'close' to the case in which the two procedures are equivalent. Adding more future periods would tend to widen the gap between the two, since the further into the future we go, the greater the difference between discounting at ρ and discounting at $R > \rho$.

Given that the two procedures will in general yield different net present values and possibly conflicting decisions, the question then arises of which is correct. Given the value judgements which underlie the analysis, the answer is without doubt that the second procedure, which discounts at the time-preference rate and calculates the opportunity cost of the public investment, is the correct one. The value judgements of course are those of Pareto optimality, extensively discussed earlier, in chapter 3. In the present context, they imply that investments should be appraised in terms of *consumers' valuations* of the net consumption time-streams to which they give rise. This clearly implies in turn that all discounting should be done at the consumers' rate of time preference and the opportunity cost of an investment is the present value of the consumption it displaces. Some other procedure, such as discounting at the weighted average rate, is acceptable only insofar as it gives equivalent results but, as we have seen, this cannot be guaranteed when investments have lives extending two or more periods into the future. We shall return to this issue in the concluding section of this chapter.

All the discussion so far has implicitly assumed that the outputs of both public and private investments are entirely consumed. This is unrealistic. We would expect consumers to save some of their income next period, thus permitting reinvestment of next period output to generate further output in the following period. The consumption time-streams will therefore differ from those so far considered. The three-period model of this section is a convenient context in which to consider this problem. We shall consider only the modification required to the time-preference rate/opportunity cost of capital procedure.

Under this procedure, all discounting takes place at ρ. The main problem therefore is to work out the shadow price of public investment, k. We proceed as follows. The displaced marginal private investment Δy_p would have generated an output stream Δx_{p1}, Δx_{p2}, as defined in (9.32). Let s_p denote the proportion of the period 1 output which would have been saved and reinvested, so that $(1 - s_p)$ is the proportion consumed. We take it that this reinvestment would earn the marginal private-sector rate of return m'_p. Thus, the reinvestment of $s_p \Delta x_{p1}$ in year 1 would return $(1 + m'_p)s_p \Delta x_{p1}$ in year 2. Thus the *consumption time-stream* which would have resulted from the displaced private investment is:

Year 1	*Year 2*
$(1 - s_p)\Delta x_{p1}$	$\Delta x_{p2} + (1 + m'_p)s_p \Delta x_{p1}$

The present value of this consumption time-stream is then found as:

$$v_p(s_p) = \frac{(1 - s_p)\Delta x_{p1}}{1 + \rho} + \frac{\Delta x_{p2} + (1 + m'_p)s_p \Delta x_{p1}}{(1 + \rho)^2} \qquad (9.40)$$

and $v_p(s_p)$ is then used to define values of λ and k exactly as before. The reader should confirm that with $s_p > 0$ and $m'_p > \rho$, we obtain a higher present value of displaced consumption than if the reinvestment of period 1 output had been ignored.

In appraising the public investment, we also have to take into account the possibility of reinvestment of part of the public-sector output since, provided this yields a rate of return which differs from the time-preference rate, the present value of the consumption time-stream will be affected. Moreover, it need not be the case that reinvestment takes place only in the public sector: the public output flows to consumers as income, part of which may be reinvested in the private sector at a rate of return m'_p. Thus it will be necessary to estimate the net time-stream of consumption flowing from the public investment taking into account both kinds of reinvestment possibilities. This time-stream should then be discounted at the time-preference rate ρ, to obtain a present value which should then be compared, as before, with $k\Delta y_g$, the opportunity cost of the marginal public investment. The shadow price k will of course, as already indicated, reflect the reinvestment of returns from the displaced private investment.

This discussion suggests that there are no problems *in principle* in defining an investment appraisal procedure which takes reinvestment possibilities into account. However, there are substantial problems of information and estimation which then arise. This is part of the general question of the usefulness and applicability of the appraisal procedures discussed in this chapter, to which we now turn.

9.3   Conclusions

In this concluding section we shall examine the problems which arise when we seek to apply the ideas discussed in this chapter. The crux of the problem can be stated as follows: given the scale and significance of public enterprise investment, it is impossible to ignore the question of the appraisal procedures which should be used. The logic of the economic models we construct to analyse this question leads to the identification of certain key parameters – the time-preference rate, the marginal private-sector rate of return, the displacement effects of public investment, the proportion of future returns reinvested – which, inescapably, should be central to any appraisal procedure. But when we come to apply the logic to real cases, we find either that the key parameters are very hard to measure or, even worse, that no exact empirical counterparts to them exist. Thus very rough and ready approximations have to be adopted in practice, and the information available may be insufficient to allow us even to judge that one approximation, which may be closer to the theoretically ideal procedure than another, is actually better.

Consider first 'the' time-preference rate and 'the' marginal private-sector rate of return. In point of fact the imperfections of capital markets are such that different consumers will be in equilibrium at different interest rates and hence there is no single consumer time-preference rate. This is partly because individual tax rates differ, and consumers will equate time-preference rates to after-tax interest rates; and also because consumers will have differing degrees of credit-worthiness which influence the terms on which they can borrow. Moreover, the existence of transactions costs, for example in buying stocks and bonds, may affect individuals' access to capital markets. In fact, once we begin seriously to address the issue of consumer equilibrium in real-world capital markets, we cannot ignore the existence of risk and uncertainty, which have been absent from the models of this chapter. One consumer may be in equilibrium at a guaranteed real interest rate of 3 per cent which he obtains by putting all his money into index-linked government securities. Another may anticipate an *average* rate of return of 8 per cent, because he includes risky shares in his portfolio which *could* turn out to earn much less than that. A consumer may be in a borrowing equilibrium at a real interest rate of 2 per cent, because he borrows on mortgage against the collateral of his house, has a high and safe income, and obtains tax relief on his interest payments. Another may be in a borrowing equilibrium of, say, 18 per cent, because, at the margin, he borrows on his credit-card account without security.

Strictly speaking, to estimate on overall time-preference rate, we would have to take a weighted average of all consumers' equilibrium time-preference rates, where the weights would be the reductions in current consumption consumers experience as a result of the public investment. This is clearly an impossible task, and some rough and ready average estimate will usually have to be arrived at in practice.

Similarly, at any point in time, firms will be undertaking investments which, at the margin, have different *expected* rates of return (again uncertainty implies that *ex post* rates of return could differ from those *ex ante*). Because of different tax rates and financing opportunities, the tax-adjusted cost of capital (r' in this chapter) may vary across firms. Moreover, it will be very hard to observe firms' *marginal ex ante* rates of return: available information may be restricted to *average ex post* accounting rates of return on all assets, old and new, which are clearly not those required by the theory set out in this chapter. Again, therefore, the marginal rate of return on private investment, or the future consumption time-stream resulting from the displaced private investment, will have to be estimated in a rough and ready way.

Severe difficulties of estimation also surround the displacement effects of marginal public investment and the rate of reinvestment of future returns. As we noted in the course of the discussion of the former, they will in general depend on the way in which the marginal public investment is financed, as well as on parameters of consumers' and firms' behavioural relationships such as the interest-elasticities of saving and investment, marginal propensities to consume out of disposable income, and so on. The reinvestment rate, since it relates to future decisions, *cannot* be known with certainty.

The purpose of pointing out the practical difficulties which confront the theoretical models of this chapter is not to argue against their application, but rather to suggest that controversy over finer points of theory is probably misplaced, since the practical impact of this may be small compared to the margins of error (relative to some unknowable 'true value') involved in quantifying the parameters. For example, we saw in the preceding section that the weighted average rate of return procedure may well give results which conflict with the time-preference rate/shadow price of capital procedure. Yet the differences between these could be insignificant compared to those resulting from variations in the estimates of the time-preference rate, marginal private-sector rate of return, displacement effects and reinvestment ratios.

Chapter 10

Pricing and investment under uncertainty

Consider the following planning problem:[1] the planners in the electricity supply industry must choose, in year t, an investment programme which will make new capacity available for production in, say, year $t+7$. The aim will be to provide capacity to meet the peak demand expected in that year. Two problems confront the planners: the first is that the peak demand cannot be known with certainty; and the second is that cost curves cannot be known with certainty, not only in respect of the level of costs, but also in respect of the capacity output which is attainable from any given amount of *installed* capacity. The uncertainty concerning demand arises from its dependence on variables such as income, prices of complements and substitutes, weather conditions, consumer durable technology and ownership, and so on, whose future values cannot be known in year t. The uncertainty about costs and output availability arises because future input prices, productivities, and incidence of plant failures cannot be known in year t. How then should the planners approach the problem of choosing prices, outputs and investment programmes? This chapter is concerned with a general theoretical approach to that question.

In terms of the analysis of marginal cost pricing carried out in chapters 4, 5 and 6, the problem can be put in the following way. We saw in chapter 4 that in the current period, price is always set at short-run marginal cost while, for the future period, plans are based on setting price at long-run marginal cost. *If* demand and costs can be predicted with complete certainty, the plans made now are fully realized, capacity will be optimally adjusted for the future output level, and the 'short-run marginal cost price' which will actually be set will be precisely the same as the 'long-run marginal cost price' which was planned – there is no conflict between them. Only if demand (or costs, though this was not investigated in chapters 4 and 5) turns out to be different than expected will price be other than that planned, so that 'marginal cost pricing' implies a price unequal to long-run marginal cost.

Now, realistically, future demand *cannot* be known with certainty, and it is quite likely that actual price would differ from that planned. It is then surely inconsistent to ignore this in planning for the future. The possibility of a range or distribution of possible future demand curves should be explicitly taken into account at the planning stage, and the question of pricing and investment policy reformulated as a *decision under uncertainty*. This will be the approach adopted in this chapter.

We shall proceed in three steps. First, in the following section, we examine how the planners in the electricity supply industry solve their planning problem. The broad approach is typical of all those industries which try to take explicit account of uncertainty in their planning, and the electricity industry is chosen mainly because its methods have been well documented. Our conclusions on this approach will be rather critical. We then go on to reformulate the problem in a more fundamental and useful way; as an extension, in fact, of the model of peak-load pricing in chapter 5. We show that the general form of the solution to the problem is very similar to that of peak-load pricing. However, it could be argued that there are practical difficulties in the way of implementing the solution we derive, and so we conclude by re-solving the problem in the light of the constraints which arise out of these practical considerations.

10.1 The capacity margin problem

We consider here how the planners in the electricity supply industry solve their decision problem under uncertainty. Their first step is to construct a probability distribution of peak demands for year $t+7$. This is done by combining two other probability distributions. A forecast of the most probable demand, given '*average cold spell*' weather conditions, is made for year $t+7$. This forecast is obtained by putting best estimates for future incomes, prices, etc. into an equation which relates these to demand, and solving for future demand. Then, taking a probability distribution of forecasting errors and applying this to the forecast demand, the first probability distribution of future demands is obtained. From past evidence on the relationship between deviations in demand from the 'average weather condition' level, and deviations in weather conditions from this standard, together with a probability distribution of weather conditions, the second probability distribution of demands can be generated. Combining these two distributions using standard probability laws then gives an overall probability distribution of demands in year $t+7$. Figure 10.1 illustrates this distribution, $f(q)$, on the assumption that it is normal. Demand in year $t+7$ is denoted by q, and the most probable demand is $\bar{q}$.

The planners now see themselves faced with the following problem: let K_0 be the level of installed capacity which will be available in year $t+7$, as a result of past investment decisions. The investment plan to be chosen in year t will bring installed capacity up to some value K^* in year $t+7$. Now, the question is should K^* be just sufficient to enable the system to meet the most probable demand, $\bar{q}$, or should it be greater? In other words, should there be a *margin of capacity* over and above that required to meet the most probable demand, and, if so, how great should that be?

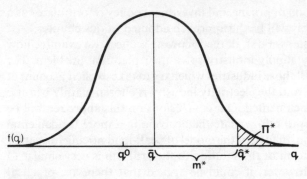

Figure 10.1

Thus the problem of investment planning resolves itself into that of determining the appropriate size of the *capacity margin*.

The capacity margin is chosen as follows: referring to Figure 10.1, suppose that the investment plan adopted in year t was just enough to increase capacity output from q_0 to $\bar{q}$. In that case, since half the distribution lies above $\bar{q}$, there is a 50 per cent chance that peak demand will actually exceed $\bar{q}$. The consequence of excess demand would be 'load-shedding' – some consumers have to be completely deprived of supply for the duration of the excess demand (which may be only a few hours of the year – but also the coldest hours) so that output is restrained to capacity. If planned capacity output were to exceed $\bar{q}$, however, the risk of excess demand is less, since the area of the distribution above it will be smaller. Given the precise parameters of the probability distribution $f(q)$, we can find, for each possible level of capacity output, $\hat{q}$, the probability that demand will exceed it. The planners then choose a critical 'risk level' or probability that demand will exceed capacity, shown by the area π^* in Figure 10.1, and find the capacity output corresponding to this, which we call $\hat{q}^*$. This is then the output level for which capacity will be installed. The procedure is illustrated in Figure 10.2. The curve $F(\hat{q})$ shows the relation between capacity output, $\hat{q}$, and the probability that demand will exceed it, π, derived from the probability distribution $f(q)$.[2] As we expect from Figure 10.1, the value of π ($=$ the area under $f(q)$ to the right of $\hat{q}$) falls rapidly at first as $\hat{q}$ increases, but then approaches zero asymptotically. Then, in the figure, the chosen risk level π^* determines the capacity output $\hat{q}^*$, and hence the margin of capacity output over most likely output, $m^* = \hat{q}^* - \bar{q}$. Consequently, there is a margin of installed capacity over the capacity most likely to be required, $K^* - \bar{K}$. At the present time, this capacity margin is roughly 28 per cent of the value of $\bar{K}$, the capacity required to meet $\bar{q}$.

   The interesting question is: on what basis is the choice of π^*, the risk level, made? To quote Berrie (1967) the planners 'must, in practice, choose a risk standard which enables the good image of electricity with consumers at large to be maintained, but without committing those consumers to too heavy a capital burden'. Thus, there is a trade-off between cost and risk: the greater the capacity margin, the greater must be total capacity costs, and so given the financial target the higher must be electricity prices; while a greater margin implies lower risk that consumers will lose supply, with consequent benefits. It is this latter part of the trade-off, however, which is put rather vaguely in the quotation. To explore this further, let us retrace our steps, and approach the problem from a different, and more general point of view.

   The capacity margin problem is essentially an inventory problem. In general, a firm would confront the problem of uncertain demand by determining a capacity level and a level of inventory of finished goods, where the latter would absorb the uncertainties. In determining its inventory level, the firm would weigh up on the one hand the costs of carrying inventory, and on the other the loss of profit from failing to meet demand. The latter has two aspects: there is the direct result, that the firm will lose the profit it might have got from making a sale, if output had been available; and the more conjectural, long-term result, that the firm may have permanently lost

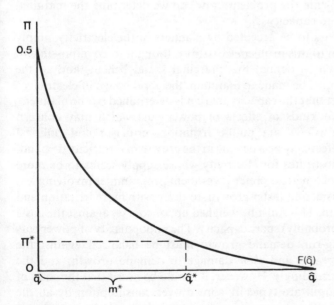

Figure 10.2

a customer because of its failure to meet the order. Given the firm's estimate of the probability distribution of future demand, it will weigh up the cost of an addition to inventory, with the expected loss it would incur if it did not make that addition to inventory. We expect it to end up roughly at a point at which the cost of the marginal addition to inventory is just about equal to the expected loss of not making that marginal addition. We now consider how this relates to electricity supply.

The first difference is that, because of its technology, electricity can only be 'stored' in the form of the capital equipment required to generate it, so that the inventory must consist of capacity, and not output. In general, this is a more expensive way of holding inventory than is the type of storage facility required for most goods. Nevertheless, in terms of finding a solution, it is quite possible to quantify these costs and so this aspect of the calculation is essentially unchanged.

The important difference arises in *valuing* an increment in the capacity margin. In the case of electricity supply, the direct loss of profit from failure to meet demand is negligible. In any case, of course, profit is not the objective of a public enterprise. If the objective of the investment is to maximize net social benefit, then we can suggest the general form of the solution: capacity should be increased up to the point at which the marginal social benefit of the reduced risk of supply interruption just equals the marginal cost of adding to capacity. This formula does not get us very far, but at least it forces us to state the problem: how can we determine the marginal social benefit of additions to capacity?

The answer which appears to be accepted by planners in the electricity supply industry is that no solution to this problem exists. It is thought to be impossible to measure (and perhaps even to define) this marginal social benefit, and so the capacity margin decision must be made to maintain 'the good image of electricity'. This seems to mean in effect that the capacity margin is determined by the planners' preferences. There are two kinds of effects of power cuts which may concern planners. The immediate effects are public irritation, criticism and political pressure. The longer-run effect may be a decline in the growth of electricity demand, as consumers switch to substitutes for electricity whose supply seems to be more reliable. We would expect planners to prefer investment programmes involving less public irritation and criticism, and faster growth, to those with more irritation and criticism, and slower growth. This must be weighed up, of course, against the costs of providing a margin of (probably) spare capacity. The unpopularity of power cuts and their damage to long-run demand growth must be balanced against the unpopularity of price increases and *their* damage to demand growth, and the 'security level' π^* chosen accordingly. However, it should be noted that the costs of providing the capacity margin are typically spread over consumption by all the consumers at all times, and are not imposed only on peak demand, the uncertainty of which is essentially the source of the need for a capacity margin. Thus, the relevant group of consumers is not made to bear the cost of their being provided with the degree of supply reliability they enjoy, and we would expect as a result that it is over-demanded – in part because they are not induced to substitute cheaper ways of providing their peak energy demands.

The 'capacity margin problem' is a very restricted and limited way of approaching the *general* problem of choosing capacity and price for a non-storable good. This problem arises in other public enterprises, the nature of whose technology is such that inventories must be held in the form of capacity rather than output. This is true of virtually all transport and communications services, but not of steel, coal and gas, whose outputs can be stored. For example, telephone connections at 4.30 pm on 15 April cannot be produced at 4 am on the previous 10 August and stored. Similarly trips from Alpha to Omega by rail, sea and air cannot be produced at one point of time and consumed at another. Inventories can only exist when production and consumption are separable in time, and are the means by which stable production can be reconciled with fluctuating and uncertain demand.

There is an important set of differences among public-sector outputs concerning the way in which excess demands can be coped with (assuming for the moment that price adjustments are not used to eliminate them). In the case of outputs such as coal and steel, available output could be rationed among consumers in a way which implies *marginal* reductions for all consumers. Excess demand for transport and communications services, on the other hand, is generally coped with by queuing: the time-profile of demand accommodates itself to the time-profile of capacity as consumers adjust to the delays with which their demands will be met, and the costs of the excess demand are borne by consumers as time costs. Electricity, and to a lesser extent gas, differ in yet another respect: excess demand results in complete withdrawal of supply from some consumers, and maintenance of full consumption by others. The total welfare loss is likely to be greater in this case than in any other, because of the difference in *marginal* and *total* utilities. Thus, suppose a cut in electricity consumption of x kWh were spread evenly over all consumers. Then, since each consumer is able to make a marginal reduction in consumption, and since the value of the marginal unit to each consumer is approximately equal to its price p, per kWh, then the welfare loss in this case is measured approximately by the loss of revenue, px, which we already know to be negligible in practice. On the other hand, if the cut is imposed on a group of consumers who suffer a total loss of consumption, then the welfare loss is equal to the total amount of their 'consumers' surplus' which, in the middle of winter, may be very high.

The obstacle to choosing capacity in a way which maximizes net social benefits appears to consist largely in the problem of measuring these surpluses. There is an important problem here of quite a general kind: 'reliability' of supply is a public good, in that no consumer can be excluded from enjoying it, and one person's consumption of it does not reduce that of someone else. The choice of a particular capacity margin determines the risk of failure to meet demand, and hence of power cuts, and a reduction in this degree of risk benefits everyone. The attempt to find, by consulting consumers, the appropriate level of provision of this public good 'reliability', therefore, encounters the general public good problem: it pays individual consumers to conceal their *true* preferences, in a way which influences the final choice in the direction they desire. For example, if a man from the electricity board were to go around asking consumers how much they would be prepared to pay to avoid power cuts, and the consumers know: (a) that they will not actually have to pay whatever sum they state; (b) the risk of power cuts will be smaller, the greater this sum; then clearly each consumer will rationally overstate his willingness to pay for the reduced risk of power cuts. In this situation, we may be forced back upon the planners' judgements, and preferences, as the second best. This also provides one way of rationalizing the belief that current capacity margins are too high: it pays individuals to pressurize, express extreme irritation, and vote for higher capacity margins than those for which they would be prepared to pay, if payment were related to benefit.

10.2 A model of price and capacity choice under uncertainty

In this section, we examine a model which deals simultaneously with pricing and investment policy. It can be regarded as the extension of the fixed-capacity model of chapter 5, to situations in which demand is uncertain. We shall set out the analysis,[3] and then consider its implications for the issues discussed in the previous section.

The situation is as follows: the enterprise, at the first instant of year 0, must choose an investment plan, which will determine capacity in year 1. Costs in year 1 are known with certainty, but demand is not. There are two possible states of the world which may prevail in year 1, in each of which there will be a demand curve. Each state will occur with probability $1/2$. The demand curves, D_1 and D_2, and cost curves relating to the optimal capacity, q^*, are drawn in Figure 10.3. The cost curves take the form familiar from the analysis of the fixed-capacity case in chapter 5. Note that for simplicity we have assumed that there is no peak-load problem: q measures the annual rate of output in year 1, with a uniform level of demand throughout the year. It is straightforward to relax this assumption to obtain the realistic case, and this is done once the basic results have been derived.

The following two assumptions are substantive rather than simplifying, and are basic to the model:

I. Price is set at the first instant of year 1, when demand will be known with certainty, and is always set in such a way as to restrain demand to capacity.
II. The value placed by a consumer, at the first instant of year 0, on the marginal unit of consumption in state s, $s = 1, 2$ is $\frac{1}{2}w_s$, where w_s is the value he will place on that unit when he knows that state s has occurred.

Each of these requires further discussion. The first is not entirely unrealistic. Prices do not normally have to be set at the time at which investment plans are being made, but rather can be announced relatively soon before peak demand. For example, prices of electricity are not set seven years in advance, but rather within, at most, twelve months of system peak. This seems generally true of other public enterprises. The degree of uncertainty confronting pricing decisions is therefore very much smaller than that for investment decisions, and assumption I sets it equal to zero.

The second part of assumption I may be invalidated by constraints placed on the levels of prices, and on the extent of price adjustments, which may well exist in

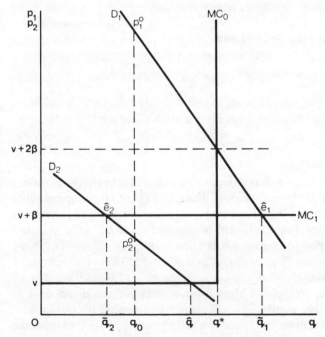

Figure 10.3

practice. By assuming the possibility of rationing by price initially, however, we are led to some interesting conclusions about the source and nature of the welfare losses due to supply interruptions.

Assumption II can be illustrated as follows: assume that the good concerned is electricity, and that state 1 corresponds to cold weather and high income for a consumer, while state 2 corresponds to mild weather and low income. Given some level of his consumption in state 1, say $\hat{q}_1$, suppose that the consumer is prepared to pay 50p for the marginal unit, when he knows that state 1 prevails. Likewise, he would pay 10p for the marginal unit of consumption when he knows state 2 prevails. Then, if the probability of each state occurring is $1/2$, the assumption says that at the first instant of year 0 he would be prepared to pay 25p to assure himself of the marginal unit of consumption *if* state 1 occurs, and 5p to assure himself of the marginal unit if state 2 occurs. It also follows that he will pay a total of 30p to assure himself of the marginal units of consumption in both states. The assumption, therefore, implies that, in year 0, the consumer is willing to pay for an increment of consumption in each state, an amount equal to the *expected value* of what he would pay when he knows for certain which state exists. A justification for this assumption, based on an explicit analysis of consumer choice under uncertainty, is given in the Appendix to this chapter.

In Figure 10.3, we analyse the determination of the optimal price and capacity level, q^*. It can be shown that the general necessary condition for optimal capacity is

$$\tfrac{1}{2}(p_1^* - v) + \tfrac{1}{2}(p_2^* - v) = \beta, \qquad p_s^* \geqslant v, \qquad s = 1, 2 \qquad (10.1)$$

where p_1^* is the optimal price which will be set in state 1, and p_2^* that which will be set in state 2. If, as in the present case, we have $p_2^* = v$, then equation (10.1) becomes

$$p_1^* = v + 2\beta \qquad (10.2)$$

as in the figure.

The argument underlying this result is straightforward, and takes a form familiar from the earlier analysis of peak-load pricing. Thus, in Figure 10.3, suppose that capacity is initially at q_0. Then, in state 1, the marginal value of output to consumers is shown by the price corresponding to point p_1^0 on demand curve D_1; while in state 2 the marginal value of output to consumers is shown by point p_2^0 on D_2. Now consider the differences between these prices, p_1^0 and p_2^0, and v. These differences, $p_1^0 - v$, and $p_2^0 - v$, can be thought of as the amount consumers would pay for an increment of output in each respective state, over and above the direct cost of producing the output. In other words, $p_1^0 - v$ measures, at capacity q^0, consumers' willingness to pay for an increment in capacity in state 1, while $p_2^0 - v$ measures the same thing for state 2. But from assumption II, we have that at the first instant of year 0, when the future state of the world is unknown, consumers' valuations of the increment of output in each state are $\frac{1}{2}p_1^0$ and $\frac{1}{2}p_2^0$, respectively. It follows from this assumption that their willingness to pay for the increment in capacity, at the first instant of year 0, is $\frac{1}{2}(p_1^0 - v) + \frac{1}{2}(p_2^0 - v)$. Note that here we again have a case of *joint products*: an increment of capacity will enable an increment of output to be produced in *each state*, and so its value, *before* the state of the world is known, is the *sum* of its values across states.

From this reasoning, it follows that an increment in capacity can make everyone better off, as long as

$$\tfrac{1}{2}(p_1^0 - v) + \tfrac{1}{2}(p_2^0 - v) > \beta. \tag{10.3}$$

By rewriting this condition as

$$p_1^0 + p_2^0 > 2(v + \beta), \tag{10.4}$$

we can see from Figure 10.3 that the inequality is satisfied at capacity q^0, since $p_1^0 > v + 2\beta$, and $p_2^0 > v$. Hence, everyone can be made better off by increasing capacity. The inequality in (10.4) is clearly satisfied right up to output $\hat{q}$. Since at this point $p_2 = v$, we know that output in state 2 should not exceed $\hat{q}$. If output in state 2 *were* to exceed $\hat{q}$, that would imply that resources at the margin are worth more in other uses than they are to consumers of this good in state 2. However, it is still the case that at capacity $\hat{q}$, $p_1 > v + 2\beta$, or alternatively, $\frac{1}{2}(p_1 - v) > \beta$, implying that consumers still value an increment of capacity at an amount greater than its cost, because of the *expected value of its benefit to them in the 'cold weather, high income' state* 1. Hence, even though no benefit will be derived from it if in fact state 2 occurs, everyone can be made better off by an expansion in capacity before the state of the world is known, because of its expected benefits if state 1 occurs. This clearly continues to hold up to capacity q^*, at which point $p_1^* = v + 2\beta$, or $\frac{1}{2}(p_1^* - v) = \beta$, and the expected value of benefit from a capacity increment is just equal to its cost.

Associated with this solution for optimal capacity choice is a pricing policy which is *conditional on the state of the world*. If state 1 occurs, then price will be set at $p_1^* = v + 2\beta$, since, following assumption I, this rations demand to capacity. If state 2 occurs, then price will be set at $p_2^* = v$, implying output $\hat{q} < q^*$, and this of course corresponds to the usual optimal pricing rule for given capacity. If state 1 occurs, the enterprise will make a profit, of the amount

$$P_1 = p_1^* q^* - (v + \beta)q^*, \tag{10.5}$$
$$= (v + 2\beta)q^* - (v + \beta)q^* = \beta q^*, \tag{10.6}$$

whereas if state 2 occurs, the enterprise makes a loss of

$$P_2 = p_2^* \hat{q} - v\hat{q} - \beta q^*, \tag{10.7}$$

$$= -\beta q^*. \tag{10.8}$$

It follows that the *expected value* of profit,

$$\bar{P} = \tfrac{1}{2}P_1 + \tfrac{1}{2}P_2, \tag{10.9}$$

is exactly zero, implying that in the long run (taking one year with another) the enterprise will break even.

Given the two assumptions underlying this model, therefore, we have a complete solution for the pricing and capacity choice problem, which is formally identical to the peak-load pricing solution, and can be generalized and operationalized in a similar way. Indeed, it is possible to consider a further case, analogous to the 'shifting-peak' case, in which, if state 2 occurs, output will also equal capacity, and $p_2^* > v$. It is in this case that the general condition in equation (10.3) applies. The details of this extension are left for the reader to supply.

It is instructive to compare the solution just derived to the 'planners' solution' to the capacity margin problem given earlier. The essential difference lies in the role of price. In the planners' procedure which determined the capacity margin, a future price was assumed in generating the central estimate of future demand, and prices then vanished from the analysis. In the present case, because of assumption I, pricing policy and capacity choice are interdependent. The use of price to ration output means that in each state of the world, price measures the marginal value of consumption, and this, in conjunction with assumption II, provides us with the valuation of the benefits of increments in capacity which eluded the planners. Thus, we have the result that *if* pricing policy is used optimally, then we also have the basis of a solution to the investment planning problem.

We can apply our solution to consider the conditions under which, *given our assumptions I and II*, the planners' solution to the capacity margin problem will be optimal. First, suppose that there are now three states of the world, which again will occur with equal probability. Extending the earlier reasoning, the optimality condition will now become

$$\tfrac{1}{3}(p_1^* - v) + \tfrac{1}{3}(p_2^* - v) + \tfrac{1}{3}(p_3^* - v) = \beta, \qquad p_s \geqslant v, \qquad s = 1, 2, 3. \tag{10.10}$$

In Figure 10.4 we show two possible solutions to the capacity choice problem. In both (a) and (b), the demand curves in the three states are shown as D_1, D_2 and D_3, and optimal capacity is q^*. In (a), we have that at the optimum, $p_2^* = p_3^* = v$, and so the necessary condition in (10.10) is satisfied with $p_1^* = v + 3\beta$. In (b), we have that $p_2^* = v$, and so $\tfrac{1}{3}(p_1^* - v) + \tfrac{1}{3}(p_2^* - v) = \beta$. We now need to characterize the capacity margin solution in these cases.

Suppose that the planners choose as their *given* price level the value $v + \beta$ ($=$ long-run marginal cost) so that in Figure 10.4(a) they generate the 'demand forecasts' q_1, q_2 and $\bar{q}_3$, and in (b) the same. By construction, $\bar{q}_3$ is, in each case, the expected value of the forecast demands. Hence, in each case, the capacity margin approach chooses some arbitrary risk level and installs capacity above $\bar{q}_3$. In case (a), we see that a capacity margin of the amount $q^* - \bar{q}_3$ is justified. At a capacity of $\bar{q}_3$, we have that the expected value of the benefits in states 1 and 3, of a capacity increment, exceeds the cost of the increment, and so everyone can be made better off by a positive 'capacity margin'. In (b), however, this is not the case: it happens that the optimal capacity level q^* is just equal to $\bar{q}_3$, and so no capacity margin is implied.

In terms of our figure, everything clearly depends on the height and slope of the demand curve D_1 relative to D_3: the higher and steeper this curve, the more likely it is that a positive capacity margin will be implied. To put this in economic rather than geometric terms, what matters is the value of marginal consumption in higher demand states of the world: where this is high relative to the 'mean' state of the world, a positive capacity margin is likely to be implied, whereas when this is low, no margin may be implied.

This statement could be a 'shattering glimpse of the obvious', were it not for the

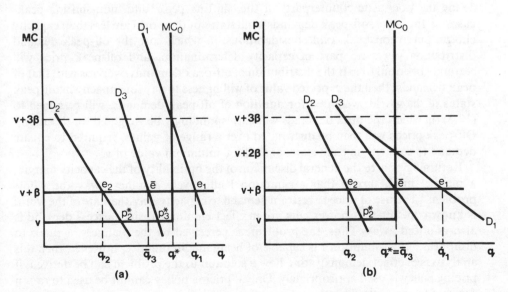

Figure 10.4

operational implications. The solution tells us that we can compute the optimal capacity margin by finding those prices which ration demand to capacity in each state of the world. Given these prices, we can also define a simple qualitative test to determine whether the existing capacity margin is too large. This test can usefully be stated in its most general form. Thus, let $p_s(q_s)$ be the (inverse) demand function in state s, where $s = 1, 2, \ldots, S$, and π_s the probability of occurrence of state s. Denote the capacity output under the 'planners' solution', by $\tilde{q}$. Finally, let S_1 be the set of states of the world, which have the property that

$$p_s(\tilde{q}) > v, \qquad s \in S_1. \tag{10.11}$$

In other words, at the chosen capacity level, the prices which equate demand to that level exceed marginal running cost for all states in $S_1 \subset S$. Then, capacity $\tilde{q}$ is too large if

$$\sum_{s \in S_1} \pi_s [p_s(\tilde{q}) - v] < \beta, \tag{10.12}$$

which means that the expected value of willingness to pay for the marginal unit of capacity, over those states in which consumers benefit from it, is less than its cost.

The discussion so far relates essentially to *peak* demand. If we explicitly incorporate peak-load considerations, then the conditions can be generalized in obvious ways. Given the probability distribution of off-peak demands, we can define the stochastic counterparts of the 'shifting peak' and 'non-shifting peak' cases. In the latter, off-peak demands in all states of the world are less than capacity chosen purely on peak-load considerations, in which case the off-peak demand distribution plays no part in capacity determination, and off-peak price will certainly be equal to v. If the distribution of off-peak demands overlaps with that of peak demands, then the expected value of willingness to pay for capacity in off-peak states of the world, weighted for duration of off-peak demands, will be added to (10.3) (in which the peak demands will correspondingly be weighted for duration). Off-peak prices will then be distributed over a range of values, required to equate demand to capacity in each state, and with a minimum value of v.

Returning now to the general discussion of the optimality of the capacity margin, a planner might argue that assumption I effectively assumes away the whole problem.[4] The use of price to restrain demand to capacity *once* the state of the world is known, means that power cuts are in effect eliminated, since excess demand is always priced away. Thus, the problem, as perceived by the planners, is made to disappear.[5] If assumption I is capable of being met in practice, however, then this analysis is in effect demonstrating how a solution to the problem can be derived, if pricing policy is used appropriately. Only if pricing policy cannot be used to ration demand to capacity, does the solution fail.

There are a number of reasons for the failure of assumption I to hold. It may not be possible technically to set a price when the state of the world is known: there may still be significant demand uncertainty confronting the pricing decision. Alternatively, there may be constraints on the level to which price may be raised, or on the size of any price adjustment. Referring back to Figure 10.3, it is clear that quite wide price variations might be necessary from year to year, if price is used as a rationing device. Suppose, for example, that state 2 has occurred in year 0, so that price equals v. Then, if state 1 occurs in year 1, price will have to rise to $v + 2\beta$, while if state 2 occurs again in year 2, price will fall again to v. These price fluctuations might be regarded as too extreme, although whatever costs are associated with this 'extremeness' would have to be weighed against the costs of power cuts, and possibly excess capital expenditure, which occur when price rationing is not adopted.

There are clearly many cases which could be analysed. We might assume that price variation may take place between v and some upper limit below $v + 2\beta$; or that it may take place between bounds which lie within v and $v + 2\beta$; or that a uniform price must be set, which will prevail in all states of the world. Furthermore, we could assume that the constraints on pricing policy are arbitrarily given, or that we may choose them in some way which minimizes the welfare loss they generate. Limitations of space preclude analysis of all of these. We now consider what appears to be a representative case.

10.3 Uniform pricing of uncertain demands

Let us take the case in which a price is to be specified before the state of the world is known, with no adjustment possible once the state *is* known. This would correspond either to the situation in which there is unavoidable demand uncertainty at the time at which prices are set, or to that in which there are extreme constraints on pricing policy. To begin with, we assume that the 'uniform price' – uniform, that is, across states of the world, and not necessarily over periods of the day or year – is arbitrarily set equal to $v + \beta$. We shall in a moment consider the question of an optimal uniform price.

Referring back to Figure 10.3, we see that if a price equal to $v + \beta$ is set before the state of the world is known, then, if state of the world 1 occurs, demand will be at $\tilde{q}_1$, and if state 2 occurs, demand will be at $\tilde{q}_2$. Now suppose that capacity happened to be at q^*. Then, if state 1 occurs, there will be excess demand in the amount $\tilde{q}_1 - q^*$, which will have to be met by reducing consumption by some consumers to zero. The welfare losses are then the value of these total consumptions, and these will in general exceed the losses due to increasing price to $v + 2\beta$, for reasons already discussed. Essentially, those who lose their consumption would be able to compensate all other consumers for sharing their losses with them, and still be better off than when they suffer power cuts, but the enterprise fails to organize this mutually beneficial exchange through its pricing policy.

If state 2 occurs there will also be a welfare loss, arising from the fact that price in state 2 exceeds the marginal cost of state 2 consumption, given by v. Now, the lower the uniform price, the smaller is the welfare loss if state 2 occurs, and the larger is that in state 1. At a uniform price of v, the former is zero; at a price of $v + 2\beta$ the converse is the case. Hence, the determination of the optimal uniform price follows from trading off the expected values of the two kinds of welfare loss, which of course cannot be done unless we know the welfare cost of power cuts.

Let us again assume an arbitrary uniform price at $v + \beta$, and consider the capacity choice decision as one of optimizing subject to the fixed price constraint. We again make use of Figure 10.3 to analyse this case. For any capacity greater than $\tilde{q}_2$, welfare in state 2 is unaffected by capacity choice (ignoring possible welfare effects arising from the way in which its costs are allocated). Thus, capacity choice appears to be determined *entirely* by an evaluation of the costs of capacity, on the one hand, against the welfare losses arising from non-price rationing of demand in state 1, on the other. Since the latter are the costs of power cuts, this describes precisely how planners view the problem. However, this view is seriously incomplete, even in the case where a uniform price has to be set, because *both* capacity *and* price can be used to trade off the welfare losses in the two states. Their optimal values should be chosen simultaneously, whereas the 'capacity margin' procedure fixes price without regard to this problem and then determines capacity given that price. We now consider, therefore, the problem of joint choice of capacity and optimal fixed price.

Take first a very special case, in which any amount of available output can be rationed off according to consumers' willingness to pay. That is, in Figure 10.3, the capacity output q^* could be allocated among consumers *just as if* there were a price mechanism which set price at $v + 2\beta$ in state 1, even though the actual price may differ from this and be constant across states. In effect, we are assuming costless non-price rationing: any excess demand can somehow be eliminated by getting consumers to give up *only* those units of consumption which are worth less to them than $v + 2\beta$. In this case, the first-best solution is again optimal, and the uniform-pricing constraint is ineffective. We should set price at v and capacity at q^*. If state 2 occurs, then consumers will buy $\hat{q}$ in Figure 10.3 and there are no welfare losses. If state 1 occurs, although there will be excess demand at price v, this can be eliminated without welfare loss and it is *as if* demand were restricted to capacity q^* by a price $v + 2\beta$.

The only problem which arises is that of financing the losses the enterprise will make, since only operating costs are recovered in revenues. It may be possible to cover capital costs by charging a fixed overhead to each consumer. Alternatively, the method of rationing available output q^* may itself generate enough revenue to cover losses, as we shall see in a moment. On the other hand, if a break-even constraint is imposed, and no non-distortionary way exists for financing the losses of the enterprise, then clearly the uniform price will exceed v and capacity will be below q^*, for reasons familiar from the earlier analysis of pricing under profit constraints.

We can briefly consider a type of mechanism which would fit the case of costless non-price rationing or, in effect, state-contingent pricing. Suppose the enterprise sets up a market in *options* to consume its output. That is, a consumer may buy at a price, say r, the *right* to buy a unit of output at the price v if and only if state 1 occurs (by assumption, demand in state 2 will be below capacity at price v, otherwise options could also be sold for this state). The options of course are sold *before* the state of the world is known. The equilibrium price on the option market, r^*, will be such as to ensure that the total rights to output in state 1 sum exactly to capacity. Thus there will be no *effective* excess demand in state 1. We can then show that if the option price r^* is set at β, and capacity at q^*, we have in effect the first-best solution. Moreover, the enterprise will break even.

Consider the interpretation we can place on the equilibrium price of an option to buy one unit. Each consumer will purchase options up to the point at which the expected value to him of the marginal unit of consumption in state 1, *net* of the price v he will have to pay for it, is just equal to the option price. If w_1 again denotes the marginal value of the consumer's state 1 consumption, his equilibrium purchase of options will therefore satisfy:

$$\tfrac{1}{2}(w_1 - v) = r^*. \tag{10.13}$$

He weights the value of an option to buy in state 1 by its probability of occurrence, $\tfrac{1}{2}$, because of course if state 2 occurs the option is worthless. Now if $r^* = \beta$, (10.13) becomes:

$$w_1 = v + 2\beta. \tag{10.14}$$

Since r^* is the same for each consumer, we have that marginal valuations are equalized at the equilibrium. Moreover, these marginal valuations are precisely those given by the appropriate state-contingent price which rations off output q^* in state 1 (see Figure 10.3). Thus a uniform price of v, a capacity of q^* and an option market with price $r^* = \beta$ achieves the first-best. Note finally that revenue always covers costs. Capital costs pq^* are covered by the proceeds from the options market, r^*q^*, while running costs are covered by the sale of output in whichever state comes about.

It could of course be argued that we have once again assumed away the problem:

option markets in electricity supply and other public enterprise outputs do not exist. One reason for this may be that the costs of organizing an options market are greater than the benefit which would be derived from its existence. This is probably true when there is *already* a substantial margin of spare capacity, since then the likelihood of excess demand is very small. But it is probable that the existence of an options market would lead to a sizeable reduction in required capacity, an important cost-saving which should be set against the cost of organizing the market.

A further difficulty may arise out of the need to enforce the option contracts, i.e. to ensure that a consumer's actual consumption in state 1 is no greater than that to which he is entitled by his holding of options. The electricity supply industry in the UK does not at present have the technological capability to restrict the supply of any *one* consumer, but instead has to disconnect whole groups of consumers living in a particular supply area. However, recent developments in microelectronics have led to the development of devices which can regulate consumption of individual consumers, and, by remote control, even switch off specific electric appliances such as freezers and water heaters. It is hard to escape the conclusion that the obstacle to rationing by prices in the face of uncertain demands does not lie in the absence of a technology for implementing contracts.

Be that as it may, let us now suppose that a uniform price must be set across states and that any excess demand in state 1 must be met by non-price rationing which is *not* costless: available consumption cannot be allocated according to willingness to pay. Price and capacity must now be set in the light of the costs created by the existence of excess demand in state 1. We therefore have to specify what these are, which in turn requires some discussion of the nature of the non-price rationing mechanism, i.e. the means by which excess demand is dealt with.

Here we shall consider the most relevant method, which is usually referred to as *random rationing*. As already suggested, in the case of electricity supply, when there is excess demand a subset of consumers – the size of which depends on the extent of excess demand – is totally deprived of supply, while remaining consumers are allowed to realize their demands in full. However, it is not generally known, before the excess demand arises, or, in our terminology, before the state of the world is known, precisely who these consumers will be. In general, at the planning stage, all that can be said is that if excess demand should arise, every consumer *stands a chance* of being disconnected, or rationed. The probability with which the ith consumer will be rationed is denoted π_i, and of course lies between 0 and 1. A simple special case of random rationing occurs when these probabilities are equal for all consumers, and given by:

$$\pi_i = \pi = \frac{q_1 - \bar{q}}{q_1} = 1 - \frac{\bar{q}}{q_1} \qquad q_1 \geqslant \bar{q} \qquad (10.15)$$

where q_1 is actual demand in state 1 (the high demand state) and $\bar{q}$ is capacity output. Thus the probability that each consumer will be rationed is determined by the ratio of capacity to demand, and is of course zero if there is no excess demand ($q_1 \leqslant \bar{q}$).

It will be useful to illustrate the argument from time to time with the help of this 'simple random rationing' case, but, more generally, we could simply regard the π_i as being dependent on capacity and excess demand, i.e.:

$$\pi_i = \pi_i(\bar{q}, q_1). \tag{10.16}$$

Moreover, it is reasonable to suppose that an increase in capacity, $\bar{q}$, with demand constant would reduce each π_i, while an increase in demand q_1 with capacity held fixed would increase each π_i, since the former corresponds to a decrease in excess demand and the latter to an increase. Then (10.15) is clearly a special case of (10.16).

To find optimal price and capacity, we shall need to evaluate their effects on consumer welfare arising out of the rationing mechanism. Let V_i be the ith consumer's surplus on his consumption in state 1. That is, it represents the amount he would be willing to pay for the right to buy output in state 1, rather than be completely deprived of supply. Then we can show (see the Appendix to this chapter) that the optimal price p^* and capacity $\bar{q}^*$ must satisfy the conditions:

$$\tfrac{1}{2}(p^* - v)\frac{\Delta q_2}{\Delta p} = \tfrac{1}{2}\sum_i V_i \frac{\Delta \pi_i}{\Delta q_1}\frac{\Delta q_1}{\Delta p} \tag{10.17}$$

$$\tfrac{1}{2}(p^* - v) - \tfrac{1}{2}\sum_i V_i \frac{\Delta \pi_i}{\Delta \bar{q}} = \beta \tag{10.18}$$

which are actually more straightforward than they appear at first sight. The $\tfrac{1}{2}$s in the conditions refer to the probabilities of states 1 and 2, which is why they have not been cancelled out (in general these probabilities need not be equal). $\Delta q_2/\Delta p$ and $\Delta q_1/\Delta p$ are the slopes of the state 2 and state 1 demand curves respectively, with respect to the price axis. Condition (10.17) refers to choice of the optimal uniform price p^*. It can be explained with the help of Figure 10.5. The condition says that the optimal price is just such as to equate the *expected marginal benefit* of a small price reduction in *state 2* (the non-rationed state) with the *expected marginal cost* of this small price reduction *in state 1* (the rationed state). The former consists essentially of the net benefit of the extra consumption induced by the price cut in state 2, which is $p - v$. The latter consists of the welfare loss to consumers of the increased risk of being rationed, because of the increase in excess demand induced by the price reduction. Thus, in Figure 10.5, consider the price p^* and the effects of a small reduction Δp in it. This would induce an increase in consumption which would yield a benefit to consumers of approximately p^* but cause an increase of costs of v, and hence a net benefit of $p^* - v$. Since state 2 occurs with a probability of $\frac{1}{2}$, the net expected benefit of the price cut is $\frac{1}{2}(p^* - v)$. The fall in price would have no effect on actual *consumption* in state 1, since this is fixed at capacity output, $\bar{q}^*$. However it would increase desired demand and also increase excess demand by the same amount. Then each rationing probability will increase, so the $\Delta\pi_i$s are all positive. The *total* welfare cost of this is found by weighting each $\Delta\pi_i$ by i's willingness to pay for consumption in state 1, V_i, and adding over consumers. Thus $\sum_i V_i \Delta\pi_i$ gives the total welfare cost of the increased risk of being rationed caused by the fall in price, and since state 1 will occur with probability $\frac{1}{2}$, the right-hand side of (10.17) gives the expected value of this welfare cost.

Condition (10.18) relates to the optimal choice of capacity, and says that the expected marginal benefit of capacity to consumers must equal its marginal cost, β. The marginal benefit of capacity is zero in state 2, because, by assumption, demand is less than capacity at the optimum. Its marginal benefit has two components in state 1, as shown by the left-hand side of (10.18). First, with price fixed at p^* in Figure 10.5, an increment of capacity permits an equal increment of consumption in state 1, the net marginal benefit of which is $p^* - v$. But in addition, the increment in capacity, $\Delta\bar{q}$, results in a fall in the probabilities with which consumers will be rationed, this effect being given by $\Delta\pi_i/\Delta\bar{q}$, and the aggregate value of this is found by weighting each $\Delta\pi_i/\Delta\bar{q}$ by the consumer's willingness to pay to avoid being rationed, V_i, and summing, to give the second marginal benefit term in (10.18).

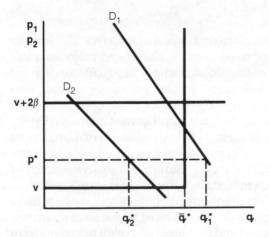

Figure 10.5

(Since $\Delta\pi_i/\Delta\bar{q} < 0$, i.e. an increment in capacity reduces the rationing probabilities, the two terms on the left of (10.18) are in effect being added and not subtracted.)

The implications of these conditions for the optimal price can be found by rearranging them to obtain:

$$p^* - v = \left[\sum_i V_i \frac{\Delta\pi_i}{\Delta q_1}\right] \frac{\Delta q_1/\Delta p}{\Delta q_2/\Delta p} > 0 \qquad (10.19)$$

$$p^* - (v + 2\beta) = \sum_i V_i \frac{\Delta\pi_i}{\Delta\bar{q}} < 0. \qquad (10.20)$$

Thus the optimal price lies between the two state-contingent first-best values, v and $v + 2\beta$, which implies that over time the enterprise can expect to make losses. The optimal uniform price lies between the two values because it is trading off the marginal welfare loss in state 1 of having price below its first-best value of $v + 2\beta$, with that in state 2 of having price above its first-best value of v. However, the precise value of p^* is clearly dependent on the V_i values, the consumers' willingness to pay to avoid being rationed in state 1, as is the optimal level of capacity $\bar{q}^*$. It is now therefore time we discussed these.

We already noted, in the discussion in section 10.2, the 'public goods' nature of supply reliability. This is further brought out by the expressions $\sum_i V_i(\Delta\pi_i/\Delta q_1)$ and $\sum_i V_i(\Delta\pi_i/\Delta\bar{q})$ in conditions (10.17) and (10.18). A change in price or capacity affects the welfare of all consumers, and the overall marginal valuation is the *sum* of the individual marginal valuations. We would therefore expect the usual 'public goods problem' of false revelation of preferences if we were to question consumers directly in the hope of eliciting their V_i values. On the other hand, in contrast to the public goods case, the basic commodity, the public enterprise output (e.g. electricity), is sold on a market and its demand curve could, at least in principle, be estimated. In fact it can be shown that an approximate value for V_i could be obtained from the standard measure of the Marshallian consumer surplus for that consumer (see Appendix to this chapter). This might not be of much help since it is the market demand curve, rather than the individual consumer demand curves, which we could at best hope to estimate. However, if the $\Delta\pi_i/\Delta q_1$ and $\Delta\pi_i/\Delta\bar{q}$ terms are approximately the same for all consumers (as they would be of course under *simple random rationing*), then all we need is the value of the sum of willingnesses to pay, $\sum_i V_i$, which can be deduced from the area under the market demand curve in state 1.

An alternative approach[7] is suggested by the observation that many public enterprise outputs, particularly electricity, are essentially intermediate goods or inputs into a household production process. The household owns a stock of consumer durables and combines with them bought-in inputs to produce certain consumption services, for example warmth, light, hot water, entertainment, and so on. This suggests a 'production cost' approach to the estimation of the V_i values which may turn out to be more practicable than direct questioning of consumers or demand estimation. The approach can be illustrated with the help of Figure 10.6. Let Z_1 denote the output of the consumption service in state 1, and C_1 the consumer's expenditure on 'producing' Z_1. The curves C_1^+ and C_1^- in Figure 10.6 then are conventional cost curves. C_1^+ shows how the cost of producing Z varies with output, given the consumer's durable goods stock and given also that he is able to buy the public enterprise output, e.g. electricity, in state 1. C_1^- on the other hand shows the relationship between cost and output on the assumption that the consumer is rationed in state 1, e.g. he is subjected to a power cut. C_1^- lies above C_1^+ because the rationing is effective – it forces the consumer to a second-best production process. In the figure, Z_1^* denotes the level of consumption service he chooses if he is not rationed, and C_1^* is its associated cost. If he is rationed, but makes the same expenditure on Z_1, his output will fall to Z_1^0, while if he maintains output at Z_1^* his expenditure must rise to $\hat{C}_1$. We could then use these cost values to define approximations to V_i. Thus, we could interpret:

(a) $\hat{C}_1 - C_1^*$ as an amount by which we could compensate the consumer to restore him to the level of welfare he would enjoy if he were not rationed in state 1, since with an expenditure of $\hat{C}_1$ he could achieve the consumption level Z^*;

(b) $C_1^* - C_1^0$ as an amount the consumer would be willing to pay to avoid being rationed, because if he were to pay this sum, and were not rationed, then he could achieve consumption level Z_1^0, which is the level he will be at if he is rationed.

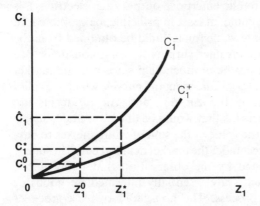

Figure 10.6

In general the two values will not be equal, because of the differing slopes of the curves. Indeed, in many cases the first measure, $\hat{C}_1 - C_1^*$, may not be defined, because the best alternative production process in the presence of rationing may not be capable of delivering an output Z^* at any cost: the curve C_1^- becomes vertical at some point to the left of Z^*. For example, it may be impossible, using whatever means are at one's disposal, to achieve the usual degree of warmth in the home during an electricity power cut. The second measure, on the other hand, does not even require the existence of an alternative production process, though clearly it will be smaller the better the available alternative.

The advantage of these cost-based measures of consumer surplus is that they can be objectively estimated. Given some assumptions about the durable-good stock and technology, it should be possible to construct the cost curves in Figure 10.6 for representative groups of consumers. Data on durable-good ownership and chosen Z values for consumers would then allow aggregate estimates to be made.

10.4 Conclusions
In this chapter we first considered the problem of capacity choice under uncertainty as perceived by planners in the electricity industry, the 'capacity margin problem'. Both the formulation and solution of this problem have serious weaknesses from the economic point of view. The role of price in rationing demands and conveying information about marginal values of output is ignored and no serious attempt is made to obtain measures of the benefit consumers derive from supply reliability. We then showed that if price can be set once the state of the world is known, a complete and straightforward solution to the problem is available, which bears a close resemblance to peak-load pricing. If, for some reason, price must be uniform across states, it is still possible to develop quite straightforward principles for pricing and capacity choice. The main difficulty here is that implementation of them requires information on consumer surpluses. This information may be obtainable from demand curve estimation. Alternatively, given the nature of electricity (and many other public enterprise outputs) as an input into a household production process, it may be possible to construct cost functions which will yield estimates of the required valuations. We should not of course underestimate the difficulties of developing and applying principles of efficient pricing and investment under uncertainty. Nevertheless, a great deal could be done to improve upon the existing planning procedures.

Appendix to chapter 10

1 State-contingent pricing

We here generalize the analysis of section 10.2 and derive the main results given there. States of the world are indexed $s = 1, \ldots, S$, p_s is the price to be set in state s, $p_s = D(q_s, s)$ is the (inverse) demand function, and $B_s = B(q_s, s)$ is the corresponding consumer benefit function, with, as before, $\partial B_s / \partial q_s = p_s$. π_s denotes the *ex ante* probability of occurrence of state s, with of course $0 \leqslant \pi_s \leqslant 1$, and $\sum_s \pi_s = 1$. We adopt as the objective function the expected value of net benefit:[8]

$$\bar{N} \equiv \sum_s \pi_s [B_s - v q_s] - \beta \bar{q} \tag{A.10.1}$$

where v is, as before, marginal operating cost, β is marginal capital cost and $\bar{q}$ capacity output. We also have the S constraints:

$$q_s \leqslant \bar{q} \qquad s = 1, \ldots, S. \tag{A.10.2}$$

Note that, in line with the exposition of this chapter, *only* demands are state-contingent: costs and capacity do not vary across states. This is, however, easy to generalize, and the reader is invited to do this.

Maximizing $\bar{N}$ with respect to q_s and $\bar{q}$, and subject to the capacity constraint, yields:

$$\pi_s (p_s^* - v) - \lambda_s^* = 0 \qquad s = 1, \ldots, S \tag{A.10.3}$$

$$\sum_s \lambda_s^* - \beta = 0 \tag{A.10.4}$$

$$q_s^* \leqslant \bar{q}^* \qquad \lambda_s^* \geqslant 0 \qquad \lambda_s^* (q_s^* - \bar{q}^*) = 0 \tag{A.10.5}$$

where λ_s^* is the shadow price of capital in state s and asterisks denote optimal values. For some s in which $q_s^* < \bar{q}^*$ (e.g. state 2 in Figure 10.3), $\lambda_s^* = 0$ from (A.10.5), and so $p_s^* = v$ for that s. Let S_1 denote the subset of states for which $\lambda_s^* > 0$ so that $q_s^* = \bar{q}^*$, $s \in S_1$. Then (A.10.3) and (A.10.4) imply:

$$p^* = v + \lambda_s^* / \pi_s \qquad s \in S_1 \tag{A.10.6}$$

and

$$\sum_s \pi_s(p_s^* - v) = \beta \qquad \text{(A.10.7)}$$

which are the general forms of the conditions given in equations (10.1) and (10.2) and discussed in some detail in section 10.2. λ_s^* clearly measures the expected marginal willingness to pay for capacity in state s, which will be zero in any state in which the capacity constraint is non-binding. Moreover, λ_s^*/π_s could clearly be interpreted as the appropriate price to charge for an option to buy one unit of output if and only if state s occurs. Optimal capacity is determined by the condition that the sum across states of expected marginal willingness to pay for capacity be equal to marginal capacity cost (in (A.10.7)). Alternatively the option prices could be used to optimize capacity. Finally, note that the conditions imply:

$$\sum_s \pi_s p_s^* q_s^* = v \sum_s \pi_s q_s^* + \beta \bar{q}^* \qquad \text{(A.10.8)}$$

and so the enterprise breaks even in the sense that the expected value of revenue equals the expected value of costs. This is, however, due to the constant-cost assumptions. If marginal cost is increasing, expected profit would be positive, if decreasing, negative. The reader can confirm that imposing the constraint that expected revenues equal expected costs in either of the last two cases leads simply to the inverse-elasticity pricing rule for each p_s (cf. chapter 7).

2 Uniform pricing

For convenience let us revert to the two-state-of-the-world case, in order to keep notation as simple as possible and to concentrate on the central point of interest. Some care must be taken in setting up the net social benefit function, because of the difference which arises in this case between consumers' desired demands on the one hand and actual consumption on the other. Let $V_i(p)$ denote i's *consumer surplus* in state 1, i.e.

$$V_i(p) \equiv \int_{\underline{p}}^{p^0} q_{i1}(p)d\bar{p} \qquad \text{(A.10.9)}$$

where $q_{i1}(p)$ is i's demand function in state 1 and p^0 is such that $q_{i1}(p^0) = 0$. Then clearly $dV_i/d\bar{p} = -q_{i1}$. This is of course all on the assumption that the consumer is allowed to realize his desired demand $q_{i1}(p)$. If not, his consumer surplus in state 1 is zero.

The most convenient way of formulating the net social welfare function for state 1 is as the sum of expected consumer surplus and expected producer surplus. If, as discussed in section 10.3, $\pi_i = \pi_i(q_1, \bar{q})$ is the probability that i will *not* realize his demand if state 1 occurs (note: π_i is a conditional probability), then expected consumer surplus in this state is $\pi \sum_i (1-\pi_i)V_i$, where π is the probability of occurrence of state 1. We can formulate expected producer surplus by noting that actual production and consumption will equal capacity in state 1, so that expected producer surplus (gross of capital cost) is $\pi(p-v)\bar{q}$. In state 2, we ignore rationing and so the formulation is just as before. Hence we can express net social benefits as:

$$\bar{N} = \pi\left[\sum_i (1-\pi_i)V_i + (p-v)\bar{q}\right] + (1-\pi)[B(q_2) - vq_2] - \beta\bar{q}. \quad \text{(A.10.10)}$$

We maximize $\bar{N}$ with respect to p and $\bar{q}$, ignoring the capacity constraint since this is already subsumed into the equation. We obtain the necessary conditions:

$$\frac{\partial\bar{N}}{\partial p} = \pi\left[\sum_i (1-\pi_i)\frac{\partial V_i}{\partial p} + \bar{q}\right] - \pi\sum_i V_i\frac{\partial\pi_i}{\partial q_1}\frac{\partial q_1}{\partial p} + (1-\pi)(p-v)\frac{\partial q_2}{\partial p} = 0 \quad \text{(A.10.11)}$$

$$\frac{\partial\bar{N}}{\partial\bar{q}} = \pi(p-v) - \pi\sum_i V_i\frac{\partial\pi_i}{\partial q} - \beta = 0. \quad \text{(A.10.12)}$$

These conditions then provide the basis for conditions (10.17) and (10.18) of this chapter, with one complication. Notice the first term in (A.10.11) (which was omitted in (10.17)). It can be written as:

$$\pi\left[\bar{q} - \sum_i (1-\pi_i)q_{i1}\right] \equiv \pi[\bar{q} - \bar{q}_1] \quad \text{(A.10.13)}$$

where $\bar{q}_1$ can be defined as the expected value of consumption in state 1 with respect to the rationing probabilities π_i. Now there is a sense in which this term 'ought' to be zero. The capacity level, $\bar{q}$, is the amount of *actual* consumption in state 1, and so there would be an inconsistency in the rationing mechanism if the π_i were such that the aggregate expected value of consumption were not equal to the actual consumption. The inconsistency can be put in another way. The term $\pi\bar{q}$ gives the change in expected producer surplus resulting from a price change, with output held constant at $\bar{q}$. The term $\pi\sum_i (1-\pi_i)q_{i1} = \pi\bar{q}_1$ gives the change in expected consumer surplus. Since actual consumption is also held fixed at $\bar{q}$, the change in price simply causes a transfer between expected consumer and producer surplus which has no effect on the total welfare measure (cf. the discussion of Figure 10.3). For this to be reflected in condition (A.10.11), we then require $\bar{q} = \bar{q}_1$. This condition could then be interpreted as a consistency requirement on the rationing mechanism. Note that it is satisfied in the case of simple random rationing, where $\pi_i = 1 - \bar{q}/\sum_i q_{i1}$, all i.

3   Consumer valuations of reliability

In the preceding section it was assumed that the ordinary consumer surplus measure, V_i, could be used to give the required valuations of output under uncertainty. This was consistent with the formulation of the optimal pricing and investment problem in terms of maximization of expected consumer and producer surplus. However, there is a large literature concerning the possible pitfalls of using consumer surplus measures in models which assume certainty, and we ought also to be aware of what we are doing in the present case. In this section therefore we look at the consumer valuation problem from a more general point of view.

We continue to assume the consumer faces two 'primary' states of the world, and that only in the first of them will his consumption of the good in question be rationed. This means that in the first primary state we can distinguish two substates, in one of which he is and in the other of which he is not rationed. We assume that there is a second good, a 'composite consumption commodity' whose price is always unity. The price of the good which may be rationed is also constant across states. The consumer then chooses state-contingent consumption quantities subject to budget constraints and the rationing constraint, in such a way as to maximize his expected utility. Let us now look at this problem formally.

Let $s = 1, 2$, denote the 'primary' state, so that the consumer's budget constraints are:

$$pq_s + c_s = m_s \qquad s = 1, 2 \qquad (A.10.14)$$

where q_s is the good which may be rationed in state 1 and c_s is the consumption commodity (which is never rationed). Because it is not possible to exchange income between states, each budget constraint must bind in its respective state of the world. There is a probability $r \in [0, 1]$ that the consumer will be faced with the constraint $q_1 = 0$, and so his expected utility will be:

$$\bar{u} = \pi[(1-r)u_1(q_1, c_1) + ru_1(0, m_1)] + (1-\pi)u_2(q_2, c_2) \qquad (A.10.15)$$

where π is the probability of primary state 1. He chooses q_s, c_s so as to maximize $\bar{u}$, subject to the budget constraints in (A.10.14), yielding the conditions:

$$\pi(1-r)\frac{\partial u_1}{\partial q_1} - \lambda_1 p = 0 \qquad (A.10.16)$$

$$\pi(1-r)\frac{\partial u_1}{\partial c_1} - \lambda_1 = 0 \qquad (A.10.17)$$

$$(1-\pi)\frac{\partial u_2}{\partial q_2} - \lambda_2 p = 0 \qquad (A.10.18)$$

$$(1-\pi)\frac{\partial u_2}{\partial c_2} - \lambda_2 = 0 \qquad (A.10.19)$$

where λ_1 is the marginal expected utility of income contingent on state 1 occurring *and* the consumer not being rationed, while λ_2 is the marginal expected utility of income in state 2. In general, because of the absence of exchange possibilities, these will not be equal to each other, nor to $\partial u_1/\partial m_1 \ (= \partial u_1/\partial c_1)$, the utility of income in state 1 when the consumer *is* rationed.

Clearly, these conditions can be expressed in the usual marginal-rate-of-substitution = price-ratio form. Moreover, on the usual assumptions we can solve them to obtain demand functions for q_s and c_s which can be written:

$$q_s = q_s(p, m_s) \quad c_s = c_s(p, m_s) \qquad s = 1, 2. \qquad (A.10.20)$$

Note that these state-contingent demand functions do not depend on probabilities and $\partial q_s/\partial m_t = 0, \ s \neq t, \ s, \ t = 1, 2$ (if p were not fixed across states then this would also apply to cross-price effects). It follows that in the usual way we can define an indirect utility function:

$$\bar{v} = \pi[(1-r)v_1(p, m_1) + ru_1(0, m_1)] + [(1-\pi)v_2(p, m_2)]. \qquad (A.10.21)$$

The effect on the consumer's expected utility of a change in the rationing probability r is:

$$\frac{\partial \bar{v}}{\partial r} = \pi[u_1(0, m_1) - v_1(p, m_1)] < 0. \qquad (A.10.22)$$

We could define a 'willingness to pay' for a reduction in r in three main ways:

(1) as the amount of income the consumer would give up *for certain*;
(2) as the amount of income the consumer would give up if state 1 occurs;
(3) as the amount of income the consumer would give up if state 1 occurs and he is *not* rationed.

We can obtain expressions for each of these by holding $\bar{v}$ fixed and allowing r and the appropriate income to vary simultaneously. Thus we find:

(1) $$\frac{dm}{dr} = \frac{\pi[u_1(0, m_1) - v_1(p, m_1)]}{\lambda_1 + \hat{\lambda}_1 + \lambda_2} \equiv \frac{\pi[u_1(0, m_1) - v_1(p, m_1)]}{\pi(1-r)\dfrac{\partial v_1}{\partial m_1} + \pi r\dfrac{\partial u_1(0, m_1)}{\partial m_1} + (1-\pi)\dfrac{\partial v_2}{\partial m_2}}$$

(2) $$\frac{dm}{dr} = \frac{\pi[u_1(0, m_1) - v_1(p, m_1)]}{\lambda_1 + \hat{\lambda}_1} \equiv \frac{[u_1(0, m_1) - v_1(p, m_1)]}{(1-r)\dfrac{\partial v_1}{\partial m_1} + r\dfrac{\partial u_1(0, m_1)}{\partial m_1}}$$

(3) $$\frac{dm}{dr} = \frac{\pi[u_1(0, m_1) - v_1(p, m_1)]}{\lambda_1} \equiv \frac{[u_1(0, m_1) - v_1(p, m_1)]}{(1-r)\dfrac{\partial v_1}{\partial m_1}}$$

as the willingness-to-pay measures in cases (1), (2) and (3) respectively. $\hat{\lambda}_1$ denotes the marginal expected utility of income contingent on the occurrence of state 1 *and* the consumer being rationed, i.e.

$$\hat{\lambda}_1 \equiv \pi r \frac{\partial u_1}{\partial m_1}(0, m_1) \equiv \pi r \frac{\partial u_1}{\partial m_1}(0, c_1).$$

From these expressions we can say that a payment which has to be made *for certain*, in all states of the world, will be smaller than one which is made only in state 1, which in turn will be less than one only made if the consumer is not rationed. The denominators in the above expressions decrease steadily because of the omission of marginal expected utilities of income in states in which payment does not have to be made. Note also that if r is very small, as is probably the case in practice, measures (2) and (3) will be roughly the same, and the main distinction is between the case in which payment must be made for certain, and that where payment is contingent on occurrence of state 1. Note that the former willingness to pay will be smaller, the less likely state 1 is to occur, while the latter is independent of this probability. However, a significant difference between measures (1) and (3) also requires different marginal utilities of income $\partial v_1/\partial m_1$ and $\partial v_2/\partial m_2$ in the two states. If these are roughly equal then (given that πr will be extremely small) the two willingness-to-pay measures will also be about the same. One case in which this will be true is where the consumer's utility function does not depend on the state of the world ($u_1 \equiv u_2$ in (A.10.15)) and the consumer is *risk-neutral*, so that $\partial u/\partial m_s$ is a constant for all s and all m_s. Risk-neutrality is, however, not regarded as typical of consumer attitudes to risk. A second case in which marginal utilities of income would be equal across states would be that in which the consumer has access to markets – in effect insurance markets – which allow income to be transferred between states. This then would equalize marginal expected utilities of income across states. Again, however, it is generally accepted that a system of markets which is complete, in this sense, does not exist, and so we must continue to allow marginal expected utilities of income to differ between states of the world.

We can now relate these measures to the use of consumer surplus V_i in the analysis of section 10.3. In fact, it is straightforward to show that this Marshallian consumer surplus is given simply by $[v_1(p, m_1) - u_1(0, m_1)]/\partial v_1/\partial m_1$, with $\partial v_1/\partial m_1$ *treated as constant*. To prove this, we make use of Roy's identity, which states:

$$\frac{\partial v_1}{\partial p} = -q_1(p, m_1)\frac{\partial v_1}{\partial m_1}.$$

Let p^0 denote the price such that $q_1(p^0, m_1) = 0$. Then we have:

$$\int_{\underline{p}}^{p^0} \frac{\partial v_1}{\partial p} \, d\bar{p} = -[v_1(p, m_1) - u_1(0, m_1)] = -\frac{\partial v_1}{\partial m_1} \int_{\underline{p}}^{p^0} q_1(p, m_1) d\bar{p}$$

or

$$[v_1(p, m_1) - u_1(0, m_1)] \Big/ \frac{\partial v_1}{\partial m_1} = \int_{\underline{p}}^{p^0} q_1(p, m_1) d\bar{p}$$

where of course the right-hand side is the Marshallian consumer surplus. Thus $V_i(\div (1 - r))$ is simply the negative of our third willingness-to-pay measure.

We can then draw a number of conclusions on the appropriateness of using expected consumer surplus as a measure of willingness to pay for supply reliability in determining optimal price and capacity under uncertainty. If consumers are required to pay only if state 1 occurs then, subject to the usual qualification concerning constancy of the marginal utility of income $\partial u_1 / \partial m_1$, V_i is a reasonable measure to take. If, as is more likely to be the case, consumers must pay for the increased reliability across *all* states of the world, use of V_i also requires that marginal utilities of income across states are the same. This is a rather stronger assumption, but one which we may nevertheless regard as worth making for the simplicity it may bring with it.

Notes

Chapter 1

1 My view, based admittedly on casual observation, is that 'mixed enterprises' tend to behave either as wholly owned public enterprises or as wholly owned private companies, more usually the latter. British Petroleum is a good example.

2 For further examples see the chapters by Raymond Vernon and Alberto Martinelli in Vernon and Aharoni (1981).

3 In the sense of the Pareto criterion. See chapter 3 below for further discussion.

4 These 'situations' of market failure do not provide a full explanation of *why* market failure occurs. For this we need also to consider the questions of the definition of property rights, the costs of establishing and using markets, the costs of reaching agreements, and so on. For further discussion of these points see Gravelle and Rees (1981), Ch. 18.

5 This is not to say that the public enterprise *will* actually achieve this. We should be aware of the fallacy in supposing that the alternative to imperfect markets is perfect government. This is further discussed in chapter 2 below.

6 Note that this was carried out by a Conservative government, in implicit endorsement of the 'market failure' argument.

7 September 1983.

8 See chapter 9 below.

9 Although where owners cannot monitor costlessly the activities of managers, it is possible that rents may be absorbed in generating managerial utility. See for example Williamson (1964) and Rees (1974).

10 A major factor, of course, was the history of labour relations in these industries over the period 1920–40.

11 For further discussion see Grassini (1981) and Martinelli (1981).

12 However, to assume that public enterprises have been created by socialist governments generally would be an inaccurate reflection of history in a number of countries, including Italy, Canada, Australia and Sweden.

13 This argument is set out in Martinelli (1981).

14 In particular the British Gas Corporation, British Telecom and to a lesser extent the electricity industry.

15 The economics of depletion of natural resources is examined in chapter 6 below.

16 Again, this is not to say that the optimal policy necessarily *will* be achieved.

17 See for example Pryke (1982) for the UK, Grassini (1981) and Martinelli (1981) for Italy, and Borcherding, Pommerehne and Schneider (1982) for a wide range of examples.

Chapter 2

1 This term seems to have originated with H. Demsetz (1961). Nirvaana is the Buddhist version of heaven – a state of bliss.
2 Though it should be pointed out that many of the activities considered, for example municipal refuse collection, would not be regarded as being carried on by public enterprises as such.
3 Ibid., p. 85.
4 See in particular the Commission's reports on the Central Electricity Generating Board (1981) and the National Coal Board (1983).
5 See for example Anastassopoulos (1981).
6 Borcherding, Pommerehne and Schneider (1982).
7 For a full definition of what is meant by this, see section 2.2 and chapter 3 below.
8 In the recent economics literature, this has also come to be known as the 'principal-agent problem'. For a general discussion of this problem, see Grossman and Hart (1982).
9 In particular the three White Papers, Cmnds. 1337 (1961), 3437 (1967) and 7131 (1978).
10 See Anastassopoulos (1981), Grassini (1981) and Martinelli (1981).
11 See Van der Bellen (1981).
12 David Henderson has suggested to me that this categorization of objectives may give a false picture of the tangled skein of motives which have prompted political interventions in practice. I accept this but would still argue that it is helpful for analytical purposes to have this classification.
13 One way of looking at this classification, which is quite standard in economics, is as a way of trying to pin down this very elusive concept, to which appeal is made as a justification for whatever government thinks it wants to do at any particular time.
14 See Grassini (1981).
15 Although it should be pointed out that this is due to an underlying macroeconomic policy objective – control of the Public Sector Borrowing Requirement.
16 For example, see the first part of the 1978 White Paper, Cmnd. 7131.
17 Thus in public enterprises in the UK, at least, though Board members and chairmen may not be reappointed at the ends of their contracts, this will usually be due to some general lack of empathy or some specific confrontation with a minister, rather than a systematic evaluation of the outcomes of investments.
18 For example, the policy adopted in the early 1970s of holding down their prices was, with some justice, used to explain the poor financial performance of the nationalized industries over this period, but how much of this was also due to low factor productivity and unwise past investment?
19 Once it has been made viable. This is not to say that those public enterprises in the UK which are subject to competition do not have severe problems, and most of them do have, in particular British Airways, British Shipbuilding and British Steel. Rather, the argument is that once a public enterprise has achieved efficient cost levels, competition should act as an effective device to maintain that state.
20 Thus in Labour Party politics, the political power of a union depends on its 'block vote', which is directly related to the size of its membership.

21 That is to say, they might accept lower wage increases than would otherwise be available in return for accepting lower manning levels and higher productivity.
22 See Rees (1984a), (1984b).
23 Particularly on overmanning, pricing behaviour and overestimation of the returns to investment.
24 The basic approach is to try to develop 'positive', as opposed to normative, models of public enterprise.
25 For an extensive treatment of this approach, see Furobotn and Pejovich (1974).
26 See for example Marris (1964), Ch. 1.

Chapter 3

1 See Mishan (1960). The definition given here varies slightly that due to Mishan.
2 After the economist Vilfredo Pareto (1848–1923), who is credited with having first proposed them.
3 This is an important point, also discussed in Mishan (1960). It is not usually possible to 'test' normative propositions empirically, and so we could not adopt Friedman's position (Friedman, 1953) of ignoring the 'assumptions' of a model, even if we should want to. Rather, we base our faith in the propositions on the view we have about the 'realism' of the assumptions.
4 That is to say, each individual's preference ordering over all possible consumption bundles, current and future, is known to him, and is exogenous to the analysis. This does not imply, of course, that the individual's preferences between perambulators and sports cars will not be different in year 10 than in year 0, but rather that these preferences are *known* in year 0 and do not change.
5 The resource allocations and price systems are determined as the equilibria of the market system in each period. We assume here that the conditions sufficient for these equilibria to exist and to be attained are always satisfied. For discussions of these conditions, at increasing levels of difficulty, see Gravelle and Rees (1981), Arrow and Hahn (1971), and Debreu (1959).
6 The description of the economy given here refers to a 'sequence economy', where there is a succession of market systems through time. An alternative characterization is given by the 'Arrow–Debreu' economy, in which the markets are held *only* at $t = 0$, and contracts are made at that time for sales and purchases at all future dates. The rest of the time is spent simply honouring these contracts. Given the assumptions made here, these two characterizations of the economy are equivalent.
7 Note that there is no *mechanism* by which these plans are made consistent and 'true' expectations formed, so assumption 5 is pretty heroic. In the Arrow–Debreu economy, the fact that all exchanges *actually* take place at $t = 0$ implies that the market mechanism does ensure consistency of all future consumptions and productions, but this hardly constitutes a gain in realism.
8 For discussions and proofs of these propositions, see Gravelle and Rees (1981), Malinvaud (1972), Arrow and Hahn (1971), and Debreu (1959).

9 As always, we make the two-person assumption to permit two-dimensional representation. All statements we make in this context generalize to an *n*-person world.

10 These utility values are unique only up to a positive monotonic transformation, since they
correspond to the usual *ordinal* utility functions of consumer theory. It follows that we
cannot rely on specific sets of *u*-values for any of our propositions: they have to hold for all
permissible transformations. This is true for all the propositions stated in this chapter.

11 These public enterprises may control industries with increasing returns, which would
otherwise act monopolistically. Other reasons for the existence of public enterprises are
hard to find in a first-best economy.

12 Briefly: that consumers' marginal rates of substitution between any two goods (including
inputs they may supply) be equal to each other, and to the corresponding marginal rates of
transformation of the two goods (including inputs) in production. It is assumed here that
the reader is thoroughly familiar with these necessary conditions.

13 It can be shown that application of this rule in the case of capital goods *implies* a
procedure of maximizing net present value of investment discounting at the market rate of
interest. This implication is shown to hold in chapter 4 below. Consequently, when in this
chapter we wish to draw specific attention to investment, we shall speak of the first-best
rule of maximizing net present value calculated by discounting at the market interest rate.
That is, it should be stressed, simply one aspect of condition (b).

14 If returns to scale are constant, then marginal cost = average cost, and so average cost
pricing (in the theoretical sense used here, rather than in the empirical accounting sense)
would imply marginal cost pricing. Non-constant returns imply, in general, inequality
between marginal and average costs, hence the statement in the text.

15 It seems to be the case that the analysis of uncertainty involves a more fundamental
departure from the first-best economy than any other of the 'second-best' issues. Some
aspects of this analysis are presented in chapter 10 below, where some references are also
given.

16 A note here on terminology: we use the term 'Pareto optimal' to refer to any situation such
that no one can be made better off without someone being made worse off, whether in the
context of a first-best economy, or a second-best economy. The concept of a Pareto
optimum is much more general than the specific model in which it is being applied. Some
authors seem to identify 'Pareto optimum' with 'first best', which in our view only leads to
confusion.

17 In other words, as we would expect, the public enterprise price would not be used as an
instrument of monopoly policy if in fact it does not affect the decision of the monopolist.
This case is the so-called 'behavioural separability' case of Davis and Whinston (1965).
Proposition (i) is really an application of the so-called 'general theorem of the second best'
of Lipsey and Lancaster (1956/7). See chapter 6, where the general applicability of the
theory of second best is further discussed.

18 This point was at the heart of the debate between MacManus (1967) and Bohm (1967), on
the one hand, and Davis and Whinston (1967), on the other. Their disagreement was
essentially concerned with the set of instruments a policy-maker has available, and the set
of decision-takers in the economy he is able to influence directly.

Chapter 4

1 Note that we are here assuming a competitive market for units of K. Recall the assumptions underlying the first-best economy, especially that of certain knowledge of future prices and technology; this clearly plays an important role in allowing us to regard the V_t as completely determined.

2 Note that this bears no relation to the accounting concept of the same name. The value δ_t is an attempt to capture the idea that use of 1 unit of K in production reduces its market value or earning power. Accountants' depreciation provisions are essentially means of putting money by so as to be able to meet debts and replace assets, and are heavily influenced by taxation conventions. At the same time, in a real economy, as opposed to the first-best economy, δ_t may be very difficult to estimate, certainly as a single known number.

3 This assumption, together with the later assumption of no technological change, makes the 'vintage' of K, i.e. the year in which it was installed, irrelevant. All these assumptions could be relaxed at the cost of a good deal of complexity, which would not really further our present purpose.

4 In what follows, we shall assume that year 1 is the 'planning horizon' – no plans are formed for subsequent periods. This is equivalent to assuming no interdependence between the plans made at year 0 for year 1, and the plans made at year 1 for year 2, and so on. In practice, such interdependence almost invariably exists. Again, however, in the interests of simplicity, we ignore that here.

5 This requires it to set out the various technological possibilities of transforming inputs into outputs, given the knowledge it has at year 0, of the technology which will be available in year 1. Introducing input prices then allows it to choose the least-cost process. The standard 'isoquant analysis' is one way of characterizing this procedure.

6 This assumes that 'depreciation', δ, does not depend on the rate of output actually produced within the year, i.e. on the rate of 'capacity utilization'. One unit of K 'depreciates' an amount δ over the year, however intensively it is used. This is not strictly realistic: some loss of value may occur simply with the passage of time, but some may also depend on intensity of use. Not a great deal of purpose would be served by introducing this distinction, however, and so we choose the simpler assumption.

7 Recall that the technology and input prices are those expected to prevail in year 1, and that in a first-best economy these are those which actually *will* prevail. Also, in the following analysis of the relation between year 0 and year 1 cost curves, an implicit assumption is that these input prices and technology are the same in each year. This is not a crucial assumption, and the consequences of its relaxation are considered in the Appendix to this chapter.

8 See previous note.

9 This 'fixed cost' assumes, as was already stated, that δ is independent of q_0.

10 Note that by 'investment' is always meant *net* investment, the amount of K installed over and above that required simply for replacement. Also, since it is possible that $K_1^* < K_0$, if demand is declining, investment may be negative. In that case, we are implicitly assuming that it also takes one year to reduce installed K – by scrapping, selling on the K, 'second-

hand' market, etc. In practice, the time it takes to reduce installed K may differ from the time taken to expand it, in which case we would define the 'year' differently for contracting as opposed to expanding enterprises.

11 Thus, from the necessary conditions for a utility maximum of a consumer, we have $MU_j/\lambda = p_j$, where MU_j is the marginal utility of good j, p_j is its price, and λ is the marginal utility of money. Note that permissible transformations of the utility function leave this equality unchanged, since MU_j and λ would be changed in the same proportion.

12 Thus, suppose there are three inputs, L, K and R, with L immediately variable, K requiring one year to be varied, and R two years to be varied. The contention now is that marginal cost pricing is ambiguous. Extend the analysis of this chapter to show that it is not.

Chapter 5

1 In other words the marginal product of L is constant over the output range $O\bar{q}_0$. If it was assumed instead that the marginal product of L diminished over that output range, the segment ab of the C_0 curve would be convex from below; if the marginal product of L were assumed to increase, the curve would be concave from below. There would then be corresponding implications for the MC_0 curve in Figure 5.2. The reader is invited to apply the subsequent analysis of this chapter to these cases, to show that nothing essential changes.

2 $\bar{q}_0$ is the output for which the fixed capacity K_0 minimizes cost. Given K_0, outputs $q_0 < \bar{q}_0$ are produced at non cost-minimizing input combinations, and so C_0 lies above C_1 over this range. See the discussion for the flexible plant case in the previous chapter. Note that again we are implicitly assuming unchanging input prices and technology between years 0 and 1.

3 A point on this vertical section of the curve does *not* show marginal cost at output $\bar{q}_0$, since this is undefined. The vertical section of the curve should be thought of as a diagrammatic device for helping us to analyse the pricing problem in the present case, rather than as showing the 'marginal cost' at some level of output.

4 In the case of electricity and gas, rationing would be carried out by supply interruptions on some basis of allocation determined by engineers; in transport systems it would probably be effected by queuing, so that those with lowest time valuations tend, other things being equal, to obtain relatively more of the good.

5 It has been pointed out that this problem is formally similar to that of joint production, which has been extensively analysed in economics – see Turvey (1971) and Littlechild (1970). Thus, just as putting inputs into raising sheep produces both mutton and wool, so installing electricity-generating capacity produces both peak and off-peak electricity. The importance of the realization of this kind of analytical similarity is that techniques and results established for one problem can then be directly applied to solve the other. The peak-load pricing problem had been solved before this similarity was first noted and exploited, however, and here we follow the 'traditional' approach.

6 See Mohring (1970). See also Takayama (1974), pp. 671–84, who analyses the continuous case.
7 See Craven (1971).
8 This 12-hourly interest rate r' is the solution to the equation: $£1(1+r')^{(8760/12)} = £1(1+r)$. In other words, lending £1 for 1 year at r' compounded 12-hourly is equivalent to lending £1 for 1 year at r.
9 Drawing both demand curves on one figure saves space but may be misleading. There could be two figures, one relating to period 1, the other to period 2. The cost curves would be the same in each. One figure succeeds the other at 12-hourly intervals throughout the year. Daily outputs are given by the sum of the two values on the horizontal axes, and price fluctuates from period to period. Thus Figure 5.6 takes advantage of the fact that the cost curves in each period are the same to save space, but the demand curves should be thought of as holding sequentially rather than simultaneously.
10 For a discussion of the economics of public goods, see any textbook in public finance, or chapter 18 of Gravelle and Rees (1981).
11 For a discussion of the joint products case which relates it directly to peak-load pricing, see Littlechild (1970).
12 See Littlechild, op. cit.
13 The problem was called this by Boiteux (1960), in his seminal work on marginal cost pricing, upon which this chapter has drawn heavily. Unlike many subsequent discussants, Boiteux clearly recognized the general nature of the peak-load pricing problem as one of dynamic optimization (see also Takayama, 1974), but chose the discrete period case both for realism and simplicity. He also discussed the question of load-curve decomposition, but far more succinctly than here.
14 Or, strictly speaking, the greatest optimal uniform price, since any price down to v' would suffice. If we are not indifferent to the extent of losses incurred by the enterprise, then the argument just set out would not apply, but this raises issues which are best analysed explicitly, as in chapter 7 below.
15 For a discussion of some possibilities and their consequences, see Rees (1980).
16 This analysis follows that of Williamson (1966).
17 Though the disruption would presumably *not* exist if the variations in price were fully anticipated by consumers.

Chapter 6

1 Exhaustible resources are defined as resources which are available in finite amounts and which do not replenish or renew themselves. Examples therefore would be mineral deposits, 'fossil fuels' such as coal, gas and oil, and so on. They are contrasted to 'renewable' resources such as fish stocks and forests which do reproduce themselves over time.
2 More generally, the problem could be looked upon as one of finding an optimal dynamic path of output and opportunity cost of mining labour. See Forster and Rees (1983) for an exploration of this approach.

3 Forster and Rees (1983), and the references cited there, consider the first problem, but there does not appear to be an explicit analysis of the second.
4 See Dasgupta and Heal (1979) for an extensive treatment of the economics of exhaustible resources.
5 It would usually be taken as the 'social time preference rate' or 'public-sector cost of capital'. In the UK this currently stands at 5 per cent in real terms.
6 Thus, setting V constant in (6.2) we have, for small changes Δq_1, Δq_2,

$$\Delta V = p_1 \Delta q_1 + \frac{p_2}{1+r} \Delta q_2 = 0$$

where we use the fact that price measures the marginal benefit of output. Then (6.3) follows from rearranging this and ignoring the minus sign.
7 Setting V' constant in (6.7) we have, for small changes q_1, q_2,

$$\Delta V' = (p_1 - MC_1)\Delta q_1 + \frac{(p_2 - MC_2)}{1+r} \Delta q_2.$$

Then (6.8) follows by rearranging.
8 Nevertheless, it is useful to have this generalization available in the literature. See again Crew and Kleindorfer (1979).

Chapter 7

1 See Lipsey and Lancaster (1956/7).
2 See Davis and Whinston (1965).
3 Though again, issues involved with the generation of revenue to the exchequer are lurking here, so this brief aside does not do full justice to the problem.
4 This appears to underly the approach to second-best problems of McManus (1957; 1967) and Turvey (1968b).
5 The general analytical framework for this section can be found in Rees (1968). Here, I shall be concerned with exposition and clarification rather than general validity of the results, and so a fairly informal partial equilibrium approach will be adopted.
6 The statement of this assumption tries to make as clear as possible two things: first, in discussing any second-best policy problem, we must specify the set of economic agents or decision-takers whose choices are controlled by the planner, and the nature of the policy instruments he has available – different specifications of these imply different problems with different solutions (see the debate between Bohm (1967) and McManus (1967) on the one hand, and Davis and Whinston (1967) on the other, for an illustration of this); secondly, this piecemeal approach is very narrowly constrained in its policy options – unreasonably so perhaps, but see the discussion in the previous section.
7 See the Appendix to this chapter.
8 This assumes that the tax is not an *optimal* one; if it is, then a different analysis applies. See the discussion of taxation in the following chapter.

9 Note that in general, each point on A refers to a different demand curve for q_2, since a change in price and output in market 2 causes a change in price and output in market 1, which in turn feeds back to change the demand in market 2. Thus, the curve A represents the value of the difference between price and marginal cost along a succession of demand curves for good 2.

10 Note, however, in adopting the policy, he must also adopt an appropriate redistribution policy if the change is *actually* to be Pareto preferred – see the discussion in chapter 3 on this point.

11 For the derivation, see the Appendix to this chapter.

12 This was first pointed out to me by L. P. Foldes, in a comment on Rees (1968).

13 It is not hard to picture the sequence of newspaper reports to accompany this chain of events. The public enterprise first monopolizes the industry, and then on the one hand produces at enormous losses, or on the other raises prices anyway.

14 A mistaken application of our earlier analysis could also lead to a similar conclusion. The (false) argument might run as follows: 'since outputs are homogeneous, an increment of one unit of output by the public enterprise reduces that of the private enterprise also by one unit. Hence, in equation (6.2), $\beta_1' = -1$, and so the condition is $p_1 - MC_1 = p_2 - MC_2$. The appropriate second-best policy, therefore, is to accept the price increase.' The reader is invited to expose the fallacy in the argument.

15 See, for example, Turvey (1973), and the references given there.

16 Though this assumes a zero marginal disutility of labour to coal-miners, which seems a very unrealistic assumption, given the nature of the work.

17 Nor, regretfully, with the interesting approach of Mohring and Boyd (1971), which essentially transforms the treatment of externalities into a public enterprise pricing problem. However, the case analysed in this section brings out some elements of this approach.

18 That is, the toll t^* would satisfy the necessary condition for a Pareto optimum. Our usual qualification applies here, however: if the initial equilibrium is at $\bar{q}_m$, imposition of the toll makes some people worse off, and so the *move* to the Pareto-optimal position is only justified on Paretian grounds if compensation is actually paid. On the other hand, this could well be done out of the proceeds of the tax, given by $t^* q_m^*$.

19 Note the similarity of this solution to the standard marginal cost pricing rule for a public enterprise. This gives a good illustration of the essence of the approach to externalities proposed by Mohring and Boyd (1971).

Chapter 8

1 This is not peculiar to public enterprises: J. Hicks was speaking quite generally when he referred to the major benefit from monopoly power as a quiet life. On the other hand, the monopoly would not have to be an entrepreneurial, profit-maximizing one, but one in which the 'divorce of ownership from control' is complete.

2 In actual fact targets are expressed as rates of return on capital, which can under some circumstances lead to results which differ from those given in this section. That is, as

Gravelle shows, a model in which the constraint is expressed as a rate of return on capital will generate different optimality conditions to one in which it is expressed as an absolute sum (see Gravelle, 1975). However, in my view, since financial targets are set by the policy-makers with the object of generating particular inflows into the exchequer, the expression of the target as an absolute sum is the more relevant form. The 'rate of return' formulation is simply presentational.

3 The analysis which follows is based on Rees (1968), in which is set out the general equilibrium analysis which validates the more informal partial equilibrium analysis given below. The paper by Boiteux (1956) is the seminal contribution in this area.

4 Note that the assumption of a 'break-even' profit target is easily generalized. If S is the target, then the revenue of the enterprise must equal $VC + S$, where VC is total variable cost. It follows that price (= average revenue) must equal $(VC + S)/q$, or $AVC + S/q$. Then, in the figure, we could imagine the curve AC as being derived from the average variable cost curve, by adding S/q at each output level. It has also been assumed that S is always such as to be greater than the surplus which would be generated by marginal cost pricing. The reader is invited to apply the above analysis to the case in which S is less than this.

5 See the Appendix to this chapter.

6 Strictly speaking, these ratios should be negative, since $MR_i < MC_i$, $i = 1, 2$ by the assumption that S is for less than maximum profit.

7 Thus, $[-(1 - \lambda)]/\lambda = -(1/\lambda) + 1$. Hence $\lim_{\lambda \to \infty}[-(1/\lambda) + 1] = 1$. The effect of S approaching the profit maximum is to make λ tend to infinity.

8 Again, see the Appendix to this chapter.

9 See the Appendix.

10 There is a large literature in business economics concerned with the determination of transfer prices, which could very usefully be read in connection with the public enterprise sector, despite the fact that profit and not social benefit is taken to be the maximand. See, in particular, Hirshleifer (1956) and Arrow (1959).

11 There will also be a term in each condition which represents the welfare effect of the variations in E's outputs, in the markets supplied by A and B. Since the selling enterprise must meet its profit target, this does not so much affect the general level of its prices, as the relative contributions made to it by A and B. For details of the analysis, see Rees (1968).

12 Note the importance of the assumption of an otherwise first-best economy. If one of the inputs bought from the private sector is priced above marginal cost, then there is *already* a distortion, and in general this will require a deviation of price from marginal cost of the public sector input, along the lines discussed in the previous chapter. It is important to keep distinct the case in which only profit targets have to be met, from that in which private-sector imperfections exist, to avoid confusion. The relation between them is explicitly discussed below.

13 The reader is invited to apply this discussion, and that earlier in this section, to show why (a) given that the Central Electricity Generating Board must meet a financial target, it is allocatively inefficient to load this entirely on one of its three outputs defined in the Bulk Supply Tariff; and (b) the imposition of a financial target on the CEGB is in any case allocatively inefficient.

14 Reading the literature of criticism of public enterprise policies in the middle-to-late 1950s, one can make out a third strand of opinion. This was the feeling that low profitability implied both low efficiency and an *over-absorption of resources*, leading to a fat and inefficient public sector. But, as we have already observed, in non-competitive markets relatively high profits are consistent with low efficiency; while the problem of determining the levels of public enterprise outputs and investment in a second-best world is approached by the kind of analysis carried out so far in this book, rather than a crude appeal to accounting rates of return. To make public enterprises 'as profitable as the private sector', whatever that may mean, has no obvious connection with efficient resource allocation, and sounds rather like a sublimation of the wish that no public enterprise existed.

15 See Robson (1960).

16 See Baumol and Bradford (1970), which gives a very clear statement of the optimal tax formula – together with an interesting discussion of its history – which included its rediscovery by various authors in various contexts. A more general treatment of the optimal taxation problem is given by Diamond and Mirrlees (1971), although, as Baumol and Bradford point out, their work was largely anticipated by Boiteux (1956).

17 Thus, given that

$$\frac{p_i - MC_i}{MR_i - MC_i} = \lambda,$$

and $MR_i = p_i(1 - 1/e_i)$, we can arrange to get

$$\frac{p_i - MC_i}{p_i} = \frac{\lambda}{(1-\lambda)} \frac{x_i}{p_i} \frac{dp_i}{dx_i},$$

which, using the definitions of t_i and e_i, gives the result in (8.18).

18 A corollary of this is that the analysis in Rees (1968) is a solution to the problem of optimal taxation, when one sector of the economy is nontaxable and includes monopolies.

19 Boiteux (1956) used the term 'tolls'.

20 Needless to say, these assumptions are purely for ease of exposition, and more general analyses exist. The general approach is set out in Feldstein (1972a, b); Wilson (1974) makes a useful contribution to the operationalization of the concepts; and Mayston (1975) discusses distributional questions in connection with his analysis of the optimal two-part tariff.

21 See the Appendix to this chapter.

22 This terminology was proposed by Feldstein (1972b).

23 For derivation, see Appendix to this chapter.

Chapter 9

1 See in particular Lind *et al.* (1982).

2 It is not innocuous because, as we shall see, certain equivalences between different ways of approaching public investment appraisal, which hold in the two-period case, break down when we move to more than two periods.

3 For a fuller exposition of this model of the economy, see Gravelle and Rees (1981), ch. 15.
4 This identification of borrowing and lending with bondholding is a useful simplification – to borrow £1000 can be regarded as 'issuing' 1000 £1 bonds. It need not be taken too literally.
5 See Gravelle and Rees (1981), ch. 15, for an explanation of why net-present-value maximization is (on present assumptions) in the best interest of shareholders.
6 This is simply a replica of the argument for equality of consumers' marginal rates of substitution between pairs of goods in a one-period context.
7 Note that this specification of the taxable profit assumes that interest on capital invested is not deductible from taxable profit. To make it so would effectively restore the first-best economy. It could be argued that it is 'unrealistic' to make the assumption, but this misses the point. In reality, the overall effect of the tax system is to cause before and after-tax rates of return to diverge. The present model is capturing this divergence in the simplest way possible. It is the fact of this divergence which is of most importance, and not the precise way in which it is created.

Chapter 10

1 Described with great clarity in Berrie (1967).
2 This distribution is essentially a frequency distribution of *past* forecasting errors, which are treated as random or serially uncorrelated. There are several objections to this procedure which could be made on statistical grounds, one of which is that the forecasting errors actually *are* serially correlated. A different approach was adopted in Rees and Rees (1972), where the distribution of prediction errors from the regression equation used in forecasting, provided the distribution of future demands. This seems a more coherent procedure.
3 There is now quite an extensive literature on this subject. See Johnson and Brown (1969), (1970) and (1973); Salkever (1970); Turvey (1970); Visscher (1973); Crew and Kleindorfer (1978); Panzar and Sibley (1978); Sherman and Visscher (1978); Rees (1973), (1980a), (1980b) and (1982).
4 He may refer to the 'well-known tendency' of economists to do this, as reflected in the famous joke about the economist shipwrecked on a desert island, with one can of beer but no can-opener. How did he avoid dying of thirst? He *assumed* that the can was open, and drank it.
5 The joke in the previous note has a mathematician and an engineer writing down in the sand all the equations they know, in a vain attempt to solve the problem of opening the can without a can-opener, before the economist takes over.
6 Brown and Johnson (1969) obtained the result that the optimal uniform price should be set equal to v. This followed from their assumption that, in effect, there were no costs associated with non-price rationing of excess demands: an example of opening cans without openers for which they were justly reproached by Turvey (1970).
7 This is set out more fully in Rees (1980a).
8 Though this is convenient in a partial equilibrium analysis, Rees (1982) suggests that strong assumptions are required to justify it.

Bibliography and references

Anastassopoulos, J-P.C., 'The French Experience: Conflicts with Government', in R. Vernon and Y. Aharoni (1981).

Arrow, K.J., *Social Choice and Individual Values* (John Wiley & Sons, New York, 1951, revised edition, 1963).

Arrow, K.J., 'Optimization, Decentralization, and Internal Pricing in Business Firms', in *Contributions to Scientific Research in Management* (Los Angeles, 1959).

Arrow, K.J., and F.H. Hahn, *General Competitive Analysis* (Oliver & Boyd, Edinburgh, 1971).

Baumol, W.J., *Economic Theory and Operations Analysis* (Prentice-Hall, Englewood Cliffs, New Jersey, 1965).

Baumol, W.J., 'On Taxation and the Control of Externalities', *American Economic Review*, 1972.

Baumol, W.J., and D.F. Bradford, 'Optimal Departures from Marginal Cost Pricing', *American Economic Review*, 1970.

Berrie, T.W., 'The Economics of System Planning in Bulk Electricity Supply' in Turvey (1968a) 1967.

Bohm, P., 'On the Theory of "Second Best"', *Review of Economic Studies*, 1967.

Boiteux, M., 'Sur la Gestion des Monopoles Publics astreint à l'Équilibre Budgetaire', *Econometrica*, 1956; translated and republished as 'On the Management of Public Monopolies subject to Budget Constraints', *Journal of Economic Theory*, 1971.

Boiteux, M., 'Peak-Load Pricing', *Journal of Business*, reprinted in Nelson (1964) 1960.

Boiteux, M., and P. Stasi, 'The Determination of Costs of Expansion of an Interconnected System of Production and Distribution of Electricity', in Nelson (1964) 1952.

Borch, K., *The Economics of Uncertainty* (Princeton, NJ, 1968).

Borcherding, T.E., W.W. Pommerehne, and F. Schneider, 'Comparing the efficiency of private and public production: the evidence from five countries', *Zeitschrift für Nationalokonomie*, Supp. 2, 1982.

Brown, G., and M.B. Johnson, 'Public Utility Pricing and Output under Risk', *American Economic Review*, 1969.

Brown, G., and M.B. Johnson, 'Public Utility Pricing and Output under Risk: Reply', *American Economic Review*, 1970.

Brown, G., and M.B. Johnson, 'Welfare-Maximizing Price and Output with Stochastic Demand: Reply', *American Economic Review*, 1973.

Burn, D., *Nuclear Power and the Energy Crisis* (Macmillan, London, 1978).

Coombes, D., *State Enterprise* (Allen & Unwin, London, 1971).

Craven, J., 'On the Choice of Optimal Time Periods for a Surplus Maximizing Utility subject to Fluctuating Demand', *The Bell Journal of Economics and Management Science*, 1971.

Crew, M.A., and P. Kleindorfer, 'Reliability and Public Utility Pricing', *American Economic Review*, 1978.

Crew, M.A., and P. Kleindorfer, *Public Utility Economics* (Macmillan, London, 1979).

Dasgupta, P.S., and G.M. Heal, *Economic Theory and Exhaustible Resources* (James Nisbet & Co. Ltd, Welwyn, and the Cambridge University Press, 1979).

Davis, O.A., and A.B. Whinston, 'Welfare Economics and the Theory of the Second Best', *Review of Economic Studies*, 1965.

Davis, O.A., and A.B. Whinston, 'Welfare Economics and the Theory of the Second *Review of Economic Studies*, 1967.

Deaton, A., and J. Muellbauer, *Economics and Consumer Behavior* (Cambridge University Press, Cambridge, 1980).

Debreu, G., *Theory of Value* (Wiley, New York, 1959).

Demsetz, H., 'Information and Efficiency: Another Viewpoint', *Journal of Law and Economics*, 1969.

Diamond, P.A., and J.A. Mirrlees, 'Optimal Taxation and Public Production', *American Economic Review*, 1971.

Drèze, J.H., 'Discount Rates and Public Investment: Post-Scriptum', *Economica*, 1974.

Feldstein, M., 'Equity and Efficiency in Public Sector Pricing: The Optimal Two-Part Tariff', *Quarterly Journal of Economics*, 1972(a).

Feldstein, M., 'Distributional Equity and the Optimal Structure of Public Prices', *American Economic Review*, 1972(b).

Feldstein, M., 'The Inadequacy of Weighted Discount Rates', in Layard (1972), 1972(c).

Ferguson, C.E., *Microeconomic Theory* (Homewood, Illinois, 1972).

Forster, B.A., and R. Rees, 'The Optimal Rate of Decline of an Inefficient Industry', *Journal of Public Economics*, 1983.

Foster, C.D., *Politics, Finance, and the Role of Economics* (Allen & Unwin, London, 1971).

Friedman, M., *Essays in Positive Economics* (Chicago, 1953).

Furobotn, E.G., and S. Pejovich, *The Economics of Property Rights* (Ballinger Publishing Co., Cambridge, Mass., 1974).

Grassini, F.A., 'The Italian Enterprises: the Political Constraints', in R. Vernon and Y. Aharoni (1981).

Gravelle, H.S.E., 'Public Enterprises under Rate of Return Financial Targets', *Manchester School*, 1976.

Gravelle, H.S.E., and R. Rees, *Microeconomics* (Longman, London, 1981).

Grossman, S.J., and O.D. Hart, 'An Analysis of the Principal-Agent Problem', *Econometrica*, 1983.

Harris, R., 'Some aspects of public-sector/private-sector competition in imperfectly competitive industries', unpublished, July 1981.

Hausmann, J.A., 'Exact Consumer's Surplus and Deadweight Loss', *American Economic Review*, 1981.

Henderson, P.D., 'Two British Errors: their Probable Size and some Possible Lessons', *Oxford Economic Papers*, 1977.

Hirshleifer, J., 'On the Economics of Transfer Pricing', *Journal of Business*, 1956.

Hirshleifer, J., *Investment, Interest and Capital* (Prentice-Hall, Englewood Cliffs, NJ, 1970).

Lancaster, K., *Mathematical Economics* (Macmillan, London, 1968).

Layard, R.G., *Cost Benefit Analysis* (Penguin, Harmondsworth, 1972).

Lind, R., *et al.*, *Discounting for Time and Risk in Energy Policy* (Resources for the Future Inc., Washington DC, 1982).

Lipsey, R.G., and K. Lancaster, 'The General Theory of the Second Best', *Review of Economic Studies*, 1956/7.

Littlechild, S., 'Marginal Cost Pricing with Joint Costs', *The Economic Journal*, 1970.

MacManus, M., 'Comments on the General Theory of Second Best', *Review of Economic Studies*, 1959.

MacManus, M., 'Private and Social Costs in the Theory of Second Best', *Review of Economic Studies*, 1967.

Malinvaud, E., *Lectures on Microeconomic Theory* (North-Holland, London, 1972).

Marris, R., *The Economic Theory of Managerial Capitalism* (Macmillan, London, 1964).

Martinelli, A., 'The Italian Experience: a Historical Perspective', in R. Vernon and Y. Aharoni (eds), (1981).

Mayston, D.J., 'Optimal Licensing in Public Sector Tariff Structures' in M. Parkin and A.R. Nobay (eds), *Contemporary Issues in Economics* (Manchester University Press, 1975).

Mishan, E.J., 'A Survey of Welfare Economics', *Economic Journal*, 1960.

Mohring, H., 'The Peak Load Problem with Increasing Returns and Pricing Constraints', *American Economic Review*, 1970.

Mohring, H., and J.H. Boyd, 'Analyzing "Externalities": "Direct Interaction" vs. "Asset Utilization" Frameworks', *Economica*, 1971.

Monopolies and Mergers Commission, *Report on the Central Electricity Generating Board* (HMSO, London, 1981).

Monopolies and Mergers Commission, *Report on the National Coal Board* (HMSO, London, 1983).

Nelson, J.R., *Marginal Cost Pricing in Practice* (Prentice-Hall, Englewood Cliffs, NJ, 1964).

Panzar, J.C., and D.S. Sibley, 'Public Utility Pricing under Risk: the Case of Self-Rationing', *American Economic Review*, 1978.

Pryke, R., *Public Enterprise in Practice* (MacGibbon & Kee, London, 1971).

Pryke, R., *The Nationalised Industries* (Martin Robertson, Oxford, 1981).

Rees, J.A., and R. Rees, 'Demand Forecasts and Planning Margins for Water in South-East England', *Journal of Regional Studies*, 1972.

Rees, R., 'Second-Best Rules for Public Enterprise Pricing', *Economica*, 1968.

Rees, R., 'The New Bulk Supply Tariff: Comment', *Economic Journal*, 1969.

Rees, R., *The Economics of Investment Analysis*, CSD Paper 18 (HMSO, London, 1973(a)).

Rees, R., 'Public Sector Resource Allocation under Conditions of Risk' in M. Parkin (ed.), *Essays in Modern Economics* (Longman, 1973(b)).

Rees, R., 'A Reconsideration of the Expense Preference Theory of the Firm', *Economica*, 1974.

Rees, R., 'Consumer Choice and Non-Price Rationing in Public Utility Pricing', in B.M. Mitchell and P.R. Kleindorfer (eds), *Regulated Industries and Public Enterprise* (Lexington Books, Lexington, Mass., 1980).

Rees, R., 'A Note on Peak Load Pricing and Rationing Policies', *Zeitschrift für Nationalokonomie*, 1980.

Rees, R., 'Some Problems in Optimal Pricing under Uncertainty', *Zeitschrift für Nationalokonomie*, Supp. 2, 1982.

Rees, R., 'A Positive Theory of the Public Enterprise', in M. Marchand, P. Pestieau and H. Tulkens (eds), *Public Enterprise Performance: Theory and Measurement* (North-Holland, Amsterdam, 1984a).

Rees, R., 'The Public Enterprise Game', *Economic Journal*, AUTE/RES supp. (1984b).

Reid, G.L., and K. Allen, *Nationalized Industries* (Penguin, Harmondsworth, 1970).

Reid, G.L., and D.J. Harris, *The Nationalized Fuel Industries* (Heinemann Educational Books, London, 1973).

Robbins, L., *Essay on the Nature and Significance of Economic Science* (Macmillan, London, 1932).

Robson, W.A., *Nationalized Industry and Public Ownership* (Allen & Unwin, London, 1960).

Salkever, D., 'Public Utility Pricing and Output under Risk: Comment', *American Economic Review*, 1970.

Sandmo, A., and J. Drèze, 'Discount Rates for Public Investment in Open and Closed Economies', *Economica*, 1971.

Sen, A., *Collective Choice and Social Welfare* (Holden-Day, San Francisco, 1970).

Sherman, R., and M. Visscher, 'Second-best Pricing with Stochastic Demand', *American Economic Review*, 1978.

Stigler, G.J., *Price Theory* (New York, 1966).

Takayama, A., *Mathematical Economics* (Dryden Press, Illinois, 1974).

Thomson, A.W.J., and L.C. Hunter, *The Nationalized Transport Industries* (Heinemann Educational Books, London, 1973).

Turvey, R. (ed.), *Public Enterprise Economics* (Penguin, Harmondsworth, 1968(a)).

Turvey, R., *Optimal Pricing and Investment in Electricity Supply* (Allen & Unwin, London, 1968(b)).

Turvey, R., 'Public Utility Pricing and Output under Risk: Comment', *American Economic Review*, 1970.

Turvey, R., *Economic Analysis and Public Enterprises* (Allen & Unwin, London, 1971).

Vanags, A., 'A Reappraisal of Public Investment Rules' in M. Parkin and A.R. Nobay (eds), *Contemporary Issues in Economics* (Manchester University Press, 1975).

Van der Bellen, A., 'The Control of Public Enterprises: the Case of Austria', *Annals of Public and Co-operative Economy*, 1981.

Viner, J., 'Cost Curves and Supply Curves', reprinted in AEA, *Readings in Price Theory*, 1952.

Visscher, M., 'Welfare-Maximising Price and Output with Stochastic Demand: Comment', *American Economic Review*, 1973.

Williamson, O.E., *The Economics of Discretionary Behavior* (Prentice-Hall, Englewood Cliffs, NJ, 1964).

Williamson, O.E., 'Peak Load Pricing and Optimal Capacity under Indivisibility Constraints', *American Economic Review*, 1966.

Willig, R., 'Consumer's Surplus without Apology', *American Economic Review*, 1976.

Wilson, L.S., 'Some Work on the Distributional Effects of Nationalized and Regulated Industry Pricing Policies', Ph.D. Thesis, University of Essex (unpublished), 1974.

Index